D0757999

VOICE IN MODERN THEATRE

VOICE IN MODERN THEATRE

WITHDRAWN

Jacqueline Martin

ROUTLEDGE

London and New York

First published 1991
by Routledge
11 New Fetter Lane, London EC4P 4EE

Simultaneously published in the USA and Canada
by Routledge
a division of Routledge, Chapman and Hall, Inc.
29 West 35th Street, New York, NY 10001

Disc conversion by Columns of Reading
Printed in Great Britain by
T. J. Press, Padstow, Cornwall

British Library Cataloguing in Publication Data
Martin, Jacqueline
Voice in modern theatre.
1. Voice production
I. Title
792.028

Library of Congress Cataloging in Publication Data
also available
ISBN 0 415 01256 2
ISBN 0 415 04894 X pbk

To P.D. as ever . . .
and in loving memory of S.P.

CONTENTS

ILLUSTRATIONS

ACKNOWLEDGEMENTS

I should like to thank the following individuals and institutions for providing illustrative material and for permission to reproduce the photographs and articles in this book: Gilles Abegg; ADN – Zentralbild, DDR; Sam Appleby; APN Press Service, Norvosti, Moscow; P. Baracz; the Berliner Ensemble; Birmingham Public Library (Niky Rathbone); Svenne Bordlöv; Centre International de Créations Théâtrales, Paris; DDR Kulturcentrum, Stockholm (Barbara Brädefors); Drama Centre, London; Drottningholms Teatermuseum, Stockholm (Barbro Stribolt); Frederick Eberstadt; Martine Franck; Hans Hasselgren; Kungliga Biblioteket, Stockholm; Lipnitzki-Viollet; Angus McBean; Nordic Theatre Studies; Rachel Morton; Polska Agencja Interpress; Fluvio Rolter; the Royal Shakespeare Company; Jan Rüsz; Schaubühne am Halleschen Uffer Berlin; Richard Schechner; the William Seymour Theatre Collection, Princeton University Library (Nora Q. Lin); the Shakespeare Bulletin; the Shakespeare Centre Library; Uppsala Universitetsbiblioteket; US Information Agency, Stockholm (Gunilla Gustafsson); Ruth Walz.

I also wish to express my deep appreciation to all my colleagues who have helped me over the years to define voice, and who have encouraged me to pursue its relevance in the development of the modern theatre. Last but not least, I would like to extend my gratitude to the Theatre Studies Department of the University of Stockholm for allowing me the time, as Research Fellow, to complete the writing of this book.

INTRODUCTION: SUITING THE ACTION TO THE WORD AND THE WORD TO THE ACTION

Voice in Modern Theatre is concerned with a much-neglected area of performance practice – vocal delivery. By this is meant not only the auditive sound emitted by the actor in his role presentation, but, in the duality which the very term 'vocal delivery' presupposes, the dramatic texts, artistic ideas or communicative needs which have given impetus to these utterances and their execution. In order to define the complex nature of vocal delivery more precisely, it concentrates on the problems connected with performing Shakespeare in the twentieth century, where trends and styles have replaced each other in rapid succession – all of which have been a far cry from Hamlet's advice to his players, 'suit the action to the word and the word to the action, with this special observance, that you o'erstep not the modesty of nature' (*Hamlet* III. ii).

Contemporary theatrical reviews of Shakespeare productions suggest that actors of today have lost the art of speaking verse; describing how they alternate between, on the one hand, wildly emoting without showing any respect for the poetry in the text in productions based on equally far-fetched 'readings', or how they mumble and internalize their stage speech in a manner more suited to the intimacy of the living-room and the demands of the TV screen. Certainly Hamlet's advice seems a dim echo from a past which has no place in the contemporary theatre, which is terrified of being deadly, aspires to being holy, tampers with therapy and is dedicated at all costs to being visual. This book attempts to show the factors which most probably have contributed to this diversity of vocal delivery styles in the modern theatre, where directives have come from a very wide field, and actors have been encouraged to do everything but suit the action to the words and the words to the action.

Is it true that actors have simply lost the 'art of speech', or is this the point of view held by a few traditionalists, who prefer a theatre which resembles spoken literature to a living art form? There is no doubt that the modern theatre is one where the visual has steadily assumed dominance over the audial. Perhaps one of the most significant changes has been in the role of the text. In the modern theatre, the 'performance' text has come to replace the 'dramatic' text, where the words of the playwright are only one of the 'signs' in the performance matrix, which includes costumes and scenography, lighting and sound, proxemics and kinesics. As a result, actors no longer have to carry out the instructions of the text and stage directions in order to produce a performance. Rather, trends would seem to indicate that the most outstanding productions in the modern theatre have been those which have completely gone against the playwright's instructions and created a completely different speech-act context. The part which the director has played cannot be underestimated, as his reading of the dramatic text has been the one which the actors have somehow tried to make their own.

However, in the past, before the director assumed such importance, the discipline of rhetoric dictated the principles upon which vocal delivery in the theatre is based. Here one finds that there were certain rules which determined how the actor should organize an appropriate vocal delivery – in terms of both suiting his delivery to the subject-matter and type of text, and organizing his movements and gestures. This demanded a carefully balanced treatment of voice, text and emotion. Nevertheless, changes in this balance began to appear through the ages, as actors experimented with the art of acting and declamation.

Many factors have replaced rhetoric in the twentieth century. Advertising and propaganda are typical of the new rhetoric of this century and have had a lasting effect on vocal delivery. On the one hand, external appearances and values have increasingly assumed importance, whereas on the other, one has come to mistrust the 'word' as bearing false truths. Developments in literary criticism and the emergence of structuralism have played a major role in the approach to poetics and speaking verse in the theatre. Theatrical language has also undergone radical changes over a very short space of time, as it has explored new ways of writing – ranging from naturalism through absurdism to the non-verbal utterances of the contemporary theatre. Of equal importance has been the growth of a more scientific approach to the training of the voice, which in turn has been significant for vocal delivery practices. A panorama of Hamlets illustrates the changes in style of vocal delivery which are characteristic of the modern theatre.

The ideologies of the following theatre theoreticians of the twentieth century: Stanislavski, Brecht, Artaud, the Roy Hart Theatre, Grotowski and Brook, have had a seminal influence on acting and vocal delivery style. Although their teachings have suggested widely diversified approaches, they have influenced the way actors have approached their vocal delivery in terms of voice/text/emotion and gesture/movement at different times throughout the rise of the modern theatre. A closer examination of a number of their theatre productions illustrates how these approaches have contributed to the emergence of different vocal delivery styles and the effect which they have had on the audience.

Chapters 4 and 5 are devoted to the director and his visions. Chapter 4 explores a number of major productions of Shakespeare, where the text and discursive speech still play an important part, although the role of language in the performance matrix is different in the hands of Bergman, Mnouchkine and Stein. Of particular interest are the diversified vocal delivery styles and the relationship they bear to style of acting in the Shakespeare productions of each of these three contemporary theatre directors.

In chapter 5 the non-verbal theatre productions of four directors, Chaikin, Schechner, Foreman and Wilson, are examined. Here the trends of the postmodern theatre are revealed, where the text has been 'deconstructed'. Initially through explorations with sound/movement and audience participation and later with visual experimentation and fragmented non-discursive vocal deliveries, the contemporary theatre has been demonstrating a rejection of the spoken word for modern-day communication.

How do acting schools cope with the problem of equating a programme of vocal delivery training with such a diversified theatre? In the last chapter, a number of English acting schools are examined in order to see how the subjects included in their curricula are related to ideology and what significance this has for voice/speech training. International comparisons are made with the practices of other acting schools, and contemporary voice-training approaches are explored in order to see whether these trends have a wider significance for the theatrical situation at large. Seen against the major changes in the Shakespearean ideal of the modern theatre in England, these pedagogical explorations are particularly revealing – partly by offering explanations for such a diversity of vocal delivery styles and partly by indicating the necessary link which actor training should have with the emergence of new trends in the theatre.

This book is the result of a long period of enquiry and study, of teaching and directing, of searching for answers to the question of textual interpretation and vocal delivery style in the theatre. Whereas it is undoubtedly true that actions speak louder than words, and that silence is golden, perhaps it is time to realize that in the beginning was the word, before we revert to the grunts and groans which satisfied the communicative needs of our ancestral forefathers.

FOREWORD

Cicely Berry

I was very pleased to be asked to write the Foreword to this book, for I believe it provides a much-needed overview of the place and the use of voice and diction in the theatre. I also believe it has particular contemporary relevance and will hopefully make us question our own attitudes to dramatic texts.

It is relevant now because so much of the actor's work has necessarily to be in television and film, both of which require a naturalness of speech – the more 'everyday' it sounds the better: yet when asked to do some classical work in the theatre, actors find themselves strangely unprepared. And I think it is not only the actor who is put off balance in this way, the audience too is not sure of what they should expect, or indeed of what they want to hear. The attitude of many people to Shakespeare, for instance, is ambivalent: they want it to sound like Shakespeare but they also want it to sound like everyday speech – they want both rhetoric and simplicity. So the actor has to find a way of allowing the language to seem naturalistic, while at the same time honouring the rhythm and imagery which are so much more extravagant than in modern texts. It is, I think, a continual balancing act.

By giving us this very clear picture of the styles of writing from Greek tragedy to the present day, and by an outline of how these demands were met at different periods, Jacqueline Martin reminds us that our own dilemmas are not unique. She also deepens our enquiry into the style and form of language, and makes us realize that everything which is spoken in the theatre must find its own style: this is integral to the meaning. I think the section on rhetoric is particularly important.

In a book which covers so much ground, it is not possible to go into each theatre movement in great detail, but it should serve to awaken our curiosity, and most particularly to open our minds to European theatre, and to imaginative and alternative approaches to sound and language. Nor, I think, is it possible to write with total accuracy about drama schools: they change quite radically as the teachers change, and it is therefore almost impossible to pinpoint their philosophy of voice at any given time. For instance, my own experience at the Central School in the forties under Gwynneth Thurburn was a very rich one: it was Gwynneth who informed all my teaching in later life; she was a teacher of very rare breadth and humanity, who was influential in setting up a whole area of voice training which was to become the root of much of the voice work which is done now. Also teaching in the thirties and forties was Clifford Turner, who made a vital contribution to the theatre of his time. The importance of theatre schools is something that will, I hope, be explored fully in other books.

This book is of great value not only to students of the theatre, but also to theatre practitioners – actors and directors. It should help them to define the position of heightened language in the theatre, and to develop a clear attitude to the continual tension between form and content. It gives interesting insights into the structure of poetry, and I believe it makes an important contribution to our perception of voice in modern theatre.

1

VOCAL DELIVERY IN HISTORICAL PERSPECTIVE

In order to examine the principles which have guided the way actors have spoken on stage from the time of ancient Greece to the nineteenth century, one must first look closely at rhetoric. This is a practical art based on concrete advice and rules together with a general theory about what really happens in the process of speech and how people react generally to different means of expression, intellectually, aesthetically and emotionally. According to classical rhetoric, there are five major parts: *inventio*, *dispositio*, *elocutio*, *memoria* and *actio/pronunciato*. After analysing his subject and organizing his argument (*inventio*), then arranging it according to certain principles (*dispositio*), the speaker was then required to find a suitable verbal form (*elocutio*) as well as commit it to memory (*memoria*). Finally he was to present it to an audience so that it had maximum effect (*actio/pronunciato*). The most disputed through the ages has been *elocutio*, or finding a suitable verbal form for one's argument, as the speaker has been increasingly tempted to use ornate style in order to reveal his personality to the listener.

It is not difficult to understand why rhetoric and the art of oratory reached such a high standard in ancient Greece. As reading and writing were difficult and unnatural, Greek society relied on oral expression. Consequently, rhetoric played a central role in ancient education, where, after basic training in reading, writing, arithmetic, music and gymnastics, boys were sent to the school of the rhetorician at the age of fourteen for theoretical instruction in public speaking and for practical exercises. It was the sign of intelligence aimed at producing clarity, vigour and beauty in a society where it was generally accepted that speech was a sign of wisdom.[1]

The principles of effective speech on stage can be said to have originated around 400 BC with Aristotle, whose *Poetics* and *Rhetoric* laid the foundations for defining the form and functions of tragedy in the theatre. His definition of rhetoric as 'that faculty by which we understand what will serve our turn concerning any subject to win belief in the hearer',[2] was of prime importance, not only for oratory in the Greek civilization, but later in contemplating the whole process of the effectiveness of speech on the audience in future civilizations. Aristotle deduced that this process of 'belief' was attained by projecting suitable 'passions' or emotion, and demonstrated that he was aware of the problems involved in attempting to persuade an audience by an overdone *elocutio*, when he recommended that the choice of words and government of voice and rhythms should suit each other.[3] In other words, that the content in its context was the best guide to the form or manner of speaking. An appropriate vocal delivery for an actor stemmed from rhetoric's *actio*, which demanded that voice, facial expression, gestures and posture should be in harmony with the text and lift out its content and character.

Rhetoric's influence and the well-made voice were seen in many aspects of acting in ancient Greece, partly because of the enormity of the open-air theatres and the critical nature of the audiences and partly because of the poetic and operatic nature of the Greek tragedies, which demanded that the actor be able to recite as well as sing. The basic elements of rhetoric were present in the way the chorus used gesture and moved from place to place, and in the beauty of tone and adaptability to the personality or mood of the character presented. Consequently, balancing the visual and the auditive rhetoric was a determining factor for the style of vocal delivery in the pre-Aeschylean drama, where use of hands for 'dancing a story' was of primary importance and these gestures were intimately associated with the words and rhythm in the same way as the musical accompaniment was. All of this was to ensure that the words would be heard throughout the vast theatres.

Actors did not attempt to reproduce the attributes of age or sex so much as to project the appropriate emotional tone. Brockett maintains that they were judged above all else for beauty of vocal tone and the ability to adapt manner of speaking to mood and character.[4] Although the style of acting was highly exaggerated, the actor followed Aristotle's directive to speak his lines with a suitable 'passion'. With the incentive of prizes being given for recitative, actors trained carefully, even dieting and fasting, in order to keep their vocal instruments trained. Further evidence of the important link between rhetoric and theatrical delivery can be witnessed in the way the orator Demosthenes trained by using actors' voice-production methods and by the teachings of the grammarian Pollux, who showed how actors studied enunciation, rhythm and timing.

During the Roman Empire, the art of eloquence declined along with morality. Although orators were told that rhetoric could civilize the barbarous, Kennedy notes that obsession with making money and living for pleasure contributed to a degeneration in the discipline necessary for the arts or sciences or eloquence.[5] Part of this degeneration was accredited to Cicero, who in his *De Oratore* (AD 54) outlined theories of rhetoric, where the orator was 'to win the audience's sympathies, prove what is true and stir their emotions to the desired action', particularly through the use of humour which, he maintained, 'secures good will for him for whom it is aroused'.[6] On the question of delivery and use of emotion, Cicero's teachings advocated an elaborate, ornate and impressive style, where rhetoric was to be regarded as an art of expression and not an art of persuasion only.

The greatest influence on oratory during the Roman Empire is attributed to Quintilian (AD 35–97), who became the first professor of rhetoric, and was appointed by the government in order to rectify the state of oratory in the schools. In his earlier works, he attempted to counteract the declamatory style which had flourished throughout the first century with Seneca, where bizarre subjects, swollen style and unrealistic conventions were the order of the day. In his twelve books dedicated to the theory of ancient rhetoric, *De Institutione Oratoria*, Quintilian reviewed the concept of rhetorical theory and devised a programme for the education of the orator from the cradle to retirement. He is most remembered for his views on the goodness of the child's moral behaviour as being a prerequisite to good oratory.[7] This was later extended to include the teacher of rhetoric, and was an attempt to pacify the philosophers, who feared the powers of the orator and the influence he had on his public. This was the origin of the struggle between rhetoric and logic which was to continue through the centuries. The principles which Quintilian outlined are significant in the evolution of vocal delivery:

All delivery is concerned with two different things, namely voice and gesture, by which the one appeals to the eye and the other to the ear, the two senses by which all emotion reaches the soul. But the voice has the first claim on our attention since even the gesture is adapted to suit it.[8]

On the question of good delivery and appropriate delivery, Quintilian stressed the importance of using variety, but not to the neglect of adapting the voice to suit the nature of the various subjects and the moods that they demanded. He specified a difference between true emotion on the one hand, and false and fictitious emotion on the other, and suggested acting the emotions in order to attain vocal verisimilitude:

> The main thing is to excite the appropriate feeling in oneself, to form a mental picture of the facts and to exhibit an emotion that cannot be distinguished from the truth . . . the voice is the index of the mind and is capable of expressing all its varieties of feeling.[9]

Roman teachers of oratory, including Quintilian, suggested actors as suitable models for imitation, not only for vocal clarity, but for grace of delivery. Many Roman actors received extensive technical training on the angle of the head, placement of the feet, use of the hands and vocal intonations appropriate to each emotion and type of situation. This was important as the theatres were very large, sometimes seating as many as 14,000 persons, which meant, according to Brockett, that the actor's movement, gesture and vocal prowess were probably also considerably enlarged.[10] The Roman actor declaimed to the audience with musical accompaniment and wore masks. His art lay not in naturalistically depicting people from real life, but in clear utterance, conveying the appropriate emotion supported by the appropriate gesture. He was also expected to be able to sing and dance well.

The metrical intricacies of the Roman drama, especially the wildly popular farcical comedies of Plautus, provided the Roman actor with ample opportunity for practising his skills. However, Roman audiences were interested in impressive staging, violent utterance and action, preferring pantomimes, chariot racing, gladiatorial contests, *venationes* (wild-animal fights) and the spectacular sea battles or *naumachiae*.

After the collapse of orderly civic life in Rome, rhetoric almost died with it. The coming of Christianity brought with it both a wariness of the artistry of rhetoric, in that it could deceive, and at the same time an awareness of the power of rhetoric in Christian preaching. One of its greatest exponents was the prolific Augustine, who in his *De Doctrina Christiana*, considered that the three duties of the orator were to teach, to delight and to move, but asserted that the chief function of Christian eloquence was to convert belief into works and to impel the faithful to the Christian life.[11] This was taken up by the monastic schools in the mid-sixth century and led eventually to the establishment of the French and English cathedral schools in the eleventh and twelfth centuries.

The thirteenth century was something of a low point for classical rhetoric in many parts of Europe despite the recovery of Aristotle's *Rhetoric* in Latin at that time, whereas the fourteenth century saw a renewed study of Cicero, not only in the Italian cities, but in France and England. For most English readers, the poems of Chaucer were the finest application of rhetoric in this period. The survival of the great models of Greek literature can be attributed to George Trebizond, who arrived in Italy in 1416 bringing the works of Byzantine author Hermogenes to the west. His *Rhetoric in Five Books* became the first rhetorical treatise of the Renaissance. When Constantinople fell in 1453, Byzantine scholars fled to the west taking with them the scripts on which our texts of the Greek plays are based. The Byzantine Empire, with its odd mixture of Christianity and proud Greek heritage, supported a widely diversified theatre – popular (resembling those of late Rome), religious and scholarly, according to Erbe, who maintains that there is even room to speculate over the influence which Byzantine religious drama may have had on western religious drama, and at what time that occurred.[12]

By the early Middle Ages, wandering performers were in evidence in Southern Europe as the church had issued edicts against them. In its attempts to convert Western Europe to Christianity, the church played an important role in the development of the theatre, displacing pagan festivals with Christian rites of a more elaborate nature centring around the mass. This was significant for vocal delivery.

Up to the year 1200, religious drama was performed exclusively within churches, with France and Germany being most prolific. The vocal delivery consisted mostly of chanting. These practices changed during the late Middle Ages, when the emergence of nations encouraged a transition from liturgical to vernacular language, and short plays were put together which were acted outdoors by laymen. These vernacular plays had spoken rather than chanted dialogue and encouraged non-clerical rather than clerical actors. English religious cycles date from 1375 and were performed until the middle of the sixteenth century. French cycles of a much greater number were performed in the vernacular and this strand of drama was strong also in Germany, according to Young.[13]

The style was mostly episodic, combining stylization and realism and depicting broadly humorous incidents written in verse with schematized action and minimal characterization. With the introduction of the guild system the productions became more elaborate and costly; however, it appears that in acting, 'voice' seems to have been valued above all else, with no skilled characterization, and by the beginning of the sixteenth century, a number of skilled actors were employed as coaches. Frank describes how the use of repetitive phrases in the enacting of the medieval French drama was designed to aid memory, underscore humorous lines and awaken recognition in the audience, whereas in the serious plays, these running words could be used as drum beats to heighten emotion.[14] On the question of emotion, the medieval rhetorician's concern for logic and grammar can be seen as an attempt to combat the practice of swaying a public rather than discovering truth. This dual interpretation of an appropriate manner of speaking continued into the Renaissance, concerning 'whether the orator should conceal all forms of artificiality and make his speech seem the natural expression of emotion or whether he should speak in a distinguished and elegant way, favouring a deliberate use of language which set the speaker and the speech apart from and above the norms of simple communication'.[15]

There is much reason to believe that the Elizabethan actor, following the principles of rhetoric, chose the latter. This is explained by the fact that in the sixteenth century full-scale rhetorics were found for the first time in the vernacular languages. Cicero's works and the complete works of Quintilian were among the earliest works to be printed on the printing press when it was invented, and were to have a lasting impression on education by rivalling grammar and dialectic, which had been so dominant in the Middle Ages. Further, Joseph ascertained that there was a very close connection between rhetorical delivery and stage playing in the Renaissance, maintaining that one only needed to see what was taught to the Renaissance orator in order to determine what was done by the actor on the Elizabethan stage.[16] Voices were trained for declamation and for health, *actio* had a revival and actors were expected to be able to follow a clear channel from the ideas in the author's head to their manifestation in minutely correspondent details of voice and gesture.[17] This was to be mastered by combining a thorough understanding of *sententia* (grammar, punctuation and phrasing) with what Heywood describes as an ability to 'fit his phrases to his action and his action to his phrases and his pronunciation to them both'.[18] John Bulwer's system of manual rhetoric, *Chirologia . . . Chironomia* (1644), greatly facilitated this practice, and Elizabethan audiences were able to experience the words in the theatre in the manner that literature was experienced from the printed page.

Elizabethan acting was designed to express the spirit through the physical medium of the body. The tragic actor could bring the author's character to life with a vivid grandeur of spirit and truthful intensity of emotion, and the Elizabethan audiences, well-schooled from an early age in the intricacies of rhetorical delivery, including manual rhetoric, appreciated these nuances in the text – even the groundlings could understand the difficult language by this use of gesture.[19] Actors were expected to behave in the Elizabethan theatre with a sensitivity to rank in terms of speech, gesture and behaviour. The countenance and the eye, together with the use of fingers, hand and arm, were the most important features of gesture.

In France in the 1600s, Corneille prescribed rhetoric's rules for *actio* as the ideal for his actors, and later books on the subject began to appear in French. In his *Traité de l'action de l'orateur* (1657) Le Faucheur emphasized a 'natural' action as the classical tragedians had, which meant tuning in to a text and truthfully repeating it, unaffectedly, but with the technical ability and personal inner life in the affects. Towards this end, the voice was the main instrument, facial expression increased tone, the right hand supported the rhythm, the left hand gave life to the undertext and the body was a resonating chamber. The result was a kind of recitative, closer to song than speech.

During the 1700s in England and France, Cibber reveals how some actors started to reject the declamatory style, when, in attempting to gain more truthful characterizations in performing tragedy, they began to break with the practice of following the rhythm of the verse and using the beautifully modulated voice, and to focus on more personal attributes.[20] Many books began to appear at this time which treated acting as separate from the art of oratory.[21]

French acting styles in the 1700s had a widespread influence on the English theatre, which was made manifest in the Age of Betterton (1635–1710) in what is known as the Restoration Period. This had witnessed vocal pyrotechnics and audiences had been conquered by sheer vocal quality, irrespective of the real needs of the lines. Actors had a special way of sounding their words, and novices had to learn how to handle the full musical cadence of their speaking voices. Similarly, strict rules applied to the use of gesture, as in France.

Macklin broke with the heavy declamatory tradition of Betterton, Booth and Quin. In his training of young actors at Drury Lane in 1740, he encouraged his pupils to speak their texts as they would in common life if they had occasion to use the same words, then to give them more force. He advocated a combination of feeling and elocution. These efforts were supported by John Hill's *The Actor: A Treatise on the Art of Playing* (1750) which was a translation of Pierre Rémond de Sainte-Albine's *Le Comédien* (1747), and which finally broke with the schematized rules for voice and gesture by focusing on the personality attributes of the actors – understanding, sensibility and fire.

The new acting style is now attributed to Macklin's pupil, David Garrick (1717–79), who appeared to his contemporaries as a natural actor, although not 'naturalistic' in the modern concept of the word, as Cibber's description bears witness:

> his over-fondness for extravagant Attitudes, frequently affected Starts, convulsive Twitchings, Jerkings of the Body, Sprawling of the Fingers, flapping of the Breast and Pockets: – A Set of mechanical Motions in constant Use – the Caricatures of Gesture, suggested by pert Vivacity, – his pantomimical Manner of acting, every Word in a Sentence, his Unnatural Pauses in the middle of a Sentence; his forc'd Conceits; – his wilful Neglect of Harmony, even where the round Period of a well express'd Noble Sentiment demands a graceful Cadence in the delivery.[22]

However, the effectiveness of his acting style (being able to change swiftly from one passion to another) and realistic use of the voice (at the end of the breath) had a lasting impression on his audiences and was a causative factor in Diderot's treatise on the art of acting with 'cool head and warm heart' in *Paradoxe sur le comédien* (1773).

By 1750, the strict conventions of gesture and declamation were broken in France and England, where more historical accuracy in costuming and staging was supported by more realism in acting styles, which included attempts to portray everyday feelings, by means other than a relentless grandeur of sound. A more conversational style was apparent in France as demonstrated by Mlle Dumesnil, Mlle Clairon and M. Lekain, who did much to revolutionize acting and bring more realism to the stage. The styles of acting which many individual actors demonstrated at this time can be seen, from the semiotic point of view, as the result of 'ostending' one particular aspect of rhetoric's *actio* more than others.[23]

This struggle of styles continued to the end of the 1800s, when, on the one hand, elocution in the classical mould advocated strict adherence to the verse metre, orchestrated vocal delivery, careful enunciation and attitudes derived by imitation of models. In direct contrast, the romantic ideal combined strong inner emotions, expressive face and varied tones, lack of clarity in diction, infrequent use of verse and over-use of gesticulation.

With the advent of naturalism in the theatre, a general deterioration in elocution was the result, and the attitude to speaking blank verse by strictly following the metre gave way to regarding it as prose.[24] A declining interest in the Elocutionary Movement and an increasing number of scientific experiments in speech and acting towards the end of the 1800s were responsible for elocution coming to be regarded as a science rather than an art. In Italy, Antonio Morrocchesi's experiments in the art of declaiming (1832) led him to believe that there was a suitable mimed action corresponding to every word. Later, in France, François Delsarte developed a System of Oratory (1884) which, in an effort to analyse human emotions and spiritual states and determine how they were outwardly expressed, subdivided the body and outlined rules for using each part.[25] His system, which is strongly reminiscent of manual rhetoric, is based on rhetorical principles, but unlike the classical ideal from antiquity, it relegated language to the weakest position, following thought and gesture. This system was to dominate actor training in Europe and America in the late nineteenth and early twentieth centuries.

A number of textbooks on the art of reading aloud appeared towards the end of the century, many designed for educating the young. Speech (language) study was closely associated with performances in a superior, heavy diction, which was correct and tasteful and differed enormously from general daily speech. This diction, easily recognized by its broad range and resonant tone, was cultivated even further by the declamation devotees. Actors most of all established this style owing to the size of the theatres, and it is easy to understand why many of the principles of modern voice production, such as controlled expiration and a preference for loudness, were founded at this time. Until the advent of naturalism, 'stage speech' persisted throughout the 1800s.

The influence which rhetoric has had on acting has shown itself to be significant ever since it was first established as a discipline for oratory in the early Greek civilization. Its rules determined how the actor should organize his gestures and how these were to be co-ordinated with the form of vocal delivery and the type of text used. Since then, the course of history has revealed that when practices in vocal usage, or the manner of speaking, became separate from the text, or speech content, this had an effect on the style of vocal delivery. In a similar way, the treatment of the emotional content, which the rhetoricians had consistently referred to, significantly influenced acting style. These changes in the manner of speaking can be seen as the result of foregrounding voice, text or emotion, which up to the middle of the nineteenth century had been guided by the principles of rhetoric. Since the last book on rhetoric as a separate work appeared in 1828 and trends towards realism became more obvious after 1850, when the existence of the fourth wall in the theatre was questioned, rhetoric lost its position as the major influence on vocal delivery style. In order to see what has replaced it in the modern theatre, a wide range of possible influences needs to be examined.

2

VOCAL DELIVERY IN THE TWENTIETH CENTURY

Many factors have contributed to the changing balance between voice, text and emotion in vocal delivery in the modern theatre. In the twentieth century an increasing number of voices have been raised advocating a 'new rhetoric' which would be more in line with the demands of modern-day living and modern-day philosophy. A growing awareness about the world as a series of signs and structures has given rise to a more analytical approach to the interpretation of language and literature, which has made the need for a 'new poetics' more obvious and this has consequently affected the performance of verse plays in the theatre. The language of the theatre has been undergoing major changes, while advancements in research into the nature and function of the human voice have altered the previously held attitude to vocal delivery from that of an art to a science, and this has in turn changed voice-training practices.

THE CALL FOR A 'NEW RHETORIC'

That aspect of the rhetorical tradition which has most come into dispute in the twentieth century has been *persuasio* – persuading or moving an audience. Rhetoric is essentially a social phenomenon, which has been in evidence since the time of antiquity and which has undergone changes as the intellectual and social environment has changed. Barthes maintains that in the middle classes, the art of speaking according to certain rules is a sign of social power whose value depends upon its immediate usefulness.[1] Even the

11

understanding of the rhetorical codes of literature is closely associated with social status, as was exemplified in the classical era of antiquity, when people would go to the teacher of rhetoric to learn how to decipher its codes. Twentieth-century rhetoricians have different views when explaining rhetoric's position in society. In his *Philosophy of Rhetoric* (1936) I. A. Richards suggests that instead of concerning themselves with the problems of persuasion, theoreticians should concentrate upon the causes of and remedies for misunderstanding, whereas Burke, in his *Rhetoric of Motives* (1950), views rhetoric as an instrument for literary analysis and social criticism. Many have been the attempts to keep rhetoric abreast of current needs by responding to changing psychological, logical and aesthetic doctrines and to answer each new generation's demands upon public discourse. If the function of rhetoric is, as Bryant suggests, 'adjusting ideas to people and people to ideas',[2] then one readily understands the negative reaction to rhetoric when the speaker falsifies ideas or tries to change people in some way.

Both of these trends have been predominant in the twentieth century, where psychology has often been used to stupefy an audience by a clever manipulation of their emotions rather than their reasoning powers. This has been effectively achieved by incorporating all the nuances of style and thus has involved following the teachings of the rhetoricians, who maintained that if a thing is said in an attractive manner it is more effective than if said otherwise. Nowhere have these skills been utilized so much, or to such great effect, as by advertisers wishing to sell their products quickly and profitably, and what advertising is to commerce, propaganda is to politics. The kinship between advertising, salesmanship and established rhetoric is too important to be denied, as Bryant has observed.[3] One only has to compare textbooks in salesmanship with those in basic rhetoric to see the similarities.

In a similar way, propaganda's basic techniques can be easily recognized as rhetorical techniques gone wrong. During the 1930s, Hitler in Germany and Mussolini in Italy employed highly emotionalized oratory as a major propaganda tool for promoting Fascism and arousing their nations to war.[4] On the other hand, English statesman Winston Churchill, following the old extravagant Ciceronian mode, exercised a decisive impact upon the course of events during and immediately after the Second World War through brilliant oratory and an expansive style. Equally effective, although in a different style, was the public address demonstrated by President Franklin D. Roosevelt, who took advantage of the opportunities which the intimacy of the radio provided, in his famous 'fireside chats' during the Great Depression. Using a conversational style of speaking, he was able to explain complex problems in layman's terms to the suffering populace as if he were in their own living-rooms with them. At the same time, the size of the audiences that the politicians could reach increased to millions. At a later date, using the medium of television, President John F. Kennedy could project an image of friendliness and intimacy, quite different from the 'aesthetic distance' so carefully cultivated by old-time orators. This had disastrous results for Nixon in their television debate on 26 September 1960, where according to Johannesson, he had great difficulties in trying to persuade or convince the viewing public because 'he came tired and emaciated to the studio and refused TV make up. His dark stubble made an unfortunate impression on this medium. This was in contrast to Kennedy, whose appearance radiated peace, strength and health'.[5]

The importance which had been attributed to *actio* in classical rhetoric has undoubtedly had a revival in the twentieth century, particularly with respect to the speaker's movements, external appearance and management of his voice, although the latter to a lesser degree. Advertising and propaganda have affected rhetoric's position in society in that a greater disbelief has grown in the word as 'emotion-bearer', or in its conveying the truth, as demonstrated by silver-tongued politicians and advertising jargon.

Rhetoric appears to have lost its former position in modern general education along with grammar and logic. Contemporary education, in rejecting hard and fast methods, has resorted to an acceptance of a few basic rules of grammar, paragraphing and bibliography. Gradually rhetoric has managed to separate itself from any skills in public speaking and has confined itself to the analysis of style in written composition. Given the fact that we have come a long way from the reading public of the nineteenth century and that speaking to the eye and the ear has had a revival through the modern mass media, it would appear that modern education is not keeping abreast with the demands of modern living.

THE CALL FOR A 'NEW POETICS'

Similarly, the gap between the study of rhetoric and the study of poetry has widened. Although Aristotle outlined his theories about these subjects in different treatises, he did not, however, encourage treating them differently, as he demonstrated when he referred readers of the *Poetics* to the *Rhetoric* for analyses of persuasive elements of certain speeches. Perhaps too much has been made of Quintilian's remarks about the teachers of literature not having sufficient knowledge to teach rhetoric as well,[6] although both he and Cicero advocated the study of poetry as a necessary part of rhetorical studies. Plato condemned poetry and attacked oratory because he believed they were guilty of the same crime – of persuading by deceitful means. Nevertheless the ancients were aware of the imaginative powers of poetry and the use to which it could be employed.

The study of poetry has contented itself in the twentieth century with the study of written literature, thereby providing very little chance for a speaker to attempt to recreate the work of the poet, which could be described as forcing from words meanings which are new and unique by his vivid and effective delivery of them. The enjoyment of poetry today is an internal one, as is most of the experience of literature, and this in turn has affected the speaker's use of voice, text and emotion.

One can only agree with Culler that what is needed in the study of literature today is 'a new poetics which stands to literature as linguistics stands to language'.[7] Only then will we be able to understand the process by which the content of literary works is formulated and thereby come closer to an understanding of the theory of the practice of reading and writing.

One of the greatest influences on the analysis and performance of literature has come from the change in the nature of perception, which began to take definite shape in the early years of the twentieth century and which bears the name 'structuralism'. According to this concept, the true nature of things lies not in the things themselves, but in the relationships which we construct and then perceive between them. The following ideas are fundamental to this way of thinking, according to Piaget: the idea of wholeness, the idea of transformation and the idea of self-regulation.[8]

Many of the concepts of structuralism were established with the

14

new studies of language (linguistics) and with the study of modern man (anthropology). It was through early attempts at structural analysis (1906–11) that Swiss linguist Ferdinand de Saussure distinguished between *langue* and *parole*. His major contribution was that the linguistic sign, upon which language is based, can be characterized in terms of the relationship which exists between its dual aspects of 'concept' (signified – *signifié*) and 'sound image' (signifier – *signifiant*).[9]

In order to follow structuralism's development and finally see its application in the theatre, particularly where vocal delivery is concerned, it is necessary to examine in more detail the contribution made by the following movements: Russian formalism, Czech structuralism and semiotics.

Russian formalism

The name itself was originally applied to a school of literary criticism which flourished around the time of the First World War and comprised both linguists and literature historians. Its two major centres were Moscow, where the Moscow Linguistic Circle was founded in 1915, and Petrograd, where in 1916 the Petrograd Society for the Study of Poetic Language was founded.

Early formalism built on the groundwork of the symbolists and their interest in form as an autonomous instrument of communication, which by extra-verbal, rhythmic, associative and connotative means could stretch language beyond its ordinary range of meaning. However, it fought against symbolism to free poetics, declared its way of working a 'morphological approach', and concerned itself with specifying how literary language functioned compared with ordinary language. In Hawkes's view, the Russian formalists shared a lot in common with the 'structural' linguists and 'structural' anthropologists of the future in the way they were:

> fundamentally concerned with literary *structure*: with the recognition, isolation and objective description of the peculiarly literary nature and use of certain 'phonemic' *devices* in the literary work, and not with the work's 'phonetic' content, its 'message', its 'sources', its 'history' or with its sociological, biographical or psychological dimensions.[10]

The self-determining and autonomous nature of art, according to the formalists, rendered the poem autonomous – its distinguishing features were to be found in the poem itself and not the poet, in the distinctive use of language involved and not in the subject of the poem, as had been the usual practice of positivism.

Figurative language (metaphors, symbols and so on) were only interesting to the formalists in the use to which they were put. Shklovsky assigned all the literary devices to one central use: that of 'making strange' (*ostranenie*). This led the formalists to conclude that the aim of poetry was to defamiliarize – to creatively deform the usual, the normal – to disrupt stock responses, to generate a heightened awareness: to restructure the ordinary perception of reality so that one ended up 'seeing' the world instead of numbly 'recognizing' it: so that one ended up designing a 'new' reality to replace the one that had become customary.

Russian formalism can be seen as pre-dating the Brechtian concept of 'alienation' (*Verfremdung*) whereby the object of art is seen to be the revolutionary goal of making the audience aware that the institutions and social formulae which they inherit are not eternal and 'natural' but historical and man-made, and so capable of change through human action. Defamiliarization is therefore the central preoccupation of formalism, as many of the most valuable formalist analyses of literature consist of giving an account of the means whereby and conditions in which *ostranenie* takes place. According to Hawkes they do this by examining the 'literariness' of the work produced through an analysis of the various devices or techniques which act as the agencies of this 'literariness'.[11]

In 1914 Shklovsky advocated for the first time the idea of form as an important element of artistic perception when he wrote:

> when they (words) are used in everyday speech and are not completely enunciated or completely heard, then they have become familiar, and their internal (image) and external (sound) forms have ceased to be sensed. We do not sense the familiar, we do not see it, but recognize it. We do not see the walls of our rooms, it is so hard for us to spot a misprint in a proof – particularly if it is written in a language well-known to us – because we cannot make ourselves see and read through, and we do not 'recognize' the familiar word. If we should wish to make a definition of 'poetic' and 'artistic' perception in general, then doubtless we would hit upon the

16

definition: 'artistic' perception is perception in which form is sensed (perhaps not only form, but form as an essential part).[12]

Shklovsky was influenced by futurist poetry in the way it used general linguistic thought-processes as poetic devices. This process of 'seeing an object' rather than simply 'recognizing' it was important to his idea of art as a whole, which he believed was a way of experiencing the artfulness of an object rather than the object itself. Further, he maintained that when this applied to poetic language, which is in essence deliberately self-conscious, self-aware and tends to emphasize itself as a 'medium' over and above the 'message' it contains, then the words in poetry achieve a position, not only as thought-bearers, but as objects in their own right. This, in Saussure's terms, means they change from being 'signifiers' to becoming 'signifieds' and it is the poem's alienating devices of rhythm, rhyme, metre and so on, which enable this structural change to be achieved.

Roman Jakobson supported this attitude to verbal art in his own formalistic linguistic theory:

The distinctive feature of poetry lies in the fact that a word is perceived as a word and not merely a proxy for the denoted object or an outburst of an emotion, that words and their arrangement, their meaning, their outward and inward form acquire weight and value of their own.[13]

Later formalist theory realized, however, that the 'meaning' habitually carried by words can never fully be separated from the words themselves, because no word has one 'simple' meaning. In this way poetry does not separate a word from its meaning so much as multiply the range of available meanings. A 'poetic' use of a word makes ambiguity a notable feature of its performance and it is that which alters its structural role from that of 'signifier' to that of 'signified'. When the devices of versification are also considered, they contribute to the range of available meanings. In the end the poem 'is' its devices, it 'is' its form.

Roman Jakobson extended further this theory of the multiplicity of possible meanings in his paper 'What is Poetry?' first published in 1935, when he extended the understanding of the literary system to include the overall system of social values. His work can be seen

17

as a link between the early formalist interest in the functions of language and later structuralist theories.

Although the concept of defamiliarization was not applied directly to theatre theory by the formalists, its importance is still felt today in attempting to analyse avant-garde performances. When a performance is conceived along the lines of perception, as later postmodern productions have increasingly demonstrated, with their interest in visual signs and other aspects of the performance code by which the audience is invited to 'see what is there' rather than simply to 'recognize' old forms, then the ability to be able to recognize these specific artistic devices and intentions is necessary for being able to appreciate the work and begin to understand its purpose.

Czech structuralism

Between 1928 and 1949 in Czechoslovakia, a prolific group of linguists and theoreticians of literature, theatre and music, known as the Prague School, worked out the first systematic structuralist–semiotic approach to the study of art. In 1928, the group published a collection of 'theses' which drew on Russian formalism and the structural linguistics of Ferdinand de Saussure and laid the foundations for a semiotic study of art. Concentrating primarily on the problems of poetry and literature, the structuralists gradually expanded their interest to include theatre, film, visual arts and music, as well as the problems of general theory and aesthetics.

The Prague linguists who were particularly interested in the analysis of the theatre drew heavily on the first major Czech work on theatre theory, *The Aesthetics of Dramatic Art* (1931) by Otakar Zich (1879–1934). Although Zich was not in fact a member of the structuralist school, his concerns overlapped theirs in a number of important ways. He rejected the fusion of Wagner's *Gesamtkunstwerk* to consider the mutual interaction of various elements in dramatic art and came very close to the Saussurean 'signifier' and 'signified' in his distinction between the material or physical (auditive and visual) elements and the imaginary or conceptual elements of plot.

In the key essay, 'Art as Semiotic Fact' (1934), Jan Mukarovsky (1891–1975) insists upon the elucidation of the 'semiotic' character of art as essential to the understanding of its function. Taking the sign as 'a reality perceivable by sense perception that has a relationship with another reality which the first reality is meant to evoke', Mukarovsky considers the nature of this second reality when the sign is an artistic one. Following Saussure's signifier/signified theory, Mukarovsky observes that certain of the arts, especially the so-called 'representational' ones, might use signifiers in an 'informational' way, but that all signs in art are primarily 'autonomous'. Rather than being restricted to a signified with a specific 'existential value', they refer to 'the total content of social phenomena' of any given milieu – 'philosophy, religion, politics, economics and so on'.[14] Mukarovsky's work on differentiating between the cognitive and expressive functions of literary language led to the principle that language is being used 'poetically' or 'aesthetically' when its expressive aspect is dominant, that is, according to Hawkes, 'when its language deviates maximally from "normal" usage, by means of devices which thrust the act of expression itself into the foreground'.[15] For Mukarovsky 'foregrounding' is crucial: 'The function of poetic language consists in the maximum of foregrounding of the utterance . . . it is not used in the services of communication, but in order to place in the foreground the act of expression, the act of speech itself.'[16]

Folklorist Petr Bogatyrev (1893–1970) was the first to trace the principles of theatrical semiosis and clarify some of the generalizations made by Zich. In his paper 'Semiotics in the Folk Theatre' (1938) and again in 'Forms and Functions of Folk Theatre' (1940) he advances his theory that 'transformation' is the central feature of the theatre, because there all aspects of material reality, including the actor, become something different – often only a 'sign of signs'. He maintains that this also applies to the actor's language, which retains all the properties of poetic language but in addition it becomes a constituent of dramatic actions, while the actor changes his voice into the voice of the character in the play. In these papers, Bogatyrev states that the speaker not only expresses the content of his thought in speech, but this is simultaneously a sign of his cultural and social status; that the dramatist and the actors use all these 'signs' for expressing the social and national status of the character – for example, using mistakes in language for fools; dialects to suggest rustic/peasant folk; prose for the common people and verse for nobility; or a high or low style of a particular language, in the same way that word order, syntax, the distribution of pauses and other verbal means are used to clarify the social status of the character.[17]

It is from Bogatyrev's 'sign of signs' system that the whole denotation/connotation, or specific/suggestive, dialectic has grown. By this is meant that in the theatre all the elements, including the scenography, costumes, lighting, sound system, actors' movements and speech, determine first-order and second-order sign relationships. Moreover, the usually dense sign system in the theatre allows it to appeal to a large and diffuse audience, since the same action may be comprehended simultaneously, but by different signs, 'by spectators of various tastes and various aesthetic standards'.[18]

In his 'Dynamics of Sign in the Theatre' (1940) Jindrich Honzl (1894–1953), director of the avant-garde Liberated Theatre in Prague, unites Zich's structuralist approach with Bogatyrev's emphasis on transformation, when he declares that everything that makes up reality on the stage stands for something else; thus the theatre is essentially a complex of signs, all easily transformable. A visual sign may change to an auditive one; an actor may take on the function of scenery, or vice versa. Honzl suggests that the essence of dramatic art be sought in the old idea of action, but with the realization that word, actor, costume, scenery and music may all advance the action as 'different conductors of a single current that either passes from one to another or flows through several at one time'.[19] The changes in this current reflect different performances, different styles and different periods. Honzl's later essay, 'The Hierarchy of Dramatic Devices' (1943), focuses on a particular kind of transformation, that of poetic reference into action not shown but imagined by the audience. He considers this device, common in classic theatre and relatively rare in realism, to be a major source of power, since theatrical perception is based upon 'an opposition between mental representation and reality' synthesized into an emotionally charged 'seeing' by the spectator's act of interpretation.[20] In this paper, Honzl asserts that history has shown that 'the supremacy of *dialogue* over *recitation* meant the supremacy of *action* over *narration* and meant turning already existing, familiar devices to a new purpose'.[21]

Jiri Veltrusky, in 'Man and Object in the Theatre' (1940), agrees with Honzl that the transformability of theatrical signs and the flexibility of the flow of action through different sign systems are central. He maintains that this flexibility makes the theatre particularly effective in a process akin to Shklovsky's defamiliarization.[22] However, he disagrees with Honzl about the transformability of the sign, where language is concerned. In 'Dramatic

Text as a Component of Theatre' (1941) Veltrusky emphasizes that the semiotics of theatre is brought about by the confrontation of two sign systems which are invariably present: language and acting. He maintains that the dramatic text is both 'theatre' and 'literature' and that theatre enters into a relation with literature as a whole.[23]

Veltrusky was well aware of the problem for an actor of balancing the form of his vocal delivery with the text. He maintains that the vocal performance is a direct translation of the sound contour of the text which exists before any theatrical performance and that this enables the text to predetermine, though in a variable degree, the stage figure in all its aspects. He therefore warns that the actor's creation can never fully escape the obligations imposed upon him by the dramatic text:

> The actor must adapt himself and mold the extralinguistic resources accordingly, so that they do not disrupt the sound dominant. In practice, this means that he must limit them as much as possible, so that they do not deflect attention, because of their striking materiality, from the subtle meanings conveyed by the movements of the dominant sound component. On the contrary, when the sound structure is dominated by a component such as voice coloring, the movements and specific shape of which are predetermined by the text only in a very general way, the actor's freedom to choose his means increases.[24]

Veltrusky also observes that there are two diametrically opposed sign systems in the theatre: the semiotics of language and the semiotics of acting. He warns that if the linguistic sign prevails, a tendency emerges to strip the sign embodied by the actor of its materiality, or at least some of it. If on the contrary the linguistic sign is outbalanced, its semantic potential diminishes. He advises that both sign systems not only check but also enrich each other.[25]

One of the most characteristic features of the Prague School was its unswerving insistence on the inseparability of the two 'polarities' in language, whether this is called *la langue/la parole*; language structure/speech; code/message. The key figure in the Prague School's efforts to systematize the aesthetic function of language was Roman Jakobson. In his 'Fundamentals of Language' (1956) Jakobson describes his notion of 'equivalence' which

21

can be based on either metaphor (where signifier and signified are imaginatively linked) or metonymy (the substitution of cause for effect or of one item for something contiguous to it). He even ventures to use this distinction as a way of determining literary style, maintaining that there was a predominance of metonymy in the literary schools of romanticism and symbolism, and metaphor in the so-called 'realistic' schools.[26]

These ideas form the basis of his definition of the 'poetic' function of language in his famous paper 'Linguistics and Poetics' (1958), where he asserts that poetry is not just an adornment of 'ordinary' language but that it represents almost the construction of a different kind of language: 'poeticalness is not a supplementation of discourse with rhetorical adornment but a total re-evaluation of the discourse and of all its components'.[27] In order to determine what makes a verbal message a work of art, Jakobson isolates six basic factors in the act of verbal communication: addresser, addressee, context, message, contact and code.[28] 'Meaning' according to Jakobson, is not simply an act which passes from sender (addresser) to receiver (addressee); one of the factors always dominates over the others, thus the communication may be orientated towards the context in one situation, or the code in another.[29]

Jakobson further proceeds to analyse the nature of verse which he considers 'is entirely within the competence of poetics'.[30] In so doing he underlines the significance of the 'figure of sound' making special note of syllabification and verse metre factors,[31] even maintaining that:

> metre – or in more explicit terms, *verse design* – underlies the structure of any single line – or, in logical terminology, any single *verse instance*. Design and instance are correlative concepts. The verse design determines the invariant features of the verse instances and sets up the limits of variations.[32]

On the question of how the verse instance is implemented in the delivery instance, Jakobson maintains that this 'depends on the *delivery design* of the speaker: he may cling to a scanning style or tend toward prose-like prosody or freely oscillate between these two poles'.[33] He is adamant that although rhyme, word-play and the overall poetic sound texture of the language are important, the sound should be balanced with the meaning. In accordance with structuralist principles, Jakobson's contribution has strengthened the position of appraising poetic language as 'self-regulating' and 'autonomous'.

Semiotics

The field of semiotics – or 'science of signs' – has been developing on both sides of the Atlantic at the same time since the Second World War. According to American C.S. Peirce, the framework for the existence of knowledge derives from the assertion of propositions through the second 'triad' of signs: *icon*, *index* and *symbol*.[34] One of the most powerful interpreters of Saussure has been Roland Barthes, who maintained that in myth, signification is attained from the relation of signifier (*form*) to signified (*concept*). When Barthes applied this to 'denotation' (the use of language to mean what it says) and 'connotation' (the use of language to mean something other than what is said), he asserted that connotation takes place when the *sign* resulting from a previous signifier/signified relationship becomes the *signifier* of a further one. More importantly, Barthes endeavoured to reinstate the socio-political status quo in the analysis of art in the theatre. Following the first appearance of the Berliner Ensemble in Paris (1954) Barthes wrote a number of articles suggesting the necessity of examining four levels in analysing the new Brechtian theatre, which Carlson summarizes as follows:

> The first is sociology, the means by which various contem-
> porary publics attempt to deal with Brecht. The second is
> ideology, not the 'message' of the plays but the general
> method of explanation. The third is semiology, especially
> interesting in Brecht because of the distance he puts between
> signifier and signified in his rejection of illusion. Finally
> comes morality, involving for Brecht analysis of a historical
> situation in the light of a belief in the potential for change.[35]

In a series of essays entitled *Sur Racine* (1960) Barthes examines the complex nature of interpretation and concludes that the would-be interpreter of Racine must be aware of the full impact of his ultimate choices including vocal delivery style, historical accuracy and so on. In the second essay, 'Dire Racine', Barthes condemns traditional delivery in which the actor, instead of simply abandoning himself to the rhythm of the alexandrine, attempts to 'sing' the lines or to 'analyse' them for the audience, losing the effect of the whole in the concern for detail. He suggests that if one wishes to experience the power of Racine, one should accept the strangeness rather than attempting to make him familiar.[36]

Barthes did not believe that writing existed which was not based on style. This prompted him to examine how texts are read and he divided the act of reading into two types, one which gives the reader a role and one which leaves him idle. As a result he divides texts into the categories 'readerly' and 'writerly'. He maintains that the former (usually classics) read themselves and perpetuate an established view of the world which is 'frozen in time' like most bourgeois values, whereas the latter involves us in an engaging way to create our world now, together with the author as we go along.[37] The work of Roland Barthes was a direct reaction against, and criticism of, the principles of New Criticism which flourished in Britain and America in the thirties and forties and which by the mid-fifties had become doctrine in the English-speaking world. Taking its impulses from T.S. Eliot, New Criticism proposed that art should be regarded as autonomous and should not be judged by references beyond the 'words on the page'.

In summary, Barthes rejected the principles of the 'innocent reader', the 'objective' text with a preordained 'content' stored within it, that reading and writing are 'natural' processes, and proposed that all critical positions and judgements masked a complex political and economic ideology.[38] The latter point, stemming from Marxist theory, sees New Criticism, with its insistence on taste and sensitivity, and with its admiration of complexity, balance, poise and tension, as characteristic of the bourgeois concern for 'fixed' and unchanging reality and one of the ideological outgrowths of capitalism.[39]

A renewed interest was shown in the system of signs in the theatre in the sixties which has concerned itself more and more with the role of language in the performance matrix. In his essay 'The Sign in the Theatre' (1968) Tadeus Kowzan isolates thirteen theatrical signs: word, tone, mime, gesture, movement, make-up, hairstyle, costume, accessory, decor, lighting, music, sound-effects. By placing the 'spoken text' first, Kowzan indicates his preference for the fable or plot as instigator for the rest of the performance, although on the whole the number of visual signs outweigh the auditive ones. Later he acknowledges the importance of space and time in the analysis of the performance, although he does not include the audience in his model.

Other voices were raised in the sixties of a different note by certain theoreticians who challenged the Saussurean assumption of language as a signifying system of primary importance for the theatre. The first of these was Jacques Derrida, who is recognized as being one of the forerunners of the 'deconstruction' movement, which rejects the practice of structuralism and semiotics in settling on stable, definite meanings and systems.

André Helbo emphasizes the importance of the 'code' over the 'message' in the theatre in 'Le Code théâtral'. However, Umberto Eco in 'Semiotics of Theatrical Performance' (1977) stresses the 'complexity and variability of the theatrical sign, depending on the theatrical context with its many possible connotations and on the varied strategies that spectators bring to the decoding of this phenomenon', according to Carlson.[40] Eco, like American Richard Schechner, looks to recent research in kinesics, proxemics and paralinguistics to help in the reading of the 'signals'. He believes that *ostension*, or 'showing', is 'the most basic instance of performance'.[41]

A voice, raised by Italian Marco de Marinis (1975), summarizes the failure of semiotics in the theatre, in particular referring to Anne Ubersfeld's *Lire le théâtre* (1977) and concludes that too much emphasis is placed on the written text and not enough on the spectacle. These misgivings are shared by Patrice Pavis in *Problèmes de sémiologie théâtrale* (1976) who later applied his theories to a performance analysis of Lewis Carroll's *The Hunting of the Snark* at the Centre Pompidou, Paris (1979).[42]

Two works which appeared at the end of the seventies reflect the real contemporary interest in the field of semiotics. The first, *L'Univers du théâtre* (1978) by Girrard *et al.*, defines theatre as a 'social place' emphasizing the complexity of 'decoding' the dramatic work, and can be seen as an indication of the trend towards giving priority to theories of communication in the analysis of performance. In *The Semiotics of Theatre and Drama* (1980) Keir Elam focuses more directly on semiotics although with special reference to speech-act theory and sees the dramatic dialogue as primarily a mode of praxis 'which sets in opposition the different personal, social and ethical forces of the dramatic world'.[43]

Perhaps deconstruction is best summed up by Anders Olsson, who in *Den okände texten* (1987) has expressed the situation as follows:

25

If 'hermeneutics' began with the meaning of the work in its interpretations then 'deconstruction' questions meaning's dominance over sound, word pictures or rhetorical effects. If hermeneutics emphasizes the text's unity and inner context, then deconstruction places its finger on cracks and openings, patterns and discrepancies. If the first will explain and make the meaning in a text clear, then the latter attempts to emphasize contradictions and ambiguity as nothing makes such clarity.[44]

Marvin Carlson has indicated the predominance hitherto of methods of dramatic analysis which have been developed for non-dramatic literary texts and emphasizes the need for a reappraisal of the theatrical event as a 'spectacle text' which employs the written text as only one element in the multicoded, multidimensional and pluralistic new textual system. He maintains that an important part of the unique power of the theatre has always derived from what he calls 'psychic polyphony', the simultaneous expression of a number of different psychic lines of action, allowing the spectator a choice of focus and a variety in the process of combination.[45]

With the emphasis now placed more upon reception theory and audience research, where the performance text replaces a literary text, and a 'theatre of energies' has precedence over a 'theatre of words', modern trends in theatre semiotics are concerned with understanding 'action'. Ascribing the failure by previous theatre semioticians to understand this process to Saussure, whose signifier/signified model never paid attention to the interpretent – the audience – contemporary theoreticians are building more on Peirce's definition of the sign, which included an audience, and are concerning themselves with attempting to analyse and understand the act of theatrical communication. As the postmodern theatre continues to move further away from the practice of using language as a means of communication either between characters or with the audience in its preference for an 'irrational' theatrical form, a crucial need has arisen for finding suitable methods for analysing the performance act.

Erika Fischer-Lichte finds similarities between the postmodern theatre and the modern theatre (in particular the Dada movement) where again 'speech' has become deconstructed.[46] She maintains that both movements reveal a disintegration of individual characters in a world where identity has become uncertain and that both indicate an indeterminacy – where fragmentation becomes the action.[47] She recommends a semiotic approach in performance analysis where the goal is 'understanding', and believes this will lead to a new perception on the part of the audience.[48] This can be seen as a welcome step towards combining semiotics with hermeneutics, while at the same time bearing in mind audience reception – a promising approach, which she has applied to her analysis of theatre performances of Shakespeare.[49]

LANGUAGE IN THE THEATRE

Together with the changes which have been made in methods of interpreting language and literature in the modern theatre, many changes have taken place in the nature of the language used. These changes very often reflect the ideology which lies behind them, such as realism, naturalism, symbolism, expressionism, surrealism, absurdism, and the epic theatre. Consequently they make special demands on the actor's vocal delivery in the way they influence the voice, text, emotion ratio. The twentieth century has also witnessed the revival of the practice of improvising the performance, where the text (if there is one) is ruthlessly cut up and the language used is often reduced to sounds. P. N. Campbell sums up the situation as follows:

> For much of the 20th century, the nonverbal aspects of theatre have been emphasized. Theorists have proclaimed the importance of the nonverbal: Brecht, Artaud, and Grotowski have all dealt in important ways with the nonverbal, and at times Artaud seemed almost to do away with language entirely. Theatre practitioners have emphasized nonverbal elements in their productions; one factor that has made this emphasis possible is the increased importance of the director, who has rivaled, if not displaced, the playwright as 'author' of the staged work. Finally, the desire of many theatre people to occupy an independent realm, to escape what they have viewed as the inferior position resulting from the concept of drama as a literary genre, has led them to deny the primacy of language and to highlight the nonverbal dimensions of theatrical works.

Since the emergence of naturalism in the theatre, the nature of dramatic language has undergone enormous changes. Initially it attempted to show people using speech on stage as in real life and to change the style of declamatory acting which had been prevalent in romantic acting. Zola, the father of naturalism, maintained 'the new dialogue should be flexible and precise and convey the tone and feeling of a character's individuality'.[51] As a result, in naturalistic plays, the artistic form came to be seen as the organic expression of its content.

The social plays of Ibsen took up the banner for more realism and a more truthful vocal delivery style from all the characters – a practice which was to influence Shaw. Ibsen himself had instructed Lindberg, who directed *Ghosts*:

> The dialogue must seem perfectly natural, and the manner of expression must differ from character to character. Many changes in the dialogue can be made during rehearsals, where one can easily hear what sounds natural and unforced, and also what needs to be revised over and over again until finally it sounds completely real and believable.[52]

Similarities are to be found in Strindberg's naturalistic tragedy *Miss Julie* (1888), where in the preface the dramatist, following Antoine's instructions for the new naturalistic theatre, explains:

> I have avoided the symmetrical, mathematically-constructed dialogue of the type favoured in France and have allowed their [the characters'] minds to work irregularly, as people's do in real life, when in conversation, no subject is fully exhausted, but one mind discovers in another a cog which it has a chance to engage. Consequently, the dialogue too, wanders, providing itself in the opening scenes with matter which is later taken up, worked upon, repeated, expanded and added to, like the theme in a musical composition.[53]

This same trend was taken up by Chekhov, who, in *Three Sisters*, depicts characters who rely on language in an attempt to communicate with each other and to find some meaning in their lives which are devoid of 'action' and purpose. At the other extreme, Pinter 'seems at pains to show characters trying to hide language almost unaware of its implications, completely aware that one can make it imply anything',[54] according to Sharp, who maintains that this is in line with the tendencies in the seventies to invoke response from an audience by moving away from verbal appeal. This trend began with Wesker, who believes that language is often incapable of expressing matters of the heart that go beyond the world of words. His characters are disillusioned by the insufficiency of the quantity of words to express the quality of emotion. Adler shows how in his trilogy Wesker 'takes the experimentation with language further – from a strictly naturalistic technique to a more poetic mode in which the action will suddenly erupt onto a higher level of symbolic reality'.[55]

This exemplifies the two different courses which language in the theatre has taken in the twentieth century, as the mounting distrust of language has given rise to the non-verbal gaining priority in creating response in an audience. The naturalist's view that dramatic speech must be exactly what the speaker would use if he were outside the theatre in the given situation, has had a strong influence on the way actors have spoken their dialogue, including verse, as though it were actual conversation. This has eliminated any attempt at using *mimesis*, or imitation, which is the foundation upon which the actor creates a character. In its place, he attempts 'to be' the character. However, the whole concept of what is 'natural' on stage has always been prone to scepticism, as each generation has given it a special meaning, dependent upon the aesthetic and cultural mores of its own time. In Styan's opinion, the manner in which to deliver such a natural dialogue is not simply to make conversation on the stage:

> A snatch of a phrase caught in everyday conversation may mean little. Used by an actor on a stage it can assume general and typical qualities. . . Dramatic speech with its basis in ordinary conversation, is speech that has a specific pressure on it. The first difference that pressure makes lies in an insistence that the words go somewhere, move towards a predetermined end. It lies in a charge of meaning that will advance the action.[56]

This 'action' is in accord with Roman Jakobson's six factors of the communicative act, which took into account the addressee as well as the emotive qualities of the addresser.

One of the most significant voices which was raised to contend the realistic approach came from the symbolists, who in the latter part of the nineteenth century maintained that deeper significance could not be represented directly, but could be evoked only through symbols, legends, myths and moods. Their chief spokesman was Maurice Maeterlinck, whose plays, produced at the Théâtre d'Art (1893–1915), set the standards for the symbolist theatre. Aiming to reach deeper realities of truth than deceptive surface appearances, they employed many theatrical devices in an attempt to find symbolic correspondences between colours and sounds. This led to multidimensional productions where, according to Innes, 'the emphasis was placed on expressive tone and pitch in speaking rather than on the sense of what was said, and the development of mime to portray psychological states in immediate, physical terms instead of describing these in dialogue'.[57]

This emphasis on the visual over the verbal marks the beginning of a trend which was to become a characteristic of the avant-garde theatre, where disbelief in the rational structures of thought is coupled with a belief that verbalizing emotion deprives it of its authenticity. Vocal delivery was often an experimentation, using singsong voice, exaggerated articulation or characters speaking past each other in overlapping monologues, while the action was located and developed on a wordless, subtextual level.

The uselessness of conversation and the deflation of language in the theatre is nowhere more characteristic than in the Theatre of the Absurd, which is essentially anti-literary. The Theatre of the Absurd realized that language had very little to do with reality, springing as it did out of a war-torn Europe, where literary theatre was regarded as analogous with the bourgeois attitudes which had given rise to the dilemma in which the world found itself. However, it was not communication which the Theatre of the Absurd considered important, only the use of logic and discursive speech. It put the language of a scene in contrast to the action by reducing it to meaningless patter and nonsense. Esslin summarizes it as follows:

> It is a theatre of situation as against a theatre of events in sequence, and therefore it uses a language based on patterns of concrete images rather than argument and discursive speech. And since it is trying to present a sense of being, it can neither investigate nor solve problems of conduct or morals.[58]

With its traces in symbolism, dada, surrealism and the principles of Antoine Artaud's Theatre of Cruelty, the non-verbal grew out of a desire to make a metaphysics out of spoken language, that is to convey what it normally does not convey – to use it in a new, exceptional and unusual way, to give it its full physical shock potential. In *The Theatre and its Double* (1938) Artaud advocated the way theatre should proceed, by breaking with the subjugation to the text and by rediscovering the idea of a kind of unique language somewhere between gesture and thought, which would work on an audience's senses.

In the Environmental Theatre movement in the late sixties, the same theories were applied to the downgrading of language in favour often of non-verbal sound. This movement was intended to criticize popular attitudes, social conditions and lifestyles. As a result all possible shock tactics, including violence and obscenity were incorporated to work on the audience in the belief, according to Beck, that 'in this way the audience would be shocked out of wanting to commit violence again'.[59] Drawing heavily from Grotowski's Poor Theatre, the playwrights and actors worked closely together, often by improvisation, to explore ideas and scenarios. A typical event from this period was Jean-Claude van Itallie's *The Serpent* (1969), which mingled events from the Bible with violence, in the way it depicted the assassinations of J.F. Kennedy and Martin Luther King, by passing from free improvised sounds to choral narration.

The last twenty years have witnessed a culmination of these trends regarding language. In the postmodern theatre, speech has no function except to show its failure as a medium of communication. Everyone plays his own 'word games' talking past each other in nonsense language in the performances of Robert Wilson, or uses text fragments, as the work of Heiner Müller and Richard Foreman demonstrates. All this fragmentation reveals an underlying feeling of helplessness and lack of contact between people – an indication of the state of the world which we have allowed to exist.

A third movement which demonstrates yet another approach to the handling of language in the theatre originated with the epic theatre. At its heart it is narrative realism, where numerous episodes around a central theme are explored by every possible means: projections, films, song, choral commentaries and narration. However, it is in the treatment of language that one can see the combination of realism, absurdism and lyricism which constitutes this style. Its chief spokesman was Bertolt Brecht, who in attempting to write for the masses – to instruct them – developed a dry language, which is at times verse and at times prose. Brecht believed that the very beauty of literature brought off the 'alienation' effect.[60] To this end, he incorporated a number of different metres, at times classical and at times free and modern, where his intention was to help underline the difference between people and force the attention of the spectators on the struggle rather than allowing them to sympathize with the characters on stage.

In conclusion, one can see that there are two distinct traditions regarding the way language has developed this century. The first favours the literary, verbal theatre, which has its roots in Aristotelian principles, where the text is the central point. The second supports an anti-literary and non-verbal theatre, and regards the text as alterable and meaningful only in its fully realized theatrical form.

SHAKESPEAREAN VERSE IN DELIVERY

As the preceding chapter indicated, one of the major problems connected with speaking verse has always been finding a way of balancing the sound level with the meaning level. On the one hand, this gave rise to the practice of declaiming, or regarding the voice as a musical instrument and the speech as a musical score. Without doubt, in Shakespeare's dramatic texts there are sufficient instances of the 'monologue' to warrant comparison with the 'aria' of opera, particularly in terms of its structure and function. However, the 'prosaic' school of performance, where the verse is treated as if it were prose, has been a frequent alternative to the former approach, and both ways have had their supporters at different times for different reasons.

Many twentieth-century performers refer to the musicality of Shakespeare's verse, even if their suggestions for methods of performing are different. G.B. Shaw advocated the singsong way: 'There must be beauty of tone, expressive inflection and an infinite variety of *nuance* to sustain the fascination of the infinite monotony of the chanting.'[61] The need to experience magic by chanting is regarded as a basic, primitive delight in the rhythms of breathing and speaking, according to Wilfred Mellers, who in discussing verse in Shakespeare's time observed: 'During the Renaissance, the word, the spoken word, the articulate and intelligible word, the communication of one individual to another became pertinent and became the very essence of song.'[62] This enjoyment in the musical utterance of verse has been seen by Burklund as follows: 'We enjoy melody because like any other rhythm it is a form of order based upon repetition. . . In the intricate blend of sound, with its repetition and contrast, its counterpoint and harmony, its magic is most pronounced.'[63] The twentieth-century practice of reading literary texts silently has eliminated the possibility of experiencing this music, which has prompted Veilleux to call for a renewed interest in *imaging*, or 'sensory-like experience', and he asks if we have become so conditioned to the symbols of language speaking to our eye without ever having to produce the sounds, that we have thereby forgotten their existence.[64]

However, suggestions have come from many sources for balancing the two levels, the sound level and the meaning level. Roman Jakobson maintained:

> How the given verse-instance is implemented in the given delivery instance depends on the *delivery design* of the reciter; he may cling to a scanning style or tend toward prose-like prosody or freely oscillate between these two poles. . . No doubt, verse is primarily a recurrent 'figure of sound.' Primarily, always, but never uniquely. Any attempts to confine such poetic conventions as meter, alliteration, or rhyme to the sound level are speculative reasonings without any empirical justification.[65]

British actor Sir Laurence Olivier also supported this 'balanced' approach when he advised against giving way entirely to the music of Shakespeare or to speaking it only as prose, instead of searching for truth through the verse. Other authors have insisted that the structure of the text used in the vocal delivery should indicate the form which the delivery is to have. Linguist I.A. Richards strongly warns against going outside the text in an attempt to give more force to the lines and advises that the poet's ideas are in the language.[66] This view is supported by Salper: 'The poem must be interpreted in its own internal linguistic content and structure. Content cannot be separated from Form'.[67] Similarly, Long and Hopkins conclude: 'An artistic utterance is ordered, structured, and performers must recognize this complexity in their preparations and performances.'[68]

A STRUCTURAL APPROACH TO THE TEXT

The problem of interpreting and performing Shakespeare is complicated but there are basic problems common to all the plays which many theoreticians advise can be solved by adapting a method of structural analysis. George R. Kernodle advocates consideration of three basic elements in the performance of Shakespeare, which are summarized below:

(i) *Poetic form.* Attention should be paid initially to the fundamental structure of the lines, their rhythm and line patterns.

(ii) *Grammatical and rhetorical form.* Phrasing, contrast, subordination and emphasis must be made clear with a carefully planned system of inflection and timing.

(iii) *Colouring.* One should render the reading of single words or whole speeches with an ever-changing range of emotional attitudes.[69]

Already in his 'Closing Statement' lecture in *Style in Language* (1960) Roman Jakobson had explained why in performing verse, syllabism, intonation, metre, rhyme and grammar were of such importance. He demonstrated the application of such a system together with Jones in their structural analysis of Shakespeare's *Sonnet 129* (1970) where, by analysing the sonnet's structure, they arrived at an interpretation. They explained their reasons as follows: 'An objective scrutiny of Shakespeare's language and verbal art, with particular reference to this poem, reveals a cogent and mandatory unity of its thematic and compositional framework.'[70] The method which these authors prescribed is summarized as follows:

(i) *External form.* The external form of the sonnet is examined first and the relationship it bears to its internal form (rimes, strophes and lines) is noted.

(ii) *Spelling and punctuation.* These two features are carefully considered.

(iii) *Interpretation.* Attention is given to the findings of modern research, particularly in the area of Elizabethan pronunciation.[71]

(iv) *Pervasive features.* Grammar and alliteration are examined.

(v) *Odds against even.* The part which rhyme plays is considered in terms of identity of sound between verse lines.

(vi) *Outer against inner.* The outer strophe's syntactical supremacy over the inner strophes is examined in relation to the part which rhythmical changes play.

(vii) *Balance in sound texture.* Consonants are weighed against vowels and monosyllables are weighed against words of more than one syllable.

(viii) *Grammatical parallels.* The use of grammar in the development of the story is noted.[72]

John Barton also recommends using a structural approach as a point of departure in the interpretation of Shakespeare and regards the verse as a guide to the performance:

> Blank verse is probably the very centre of the Elizabethan tradition and perhaps the most important thing in Shakespeare that an actor has to come to terms with – or rather I should say that an actor needs to get help from. . . It is stage-direction in shorthand – full of little hints from Shakespeare about how to act a given speech or scene.[73]

The method he advocates is therefore based upon an analysis of blank verse and his reasons for this are summarized below:

  (i) *The norm.* Iambic pentameter is the norm; any changes in the norm give added stress and heighten antithesis.

 (ii) *Long vowels and diphthongs.* These are indicators of strong stress.

(iii) *Feminine endings.* These are indicators of light stress.

(iv) *Syllabism and use of pauses.* When the count of syllables does not total ten, this indicates that a pause is built in.

 (v) *Shared lines and pauses.* When a line has only one syllable, the following lines are shared, often with a pause built in, so that the total reaches ten.

(vi) *Grammatical phrases and end-stopped lines.* Making a slight pause at the end of a line of verse, where it is not indicated by the grammatical phrasing, can often say something strong about the character.

(vii) *Caesura and phrasing.* Phrasing with, rather than against, the verse-lines by running on at the caesuras and taking a breath pause at the ends of the lines, gives the actor much more control. In this way the verse has the possibility of carrying the actor, which is particularly important in Shakespeare's later plays where the verse is more chaotic.

(viii) *Elision.* When a line is difficult to scan because it has more than ten syllables, this is usually an indication that Shakespeare has built into the verse natural elisions and slurrings as occur in our everyday speech.

 (ix) *Elizabethan pronunciation, metre and modern meaning.* Using the old pronunciation is often easier to say and it keeps the rhythm of the line better.

(x) *'-èd' endings and scansion.* When the count of syllables does not total ten, this is an indication to use the '-èd' endings so that it scans properly. It is also often much easier to say the word with the help of the rhythm.[74]

These methods, which strictly follow a structural approach in analysing Shakespearean verse, all emphasize the importance of the text as point of departure for the interpretation and performance, because it prevents the actor from what Umberto Eco calls 'overcoding' – the practice of forcing a surplus of expression on the addressee by a surplus of content.[75] They can be seen as an attempt to reinstate a form of 'poetics' upon which the vocal delivery is based.

In dealing with the dual problem facing contemporary actors, of tackling a Shakespearean text written for an Elizabethan audience and coping with modern habits of thinking, actor Ian McKellan recommends the structural approach, as it assists the actor to keep the balance between the emotion and the language, and ensures that Shakespeare is directing him.[76] Whilst the contemporary practice of staging Shakespeare in 'timeless' settings is a reaction to nineteenth-century stagings in settings of meticulous historical accuracy, it has also encouraged a free experimentation which does not always assist the actor in his acting situation. It has placed a linguistic duality on the 'relation of reference' in the act of communication, in that the actor has had to equate the character in the dramatic text with the character imposed by the director/designer's interpretation in the performance text. This practice has not been conflict-free and has often been the target for criticism as it has had a significant effect on vocal delivery style.

A STRUCTURAL APPROACH TO VOCAL DELIVERY

The other level in the communication act is the paralinguistic one – the one guiding the speaker's orchestration of his discourse, referred to by Elam as 'the material tissue of speech – the substance of expression'.[77] He isolates the following elements as constituting its structure: articulation, pitch, tempo, loudness, resonance, rhythm and control. Elam even draws particular attention to the importance of training in breath control. That these elements constitute the manner of speaking is forthcoming from an examination of the effects which voice science has had on voice training.

Since Manuel Garcia's discovery of a way to examine the action of the vocal folds with mirrors in 1885,[78] together with the further study of the larynx during phonation with the help of high-speed cinematography,[79] the nature of the vibration of the vocal folds has become clearer.[80] Numerous experiments have been conducted since then, thereby adding to the store of knowledge regarding the voice: studies on the voice as a stringed instrument; the role of the nasal cavities in resonance; the hygiene of the vocal organs; the effect of hormonal imbalance on vocal quality. Assisted by electronic engineering, research in the twentieth century has been most prolific in producing a wealth of new insights into the physiology of the voice, which has given rise to new concepts of vocal function, particularly the act of phonation. No longer can the function of the voice be regarded as an art but as a science, in which many factors are involved simultaneously, all carrying different information to different specialists – laryngologist, speech therapist, speech and singing teacher, phoniatric researcher and psychologist.

Modern voice training has been based upon the findings of voice science which maintain that the act of voice production consists of an interplay between the following four areas: breathing, phonation, resonance and articulation. These four areas have formed the basis of most textbooks written on voice training in the twentieth century, whereas the following factors have been part of the process of voice production through the ages: breathing, tone production, relaxation, pitch, quality, loudness and diction.[81]

Breathing

The relationship between proper breathing and effective speaking was recognized by the Greeks and Romans of antiquity. The practice was taken up in earnest in the Renaissance, especially in Elizabethan education, and continued to the time of the elocutionists, who placed it foremost in voice training with practices such as taking large amounts of air and sundry exercises of general callisthenics. Many of the exercises disappeared as the status of elocution declined.[82] [83] Two schools of thought have persisted even to the present, concerning the control of expiration by strenuously using the intercostal muscles or by a relaxed diaphragmatic action. Techniques for acquiring the former were not known before the late nineteenth century, while methods for achieving the latter are relatively new and still debatable.[84]

Phonation

The importance of co-ordinating breathing and tone production (phonation) was not really considered before the 1800s.[85] Up to this time vocal effects were of primary interest. However, around 1850 some elocutionists began working with whispering and yawning to maintain openness of the 'tone passage', while others later worked on the relationship between breathing and tone production.[86] Early twentieth-century teachers added empiric drills such as relaxation of the throat, the laryngeal musculature, the jaw and the back of the tongue, which later received support from the findings of the voice scientists. This area of voice production has become more popular because of the immediacy of the results on either the singing or speaking voice.

Relaxation's influence on resonance

In an effort to acquire the resonance needed for the voice to carry through a large hall, even at a low intensity, and at the same time minimize effort and avoid 'break' in the voice, a number of factors come into play which are dependent upon lack of tension. A condition of 'spontaneous relaxation' of the spine, as well as the larynx, mouth and tongue, is now considered to be of prime importance in the production of a good vocal quality; however, the idea of the body as a 'resonating chamber' is not new. Throughout history, various methods have been employed to encourage chest resonance, such as beating on the chest while speaking, however these theories have been refuted in this century.[87] Nevertheless, the old resonating chamber theory has not only received an enormous amount of attention in the training of the voice, but has been expanded this century with the influences which have come from Eastern voice-training practices. This is particularly prevalent with Grotowski, who, following Wolfsohn's findings, has incorporated many such practices in his voice-training techniques.[88] More recently, research has indicated that optimum resonance is achieved by being able to lower the larynx during voice production. In this way, the supraglottic airway is lengthened and subsequently, in Proctor's view, any vowel can be sounded 'with the most perfect clarity and beauty'.[89]

Pitch

In terms of voice training, pitch means the level at which one places or pitches one's voice in terms of height or depth of sound. A 'middle' range was prescribed as suitable by ancient Graeco-Roman writers and predominated without any scientific verification until after the Second World War. Scientists have determined that an individual's natural pitch level, which is often referred to as 'optimum', lies somewhere near the third or fourth tone above the lowest which can be produced clearly.[90] Many teachers now realize that locating this 'natural' pitch level constitutes a basic step towards improving voice and a number of methods are easily available for its determination.[91] The pitch level, particularly in women, is a trend which follows fashion – at times too high (the female ideal) and at times too low to be truly effective, as women have endeavoured to assert their social standing.

Quality

Quality has been defined as 'that element of voice which differentiates voices of identical pitch and intensity'.[92] It has been in search of this aspect of voice that one has witnessed perhaps the most questionable approaches and unfounded techniques in the history of voice training. Throughout most of the nineteenth century, teachers generally developed vocal quality by means of imitating models. The method of training was simply to imitate the teacher's voice and pronunciation as exactly as possible and there was only one ideal – the 'beautiful voice'. This method of training is not practised today, as voice science has shown the importance of co-ordinating and interrelating all parts of the vocal mechanism and teachers have discovered that the same practices used for good tone production also result in good quality.

Loudness

Great emphasis was placed on having a strong voice in the huge Greek and Roman amphitheatres and later in the nineteenth century, when it became necessary to speak to large crowds outdoors or in large auditoria. Even Quintilian's warnings against the ill-effects of vocal strain did not deter force and vigorous action of the voice from becoming popular well into the first two decades of the twentieth century. This was a continuation of the bombastic 'stage speech' practices in the enormous theatres of the turn of the century. Diverse factors have contributed to the change in this practice today, as teachers have become aware of the abuse which unnecessary strain can cause and have begun to develop carrying power by other means, 'by breath control, openness of the throat and laryngeal areas, effective vowel formation and clear articulation'[93] according to Anderson. With the advent of a more naturalistic style of acting, theatres became smaller in size, thereby eliminating the necessity for such enormous volume. In addition, the development of acoustical engineering, amplification and the use of radio and television as primary media for speech have removed the need for developing force or loudness.

Diction

The modern terminology for this aspect of voice training is 'articulation', which includes several practices in existence since the early part of the nineteenth century. It was only when elocution came into prominence that specific drills were introduced involving vowels and consonants, prepared word lists and practice on sentences following some form of phonetic analysis. Many teachers, using arbitrary standards of pronunciation, followed this general procedure as late as the first two decades of the twentieth century. There was, however, no effective way of representing speech sound or of explaining the formation of specific sounds until around the time of the First World War, when phonetic science progressed to the extent that it clarified not only symbolic representation by application of the International Phonetic Alphabet and descriptive analyses of sounds, but also standards of pronunciation. The arbitrary selection of pronunciation patterns also began to decline in practice as elocution faded in status. Towards the end of the second decade of the twentieth century, the trend was towards 'accepted usage' as teachers, realizing the fallacy of the 'one-and-only' correct formation of a sound, employed drill methods to improve both pronunciation and speech sounds within the structure of descriptive phonetics. As a result, 'ear training' replaced the former drills which remained in existence up to the end of the fifties. Since then, a student's pronunciation has been measured against an accepted standard and the specific manner in which he forms the sounds has become relatively unimportant. This trend was marked by the use of regional accents on stage for the first time in England in 1956 with John Osborne's *Look Back in Anger*.[94] Problems of elision and mispronunciation have always posed problems for the actor in both prose and verse when seeking a compromise between the original musicality of the verse and the anxiety about being modern.

However, Anderson has found that the effectiveness of the voice in terms of expression is equally important to voice training or manner of speaking, although it is harder to achieve: 'In addition, the teacher must be concerned with what the individual *does* with his voice; for vocal expression is profoundly influenced by the thoughts, attitudes and purposes of the speaker. These aspects of voice are considerably more obscure than pitch, loudness or quality.'[95] No longer does the practice of 'imitation of models' suffice in the training of the voice. Since the twenties a basic knowledge of the structure and function of the speech mechanisms has been included in voice training, whereas the trend later in the twentieth century has progressed towards 'liberating' and 'freeing', and a more psychological approach to analysis, which rejects anything to do with 'mechanical practices', as this definition of the 'voice' by Brodnitz illustrates:

In a sense, all the mechanical, accoustic and physiological forces that shape vocal function and vocal quality are but the tools with which the mind, the personality, the emotions are expressed in vocal terms. . . . Voice is more than a mechanical or accoustic phenomenon. It is a mirror of the personality, a carrier of moods and emotions, a key to neurotic and psychotic tendencies.[96]

TO 'BE' HAMLET OR TO 'ACT' HIM

The tussle between the old style of vocal delivery and the new was demonstrated at the turn of the century by a number of actors, whose performances of Shakespeare revealed all the problems of trying to marry the established technique with the new-found desire for truth. An examination of a number of English Hamlet performances from the end of the nineteenth century through into the twentieth century reveals how the style of vocal delivery has changed in the balance between voice, text and emotion.

Henry Irving (1834–1916) adopted a psychological approach to his Hamlet and appeared to 'think' his words rather than simply speak them. According to one of the critics of the day, Irving refused to 'declaim or recite the text which became thoughts aloud'.[97] His strong intellect and intense imagination, which was capable of expressing passion, produced a Hamlet at the Lyceum in 1874 which was both natural and intelligent, where according to Cain 'every speech is good and weighty, correct and dignified and treated with feeling'.[98] Irving had strong ideas on the worth of a careful elocution and an unaffected pronunciation. He demanded that the actor learned to think before he spoke:

> of course there are passages in which thought and language are borne along by the streams of emotion and completely intermingled. But more often it will be found that the most natural, the most seemingly accidental effects are obtained when the working of the mind is seen before the tongue gives it words.[99]

His acting style has been described as natural sublimated to the ideal.

The Hamlet of Herbert Beerbohm Tree (1853–1917) apparently did not achieve this blending of realism and idealization and met with criticism. According to the critics of the time, his elocution in Shakespeare tended to be monotonously declamatory: it lacked sensitivity to the music in the words; he had a throaty voice; practised 'rant' and tended to create his own character rather than performing the author's, in the best style of the romantic character actor.[100]

With his Hamlet, Johnston Forbes-Roberton (1853–1937) marked the end of the 'old style' of acting tragedy – of incorporating convention and declamation – by replacing it with 'drawing-room tone and gesture', according to Joseph.[101] Nevertheless his style impressed G.B. Shaw so much that he referred to him as a classical actor.

Forbes-Robertson did not believe that his acting was of the new 'acting-down' school, although he was proud of his training's descent from Garrick, Siddons, Macready and Phelps. He had learned how to produce his voice in the old way, using tone

42

correctly, but from Phelps he also learned how to emphasize the author's words so perfectly that they seemed entirely natural.[102] Barnes has revealed that one of the actors who played Polonius in *Hamlet* (1897) enthused that no contemporary Hamlet had read the lines as beautifully or brought out their meaning with such distinction and such distinctness; that on all sides there was acclamation of his speaking 'with the finest regard for effect and the truest emphasis', as well as for 'his exquisite voice, attuned to the expression alike of tenderness and of passion'.[103]

His ability to blend technique with truth and give classical tragic acting modern connotations, was demonstrated not only in the production of his voice, which was described as rich and resonant, but also in the speaking of verse, where he allowed the melody to come from the verse and brilliantly blended the rhythm of colloquial speech with the artificiality of metre.

John Gielgud (1904–) is another actor who believes in trying to find a compromise between a declamatory and a naturalistic style. In performance, Gielgud always demonstrates his ability to be expressive while at the same time winning admiration for his skilful craft. In creating his Hamlet, he endeavoured to use his own feelings, which he felt matched the character's, while at the same time lifting them to a high classical style. He believed he could act the part only when he experienced every word of it as he spoke. His vocal prowess, which has won great acclaim, has been described by Peter Brook as 'not just speech, nor melodies, but the continual movement between the word-forming mechanism and his understanding'.[104] Laurence Olivier paid homage to his first Hamlet, where the verse was spoken beautifully and the voice used musically, but recalled that Gielgud allowed himself to 'sing' the text more and more as time went by so that finally it was a complete aria.[105] Gielgud himself has related that in this first Hamlet, performed at the Old Vic in 1930, he threw himself into the part like a man learning to swim, and found that the text could hold him up if he sought the truth in it. This performance received acclaim from the critics, but not the revival in 1934 at the New Theatre, although it was a great box-office success. Gielgud toured America in the role in 1936 and took it to Elsinore in Denmark in 1939, where he received much acclaim. He took on the part again in 1944 and toured with it in 1945. Most critics have acclaimed his later Hamlets. The critic James Agate believed that Gielgud's 1944 Hamlet was his finest:

Mr Gielgud is now completely and authoritatively master of this tremendous part. . . He has acquired an almost Irving-esque quality of pathos, and in the passages after the play scene an incisiveness, a raillery, a mordance worthy of the Old Man. He imposes on us this play's questing feverishness. The middle act gives us ninety minutes of high excitement and assured virtuosity; Forbes-Robertson was not more bedaz-zling in the 'O What a rogue and peasant slave' soliloquy. In short, I hold that this is and is likely to remain, the best Hamlet of our time.[106]

As an actor, Laurence Olivier (1907–89) regarded himself as all earth, blood and humanity in contrast to Gielgud's spirituality, beauty and abstraction. This is evident by their different approaches to handling the verse in *Hamlet*. Although Olivier always believed that the stage actor needed plenty of voice and vocal control in his handling of the text, he tried to project the man's thoughts to people who otherwise would never have the opportunity to hear them. He was determined to give the audience a Hamlet at the Old Vic (1937) they could believe in. In his handling of the verse at that time, although he was aware of the metre and the rhythm, he did not want it to dominate as he felt had become the fashion of the day. His quest became to speak the truth:

Rhythm and timing are needed to create effects which must also appear to be spontaneous: it is the seeming absolute spontaneity of reaction which makes the audience feel a moment of recognition of new understanding. Reading may be better than nothing, but it is not the same as feeling and understanding Shakespeare's great lines through the inter-pretation of an actor.[107]

In spite of these intentions, Olivier's Shakespearean roles often met with criticism from the press, who thought that he had too many vocal and physical mannerisms with odd inflexions and voice placement. Olivier regarded all this as part of his characterizations, and persisted in giving remarkably diverse deliveries, such as a thin-voiced Richard III and an Othello with a bass resonance. He constantly fought against the 'music in the text' approach in favour of feeding in emotion and believability within the perimeter of his characterizations.

Paul Scofield (1922–   ) is another actor who is not afraid of vocal characterization. He regards preparation for a role as being important in that the communication between thinking and feeling is what informs the voice and makes it a willing instrument. Peter Brook has called him an actor of flesh and blood, where instrument and player are one, and describes his vocal work as follows:

> Scofield, when I first knew him as a very young actor, had a strange characteristic: verse hampered him, but he would make unforgettable verse out of prose. It was as though the act of speaking a word sent through him vibrations that echoed back meanings far more complex than his rational thinking could find: he would pronounce a word like 'night' and then he would be compelled to pause: listening with all his being to the amazing impulses stirring in some mysterious inner chamber, he would experience the wonder of discovery at the moment when it happened. Those breaks, those sallies in depth, give his acting its absolutely personal structure of rhythms, its own instinctive meanings: to rehearse a part, he lets his whole nature – a milliard of supersensitive scanners – pass to and fro across the words. In performance the same process makes everything that he has apparently fixed come back again each night the same and absolutely different.[108]

Theatre critic J. C. Trewin described Scofield's 1955 Hamlet, which Peter Brook directed for a tour to the Moscow Art Theatre, as touching:

> where emotion was not simply fabricated to fit the words . . . for me Scofield, with his rifted voice, one that can bring an image of light diffused and fretted across a broken classic column, has been essentially the man. Nowhere has the Hamlet that I know risen from the text more poignantly.[109]

It seems that in his handling of the verse, Scofield strove for the sense but did not lose the sound, while his concept of the character was that of a suffering, melancholy Renaissance prince. Scofield had first tackled Hamlet in 1948 at the Shakespeare Memorial Theatre, Stratford–upon–Avon.

The Hamlet of Richard Burton (1925–84) performed in New York in 1964 was, in the words of the director, John Gielgud, 'acted in rehearsal clothes, stripped of all extraneous trappings so the beauty of the language and imagery may shine through unencumbered by an elaborate reconstruction of any particular historical period.'[110] In keeping with the rehearsal format of the production, Burton varied his performance considerably from night to night and this included his vocal delivery. Most of the critics acclaimed his vocal skills, in particular his disciplined voice which could bring out the sense of each word and each line; his vocal range and eloquence. However, they were agreed upon the fact that the delivery was cold and intelligent – where soliloquies were 'reported' rather than 'delivered' by adopting pitches and radically changing speeds. His voice was criticized as lacking warmth and passion although he was praised as a technical genius who breathed new life into the old familiar soliloquies. *Time* reviewed his performance as follows:

> This is a thinking man's Hamlet, the kind G.B. Shaw might have written, and it is cool, clever, lucid, fresh, contemporary and vivid, but seldom emotionally affecting. . . His voice has gem-cutting precision and he can outroar Times Square traffic. . . His hands punctuate the speeches with persuasive rhythm and instinctive grace. He is virile, yet mannerly, as sweet of temper as he is quick to anger, and his wary eyes dart from foe to friend with the swiftness of thought.[111]

This production of *Hamlet* went on to become Broadway's longest running and most profitable *Hamlet* in stage history and the first Broadway production to be filmed while in performance before an audience.

Ian McKellen's (1939–   ) Hamlet with the Prospect Theatre Company in 1971 was awaited with anticipation, as he had already gained a reputation for a grand and mannered style of acting in the best tradition of the romantic actors of the past. Lloyd-Evans in the *Guardian*, 25 March 1971, commented that his acting was less a committal to the past than a demonstration of personal idiosyncrasies and that there were many of them, including a mannerism of speaking 'which is constantly listening to itself and his diction has moments of incredible eccentricity'. The reviews which met McKellen's Hamlet on tour were extremely positive, although this was not the case when the company returned to England. Irving Wardle in *The Times*, 16 April 1971, while admitting to improvement, criticized his conception of the part as a 'febrile juvenile capable of rousing himself into furies of self-intoxicated rhetoric'. The reception of his *Acting Shakespeare* recital in New York in 1983 was entirely different; one critic raved about McKellen's ability to play with the spoken word:

> Every syllable is enunciated with exactly the right emphasis. He rolls the words around his tongue, tastes them and produces them each with exactly the right interpretation. This isn't simply a matter of perfect diction or of playing with the various possible registers, *but a thoughtful and emotional comprehension of each word, an internalization of each phrase, profound analysis of each sentence.* In this way it is possible to play Shakespeare without exaggerated gesticulations, without unnecessary pathos and still communicate the least shadow of meaning. (Author's italics.)[112]

McKellen's views on verse speaking were shaped at Cambridge under George Rylands, John Barton and F.R. Leavis, but his own views reveal the modern man – more interested in the meaning than the music of Shakespeare:

> You have to think and have analysed in rehearsal totally so that your imagination, being fed by the concrete metaphors, concrete images and pictures, can be fed through into the body, into gesture, into timbre of voice, into eyelids, into every part of the actor's make-up, so that it does seem . . . that he is making it up as he goes along, although the actor, of course, knows that he isn't.[113]

This panorama of Hamlets reveals changing attitudes to the use of voice, text and emotion in the modern theatre. It can be seen as a reflection of the changes which this century has witnessed in rhetoric, dramatic literature, literary and performance analysis as well as voice training. Nevertheless, the modern theatre belongs as much to the director as to the actor, if not more, so it is to the role of the director that one must now turn one's attention.

3

A SMORGASBORD OF
IDEALS

During the twentieth century, the major changes in the ideals of
vocal delivery have come not from the discipline of rhetoric, or
from individual actors, so much as from a number of directors who
have evolved their own theories about the meaning and function of
theatre, which they have implemented in their productions. To
them, new attitudes to acting, including use of voice, text and
emotion, can be attributed, which both their productions and
writings have borne witness to. Their disparate ideologies have
resulted in a multiplicity of approaches to acting and to vocal
delivery and have had a widespread influence on the manner of
speaking in the modern theatre.

FROM TEXT TO SUBTEXT: KONSTANTIN
STANISLAVSKI

Stanislavski's theories on vocal delivery were closely bound to the
evolution of his system. In his early period (after 1906) he placed
emphasis on emotional memory and improvisation in his teaching,[1] while his later theories (after 1933) emphasized a Method of
Analysis through Physical Actions, where he maintained that 'the
emotional life of a character results from the actor's physical
behaviour more directly than from memory of emotion'.[2] This
factor, together with inconsistencies in translations, has caused
confusion in understanding the fundamental principles of Stanislavski's 'System',[3] and has led to misplacing emphasis on the
internal as opposed to the external factors of role creation. On the
contrary, the System was exceptionally well structured. There was
a logical process for each segment of the play, as this recent
translation indicates:

48

The actor first examines the 'given circumstances' in order to describe his character's situation. The situation poses 'a problem' [*zadacha*, in Hapgood's translation 'objective'], which his character must solve through the choice of an 'action'. The 'action' is intended to turn the situation to the character's advantage, and thus solve the problem. In sum, by carefully defining the 'problem', the actor slowly finds his way to his action. Through these logical steps, the actor finds a specific action for each segment of the play on which he can place his full attention. Stanislavski then stresses that the emotional life of the character follows as the direct and natural result of the action. By focusing solely on the action, the actor feels the emotional life of the character.[4]

The actor's vocal delivery was closely aligned to this System, because Stanislavski discovered that dialogue was situational, depending on speaker, recipient and context, and that in the theatre this included the audience. This led him to realize that words did not contain the full meaning, but that they depended on what lay beneath them – the 'subtext'. In this way the text became part of the creative process, part of the 'action', and was no longer to be regarded as a literary form. The actor was to consider the word as 'verbal action', which meant that when he spoke he was in the process of action through words,[5] providing he had a need and a purpose for saying them. The main sources of Stanislavski's teachings on speech were Volkonski's *The Expressive Word* (1913) and Ushakov's *Brief Introduction to the Science of Language* (1913). He found the former most useful, although he had reservations about Volkonski's general approach, which he thought external – drawing attention to the desired results rather than concentrating on the means by which they were to be achieved, the discovery of motivation and meaning:

> Volkonski's mistake is that he is always looking for the result and you have to decide what that is. But Volkonski is essential. To simplify intricate, complex sentences you must discard all subordinate phrases and words and preserve a single skeleton – the main idea – and express it according to the laws of speech. If it's in verse then respect the rhythm of the poetry.[6]

However, Stanislavski changed his attitude to Volkonski and to the subtext after battling with Pushkin's verse in *Mozart and Salieri*, in which he performed in 1915, when he confessed that the subtext was swamping the verse, that there were almost more pauses than words and that he was failing to hold his audience. The twelve-page text was being dragged out to inordinate lengths as he attempted to reveal the inner psychology of the character and it was only when he decided to pull all the stops out physically and vocally that he won the audience back again to listen more attentively than ever.[7]

It is not difficult to understand why Stanislavski insisted that the actor's vocal delivery was not only to consist of the 'subtext' references, as the practitioners of the 'Method' later erroneously concluded,[8] but was to convey every subtle nuance which his voice and understanding of the text could realize. This demanded a mastering of voice and text in order to convey all the full connotative and denotative aspects of speech, and necessitated regular training to improve breathing, diction and range as well as the skills required to convey the logic of speech from a careful analysis of the structure of the text. The advice which Stanislavski gave to actors, whose previous training had consisted of imitating intonations and gestures, was to train daily to free the body of unnecessary tensions and to develop the voice, so that it could express externally the delicate inner experiences of the creative process.

In order to gain more power in the voice, Stanislavski advised that the actor should be encouraged to think about the strength of the effect of his speech rather than volume, which was to be found in the intonations and range of the voice, not in loudness or shouting. Neither was the importance of range to be underes-timated, as Stanislavski insisted that the way the actor used the 'whole spectrum' of sound available to him was a way of showing the whole spectrum of the human condition and he drew the following parallels: 'To paint a picture with vivid colours an actor must use the whole scale of his voice . . . his voice must be trained like that of a singer and placed in the "masque" where the resonators are.'[9]

Working from Volkonski's theories of speech regarding diction, Stanislavski advocated the practice of learning the alphabet as a 'phonetics gourmet' where the sensation of each sound and syllable should be explored. He advised diction exercises on the consonant and vowel sounds in order to be able to fill out their content and recommended that these exercises were to be practised while singing, so that the full potential of the voice could be realized.[10]

Stanislavski maintained that understanding the logic of speech demanded a careful analysis of the structure of the text and the grammatical structure of the sentence. In this way the actor could evaluate each thought, select the key words to express them and see how intonation, pausing and emphasis should be used. This approach was not recommended as a substitute for the 'verbal action' and 'emotionally-filled' word, but seen as an obligatory prerequisite towards making the superior quality possible and even communicating the subtext, as the following statement of Stanislavski's indicates:

> The habit of speaking in measures will make your speech more graceful in form, intelligible and profound in content, because it forces you to keep your mind constantly on the essential meaning of what you are saying when you are on the stage. Until you achieve this, there is no use either in your attempting to carry out one of the principal functions of the words, which is to convey the illustrated subtext of your monologue, or even in doing the preparatory work of creating this subtext.[11]

In the same way, not all words were to be accentuated equally if the actor was to find the 'soul' or inner essence and high point of the subtext.

By the application of the rules of the language or idiomatic usage, many words and accents fell into place. By studying synthesis and the rules of grammar, one came more readily to perceive which of the words were 'key' words. These stresses were not to compete with each other, but to give perspective and it is interesting to note that Stanislavski uses the word 'foreground' here in the semiotic meaning:

> With us we have as many planes of speech which create perspective in a phrase. The most important word stands out most vividly defined in the very foreground of the sound plane. Less important words create a series of deeper planes.[12]

All of this technique was to be meshed with the super-objective of the play, along the line of the subtext and the through-line of action, and supports the contention that Stanislavski's system demonstrated the possibility of balancing the voice with text and emotion. Actors were not, as Stanislavski put it, 'to allow themselves to be carried away by the external form of poetry, its metre and completely ignore the subtext and all the inner rhythm of living and feeling',[13] or to use a vocal delivery style which was 'the result of excessive, exaggerated, over-intensified attention to the subtextual content out of all proportion to the verse', but to find a balance between the two.[14]

In rehearsal, every possible means was undertaken by Stanislavski to bring out the 'verbal action' in the play and to keep the words fresh because he believed that 'words mechanically repeated during rehearsals without meaning or justification become merely lodged in the muscles of the tongue and no more'.[15] This meant in practice that the text was rarely spoken out aloud but rather was whispered, that cuts were made in longer speeches and even nonsense language was used instead of the words of the text.

In acting plays in verse, Stanislavski advocated coupling the subtext with its inner tempo and rhythm, and the verbal verse text with its external tempo and rhythm, believing that 'it is only under such circumstances that the verse form presents no embarrassment to the actor and his emotions but even helps him to a full freedom of inner and outer action'.[16]

His changing attitude to handling the manner of speaking verse can be seen from his encounter with Shakespeare. Stanislavski realized at an early date the demands which Shakespeare makes on the voice, when in the 1896 *Othello* his voice began to give out – a sad fact which he recounted in *My Life in Art* (1924). The ensuing productions, *Much Ado About Nothing* (1897), *Twelfth Night* (1897) and *The Merchant of Venice* (1898), taught him that the methods which worked in performing Chekhov did not necessarily work with Shakespeare in spite of the fact that they worked with such detailed historical accuracy. This realization remained unchanged in the production of *Julius Caesar* which he co-directed with Danchenko (1903), where he played the part of Brutus, when he realized the failure of a naturalistic acting style in staging Shakespeare effectively.[17] Here many problems arose concerning how to treat the monologues, well-known passages and reported speech.

Before attempting his next Shakespeare production, *Hamlet*, in co-direction with Gordon Craig, Stanislavski had begun to evolve the principles of his psychological–realistic acting method, when he came to the realization that internal truth should stimulate external truth. Needless to say these ideas conflicted with Craig's concept of the actor as Über-Marionette and his main idea of the play which was 'to be in no way realistic'.[18] Craig realized these ideas in his symbolist setting which comprised shifting screens, exaggerated costuming, impressionistic music and choral effects interplaying with an expressionistic lighting. In this visually abstract world, the naturalistic acting style and handling of the text jarred on audience and critics alike – its dualism being difficult for many to accept at that time – although it was regarded as an innovation in Russian theatre circles.

The 1918 studio production of *Twelfth Night*, in its simplistic staging, witnessed the success of Stanislavski's first attempts at using his system, whereby physical tasks were used as a key to theatrical creativity.[19] At this time he emphasized verbal dexterity and manipulated the text to speed up the pace of the performance. It was on the whole very well received.

It is in the prompt-book to the Moscow Art Theatre production of *Othello* (1930) that Stanislavski's Method of Analysis through Physical Action is revealed in its completeness. On the question of dealing with vocal delivery, he advised that the practice of beginning with the text would lead the actor to the subtext 'where the writer has concealed the motives which prompted him to create the play. The text thus gives birth to the subtext in order to have it recreate the text.'[20] This process meant coupling the verse's rhythm and tempo with the subtext so that the meaning behind every word could be 'penetrated' and 'justified' to the full. In this way, the actors felt that the lines of the play were pulling them along 'logically, consecutively, down into their soul',[21] and were able to combine voice, text and emotion as a result in their manner of speaking.

FOLLOWING THE 'GESTUS': BERTOLT BRECHT

Brecht's ideal of vocal delivery was closely aligned to his theories of a non-illusionistic theatre – an epic theatre – and the direct opposite to those of Stanislavski, whom he regarded as mystical and cultish. Brecht's epic theatre was so named because of the possibilities which it opened up for description and reference and because of its technical features, such as commenting choruses and written projections. In this theatre, the dramatic situation was to be 'artistically demonstrated' to an audience, which was to be set at a distance from it in order to be able to pass judgement on it and thereby see in what way society needed to be changed.[22] It was also called epic on the grounds that it had a narrative form as opposed to the Aristotelian form, which Brecht considered degenerate – as it only perpetuated the bourgeois ideals of the 'dramatic' theatre of his era. Brecht's epic theatre did, however, agree with Aristotle in that the story is the kernel of the tragedy, and adopted a theatre of narrative realism which stood midway between naturalism and symbolism. While avoiding the cuteness of arty anti-naturalistic theatre, it offered in its place a commonsense approach by demanding that the audience accept the reality of the theatre. This theatre was to be the handmaiden of society and not of the poet's own world and the poet's words were only sacred in so far as they were true.[23]

To achieve these ends, the actor was expected to master the 'alienation effect', that is to use enough empathy in his acting to show how men behave, but not to convince by winning the audience's sympathies.[24] His acting had to express his awareness of being watched by the audience, which called upon him to look at himself with distance, 'quoting' the character played, as the actors in the Chinese theatre managed to do.[25] In order to prevent the audience from falling into a trance, the actor had to control his manner of speaking to keep it 'free from parsonical sing-song and from all those cadences which lull the spectator so that the sense gets lost'.[26]

In his writing, Brecht admitted that he always bore in mind the actual delivery, for which he had worked out a definite technique which he called 'gestus'. This meant that the sentence (whether verse or prose) was supposed to follow the 'gest', or attitude, of the person speaking. As a result, Brecht's dramatic language contains particular 'gestic' rhythms which are able to demonstrate the kind of person speaking and it was for this reason that he rejected stringent verse patterns and rhyme as these were too restrictive. For the performance of Shakespeare, Brecht was struck with the greater force of the actors' delivery when they used the almost unreadable 'stumbling' verses of the old Schlegel and Tieck translations rather than Rothe's smooth new one:

How much better it expressed the tussle of thoughts in the great monologue! How much richer the structure of the verse!

The problem was simple: I needed elevated language, but was brought up against the oily smoothness of the usual five-foot iambic metre. I needed rhythm, but not the usual jingle.[27]

In order to maintain a distance from the part and allow for the 'gest' to predominate, the actor was to adopt the third person, and the past tense, and was required to speak all the stage directions and comments while rehearsing. The director was to help by filming the performance, concentrating on the nodal points of the action and cutting it to bring out the gestus in a very abbreviated way.

Brecht's concern with the actor's ability to bring out the meaning of his lines did not prevent him from realizing that to convey this, an actor needed a flexible voice and well-developed speech – not of the 'voice-beautiful' type, however, but one which was well trained and which could express great passions without ill-effect. To this end he recommended integrating acting exercises with technical exercises so that empty, superficial, formalistic acting would be avoided. In order to portray the speech of people from all social classes, actors were encouraged to use dialects and not only High German – as was the usual practice.

On the question of emotion in the epic theatre, Brecht believed that the audience should experience through understanding. This does not mean that there is no place for emotion; rather he thought that the audience should be able to confront emotion without losing their power of reason. This means that in the epic theatre, actors do not attempt to 'share the emotions of the characters' they are portraying, but believe that these emotions none the less should be fully and movingly represented.[28] Brecht did not want his characters 'falsified' by the actors in their efforts to reach the audience's hearts – insisting that they were not a matter for 'empathy' but rather that the characters should be presented coldly, classically and objectively.[29] In this way he felt the audience would be able to make its own sense of the material by putting its reason to work.

To achieve these ends, the actor had to maintain a duality in his acting – that of the character he was portraying and that of his own personality. In this respect, Brecht's ideas can be seen as being in agreement with Stanislavski's 'perspective of the role and perspective of the actor'.[30] However, unlike Stanislavski, Brecht did not believe in applying the 'magic if' because for him making the actions fit the character and the character fit the actions was too great a simplification. This kind of acting did not allow for portraying the 'imperfect inconsistencies of real people in society'.[31]

Performing in a Brecht play meant for an actor mastering the ability to pass from prose to verse and from speech to song and at times even being called upon to speak against the music. This was demanded by the *Lehrstücke*, or learning form, whose pedagogical function was that moral and political lessons could best be taught by participation in an actual performance. The *Lehrstücke* incorporated didactic cantatas, with solos, choruses and scraps of acting, for which Brecht experimented with many different 'regular (or almost regular) rhythms', by which he endeavoured to further the 'gestic' way of putting things, particularly when accompanied by 'gestic' music.[32] One of the problems facing the epic theatre in its attitude to music was that in spite of the effort to alienate it, audiences seemed to find it impossible not to enjoy it on an emotional level.

Helene Weigel epitomized Brecht's vocal delivery ideal by demonstrating the qualities which he believed the non-Aristotelian acting style demanded, and that included a wholly unemotional and penetrating voice which always possessed an element of astonishment and lamentation. She, in turn, admitted to a daily speech-training programme, without which, she maintained, one could not act.[33]

Believing that the story was the 'heart of the theatrical performance, for it is what happens *between* people that provides them (the audience) with all the material that they can discuss, criticize, alter',[34] and that the theatre had to speak up decisively for the interests of its own time, Brecht did not underestimate the importance of the 'interpretation' or reading of the play. From his reading of *Hamlet* (1947–8) we see how he was guided by his concern for society first and foremost, 'the dark and bloody period in which I am writing – the criminal ruling classes, the widespread doubt in the power of reason, continually being misused'.[35] His interpretation can be seen as substantiating the belief that every production in the theatre has the possibility to transform society and bring about change.

From Brecht's *Modellbuch* for *Mother Courage* (which he directed together with Erich Engel at the Deutsches Theater in Berlin in

1949, with Helene Weigel in the title role), and the number of photographs and comments on individual scenes which it contained, one can learn a great deal about the production as a whole, and in particular Brecht's ideas concerning 'gestus' in language and his attempts to define emotion. These 'model' productions were to serve as definitive examples for others to work from – a practice which Brecht did not in the least fear would reduce the theatre practitioner's freedom. On the contrary, he maintained that rather than being a disgrace, copying was an art which could be learned, and recommended that the groupings should follow the 'model' as the point of departure for telling the story in rehearsal.[36]

The instructions for the staging of *Mother Courage* also made reference to the epic style of acting, which, although Brecht did not regard it to be 'equally valid for every classical work', he believed it was suitable for Shakespeare. He saw similarities between the 'chronicle' form of *Mother Courage*, in the way it was based on factual elements far removed from psychological theatre, and the Shakespearean dramatic structure.

In order to control any emotional identification with the characters in *Mother Courage*, Brecht did not allow his leading character to undergo catharsis and his repeated use of projections renounced the dramatic elements of surprise and tension, so that nothing could interfere with the audience's reasoning powers. This explains why his concept of Mother Courage met with criticism in that by the end of the play she has learnt nothing from the disasters that befall her during the Thirty Years War. Brecht's rejoinder was, however, that even if she learns nothing, at least the audience can learn by observing her.

The film version of this production clearly portrays the specific gestic manner of speaking which the epic theatre demanded, particularly as demonstrated by Helene Weigel; where, without over-emotionalizing or attempting to sing in anything resembling a beautiful voice, her character's attitudes to the many harrowing moments in the story are depicted strongly but without sentimentality. Prior to commencing rehearsals on this production, Brecht had just completed writing his theoretical aesthetic, 'A Short Organum for the Theatre', where he defines his theories about epic theatre, including ideas for staging, acting and training. The desire to establish similar 'model' productions was one of the reasons for establishing the Berliner Ensemble, where Brecht himself directed

Puntilla, *The Mother*, *Senora Carrar's Rifles* and *The Caucasian Chalk Circle*.

Although he was well aware of the need to allow some artistic freedom in the performing of these plays, realizing that no real work of art can be simply an imitation, nevertheless Brecht wanted these 'models' to serve as a way of describing 'reality' more precisely and that seems to explain how he had solved these problems himself in his productions. Following a conference on Stanislavski in the spring of 1953, this 'schematized' practice earned for Brecht the criticism that he was guilty of formalism.[37] One certainly can see how the stringent rules for dramaturgy, production, direction, stage design and acting must have contributed to this attack. However, his attitude that there is freedom within the outlines of the structure, rather than the approach of the so-called 'free artist' who revels in the sheer anarchy of his own prejudices, is not new, and has been the very backbone of many ideological and aesthetic debates of the twentieth century.

METAPHYSICS-IN-ACTION: ANTONIN ARTAUD

A new approach to vocal delivery was introduced by Antonin Artaud in France during the twenties. Coming to distrust the role which spoken language had steadily been adopting in the theatre, Artaud advocated dispensing with the 'word' in favour of other means of expressing human thoughts and emotions. These ideas finally crystallized in his manifesto for the theatre, *Le Théâtre et son double*, published in 1938. Although he was critical of speech, Artaud was really searching for another language for the theatre which was not so literary, but which was able to 'make use of everything – gestures, sounds, words, screams, light, darkness'[38] in order to be able to get in touch with life.

Artaud believed that by rediscovering its communicative powers, the theatre would be capable of exposing the audience to its own secret crimes and obsessions and thereby help it to rediscover the metaphysical, mystical meaning of life. He considered the function of the theatre to be to re-establish the subconscious links between actor and spectator, but it was not until he explored various means of achieving this, with his partner Roger Vitrac, in their newly formed Alfred Jarry Theatre (1927–9), that he discovered the way. These discoveries were outlined in his

Theatre of Cruelty manifesto and have had a seminal influence on theatre practice in the modern theatre ever since.

In its short life, the Alfred Jarry Theatre staged four productions, all of which were intended to 'restore to theatre all the freedom that music, poetry, or painting have and from which it has been strangely cut off up to now'.[39] Their aim was a revival of interest in the 'total theatre' formula, in a world which was slowly being overtaken by the newly arrived 'talkies'. Towards this end their productions fell into three categories: plays written specifically for it, adaptations of the classics and stage scenarios. Further intentions included making the theatre actual, through engaging the emotions of the audience by totally disregarding the priority of the author's text over the production.

Common to all these plays and productions was the freeing of all social form, in a world which rejected logic and reason, where the metaphysics were to be imprinted in the minds of the audience directly through the skin. To attain these effects, the theatre had to develop rhythms, both visually and audially, so that the desired state of 'delirium' could be experienced by the audience. On this point, Artaud was adamant that: 'In the theatre a play disturbs the senses' repose, frees the repressed unconscious, incites a kind of virtual revolt. . .and imposes on the assembled collectively an attitude that is both difficult and heroic',[40] where an element of danger is always present. And it was this aspect of theatre which fascinated him.

Artaud had come to despair of the fact that speech had become impotent and that the European theatre did not know how to speak the language that belonged to it. With its emphasis on psychology and role analysis in such human themes as love and duty, the theatre had lost its religious and mystical powers and simply encouraged elucidating states of consciousness and verbal exchange. The theatre of the East, on the other hand, did not deal with such psychological matters, rather it emphasized metaphysical tendencies and utilized the whole 'complex of gestures, signs, postures and sonorities which constitute the language of stage performance'.[41] Artaud termed this 'pure theatre' and called for a new approach, which would substitute this poetry of language with 'poetry in space', which meant a new approach to the *mise-en-scène* and the role of the director, rather than the supremacy of the author and the text.

An examination of the productions which Artaud staged, alone and together with Vitrac, as well as his scenarios indicates the nature of this new 'poetry of space' and his attitude to language and vocal delivery. Basically, these writings are devoid of logic and consequence, in accordance with the dictates of surrealism. There are no in-depth characters, rather de-identification is emphasized, where the dynamics of the masses have supremacy over the individual. In this universal way, Artaud believes that themes of a more serious nature can be explored, which are relevant for all of society rather than individual persons.

The language used is designed to shock, not by its inherent semantic qualities but by its use of unconventional words. It is often simplistic and repetitive, and has the effect of attaining irony, particularly when delivered in a non-realistic manner, as is indicated in the repetition of the phrase 'I love you' in different rhythms and tones of voice at the beginning of Artaud's *The Spurt of Blood*. This language, when coupled with the use of screams, shouts and cries, choking noises, dialects, ventriloquists' voices, the strange placement of pauses and above all long silences, polyphonies of speaking voices and odd, unexpected sound-effects, results in a textual performance which is rich and varied and above all never realistic or predictable.

The classics are rid of such devices as verse, reliance on dialogue, monologues and asides to carry the action. Instead, as the scenario for Strindberg's *The Dream Play*, staged by the Jarry Theatre in 1928, and *The Ghost Sonata*'s proposed plans indicate, a new audio-visual text is evolved, which treats the themes in a manner intended to reawaken what Artaud believes is the dormant fear hiding beneath the skin of the audience.

The scenarios continue this trend of using fragmentation, in a manner later adopted by the Theatre of the Abssurd and even later by the postmodern theatre, to present a wide spectrum of themes, where perversions and a change in the status quo of good and evil are used to maximum effect. In *The Philosopher's Stone* and *There is No More Firmament* (1929) dismemberment and descriptions designed to shock appear regularly and are intended to indicate the dire mental state of society. Very often puppets are utilized to give this aspect of the performance particular emphasis.

Although Artaud negated words and referred to the 'dictatorship of speech' in the European theatre, his chief concern was to reinstate the auditive aspect of the performance by what he termed 'metaphysics-in-action':

To make a metaphysics out of a spoken language is to make the language express what it does not ordinarily express: to make use of it in a new exceptional and unaccustomed fashion; to reveal its possibilities for producing physical shock; to divide and distribute it actively in space; to deal with intonations in an absolutely concrete manner, restoring their power to shatter as well as really to manifest something; to turn against language and its basely utilitarian, one could say alimentary sources, against its trapped-beast origins; and finally, to consider language as the form of *Incantation*.[42]

Believing in the shaman-like powers of the actor, who could tap his own passions, Artaud developed a series of breathing exercises to assist his craft, maintaining: 'Since breathing accompanies feeling, the actor can penetrate this feeling through breathing providing he knows how to distinguish which breathing suits which feeling.'[43] In attempting to give new life to a text, Artaud began with a distillation of the images contained therein and advocated many diversified methods of actualizing them. Frequently the recommended vocal delivery was completely at variance with any possible clarification, and was so obscure that it evoked ridicule and laughter from the audience. He often called for an actor to start a speech standing, continue on his knees and end it flat on his back, or to present his own inner states without reference to the sense of the speech, as for instance, the beautiful mother in *Victor, or the Children are in Power* (Jarry Theatre, December 1928) breaking wind every time she spoke.

In *The Cenci* (1935), where the dialogue was neither conversational nor conventionally dramatic, its reality was heightened and transposed by orchestrating it for musical effect by creating clear rhythms and capturing the audience in a net of sonorous vibrations, with exaggerated sound-effects, such as loudspeakers, metronomes running at different rhythms and music from an electric keyboard. According to Blin's production notes, the movement was also carefully orchestrated and organized, the words in the text being little more than catalysts for extended physical movement.[44] All this careful organization was intended to reveal a metaphysical world of the mind rather than physical reality and at the same time to involve the audience by means of the hallucinatory effects which this juxtaposition of the 'real' with the 'symbolic' created.

In the first spectacle of the Theatre of Cruelty, *The Conquest of Mexico*, with its erotic and orgiastic scenes, Artaud's intentions were outlined as follows:

> These images, movements, dances, rites, these fragmented melodies and sudden turns of dialogue will be carefully recorded and described as far as possible with words, especially for the portions of the spectacle not in dialogue, the principle here being to record in codes, as on a musical score, what cannot be described in words.[45]

These staging devices, or *mise-en-scène*, were in accordance with the principles of Artaud's Theatre of Cruelty – a theatre based primarily on spectacle, where images and movements were intended to reach the spirit of the audience with force and extreme action, pushed beyond all limit, and in this way it would be able to recover its former necessity.[46]

In the First Manifesto of the Theatre of Cruelty, Artaud expounded his theory of a new kind of language for the theatre, which was to be a 'unique language half-way between gesture and thought', capable of a dynamic expression in space, as opposed to the previous subjugation to the text and spoken dialogue: 'It is not a question of suppressing the spoken language, but of giving words approximately the importance they have in dreams.'[47] Artaud meant that this new language was even to be regarded as a musical cadence – and that perhaps musical transcription would be valuable as a means of transcribing voices. In this way, harmonic balance could be achieved by making particular use of intonations.

Above all else, the language of words was to give way to a language of space in the Theatre of Cruelty, which Artaud maintained was based on gesture springing from the 'necessity of speech more than from speech already formed. But finding an impasse in speech, it returns spontaneously to gesture.'[48]

With his interest in codes, signs, use of the theatrical space, allowing the performance text to predominate over the written text, structuring visual and auditive attitudes, together with his endeavours to redefine the function of the author/director as the 'unique creator upon whom will devolve the double responsibility of the spectacle and the plot',[49] Artaud must be regarded as one of the earliest semioticians of the theatre. His interest in the denotative and connotative 'codes' or possibilities of the spectacle, which he attempted to define for his Theatre of Cruelty: musical

instruments; lights and lighting; costumes; the relationship between stage and auditorium; objects, masks and accessories; the
actor and the interpretation, all support this statement. The
language of words was to be regarded as simply another code of
equal value.

Artaud maintained that in European theatre, as opposed to the
theatre of the East, the text had become everything – even
assuming some definite spiritual value, and words had become
'frozen and cramped in their meanings',[50] which explains his
argument for a new approach.

Although his actual productions were so few, and in spite of
their poor reception by audiences and critics alike, Artaud's theories
have had a lasting effect on the non-traditional, avant-garde theatre
movement. They have had a strong influence on the happenings of the
fifties and the group theatre movement of the sixties in America and
Europe, as well as on many twentieth-century directors who have
also rejected conventional proscenium-arch staging and the idea of
a theatre as a literary form of expression in their quest to make a
more immediate contact with their audiences by what is called
'The Theatre of Ecstasy'.[51] His experiments have no doubt had a
seminal influence on the vocal delivery of the non-verbal theatre
movement, which chooses to communicate through sounds rather
than words and through screams and cries rather than speech,
where the visual and physical have taken precedence over the
auditive and literary. In the words of Innes:

> On the level of technique his extension of stage language by
> emphasising symbolic gesture, patterned movement, speech
> as sound, has been developed by Peter Brook and others.
> Above all his ritualisation of theatre, with its accompanying
> aim to involve the spectator totally in the stage action, has
> become an ideal for much of the serious western drama.[52]

One thing is certain: with Artaud, the 'dramatic text' underwent a
shift of importance in the production as a whole, when the
emphasis was placed on the supremacy of the 'performance text'.

THE EIGHT-OCTAVE IDEAL: THE ROY HART THEATRE

Vocal delivery lies at the very centre of the artistic work of the Roy
Hart Theatre which evolved from the research of its founder,

Alfred Wolfsohn (1896–1962), who discovered that the voice is not the function solely of any anatomical structure, but rather the expression of the whole personality, and that through the voice all aspects of an individual could be developed.[53] In their approach to their work, the Roy Hart Theatre wants 'people' on the stage and not just actors – people who are seeking to liberate their tensions and those of the audience through sound.[54] For them, theatre is a way of life and the roles they play in performance are regarded as a way of exploring a full range of emotions through the voice. They believe that the voice and the person are one and that when one of them is expanded so will the other be. This link between the voice and the psychological growth of the individual is what is original about Wolfsohn's discoveries, as well as his theory that the actor releases emotional blocks in order to realize creative potential more fully.

Wolfsohn discovered that many sounds are produced, not by the larynx, but by different parts of the body – from energy centres in the head, chest and stomach, which are resonated through the body. He maintained that the range of the human voice could be expanded to more than seven octaves – even nine – and that restricting it to one specialized area, such as a tenor or a soprano, was artificial:

> Man has elevated the sin against nature to a dogma, the dogma of those strictly confined, neatly labeled categories: male voice and female, high voice and low, child's voice and adult's. In reality, the natural human voice comprises all these ranges and registers.[55]

Wolfsohn's experiences in the trenches during the First World War, where he discovered the potential which the human voice had through its audible expression for revealing the inner being of an individual's personality, encouraged him to devote his life to trying to discover why in most people it was shackled, monotonous and cramped.[56] His work with a wide variety of people led to some amazing developments in their usual vocal ranges and had a lasting impression on music critics, composers, Grotowski, Brook and Jean-Louis Barrault, who was a motivating force behind the group's eventual move to France.

Refuting the conventional acceptance of the vocal chords as the only reason for producing singing voices which demonstrated an extended range, Wolfsohn, along with Roy Hart, presented one of his most gifted pupils at the Zurich Laryngological Institute in 1956. Her larynx was found not to be adversely affected by the wide range of notes (five octaves and six tones) when subjected to various tests including X-ray, high-speed film and stroboscope; it was also found that other pupils could 'rumble and squeak over seven octaves'.[57] More importantly, for Wolfsohn this was proof of the degree of liberation his pupils had attained.

His successor, Roy Hart, carried this psychological aspect of the approach to work on the voice even further. As a graduate of the Royal Academy of Dramatic Art in London, Hart found in Wolfsohn all the qualities of guru and mentor, and carried his theories further by defining an 'eight-octave' ideal whereby the 'whole man' could be explored – any failure to do so being an indication of the individual's inherent fear. In every aspect of working on the voice, the Roy Hart Theatre insists on the 'humanity' of sound and not the 'beauty' of sound or 'sound for sound's sake'. In this way they see themselves as more liberated because they are simply calling on energies which are not often used in daily life, and by calling on them they feed their lives by 'singing' them. Their work is explained by one of their members, Enrique Pardo, as follows:

> The root metaphor of our work on the voice, the human voice, is the word 'singing' and involves far more than the application of technique. I believe for instance, that evils should be sung. If you don't sing evil, evil will sing you. There are forces within one, and forces outside, that can lead you into producing certain sounds, to emit energies which you would never think yourself capable of. . . Suddenly you find yourself using your voice in a way quite outside your normal experience of it. In a sense, our work is to do with the meaning of these energies behind the voice. What makes a person capable of producing certain sounds at certain moments and not at others?[58]

This ideology lies behind the Roy Hart Theatre's approach to work in the theatre. They have redefined the verb 'to sing' to mean the individual's willingness to give all the manner of voices which he is capable of producing – high, low, loud, soft, cries, gurgles, shouts, squeaks – the whole register of so-called 'ugly' unconventional voices, which, like hidden, darker forces within him, are constantly struggling to be released.[59] By learning to 'attack the sounds', the members of the Roy Hart Theatre confront their fears and learn to 'find their real feelings and not hide behind masks, which is very often a painful experience',[60] according to one of its members, Orlanda Cook.

Normal barriers, such as those to do with sexual differentiations and social behaviour, must be broken down if the individual is to realize his full potential through the human voice. In practice this means that females are encouraged to explore the deeper, masculine voices normally associated with aggression, while on the other hand, males are encouraged to confront within themselves the softer, more feminine and traditionally vulnerable sides of their personalities. These, according to the Roy Hart Theatre, are the 'forces' in every individual which need to be 'sung' and which will help him break through the convention of a 'one-octave life' in his attempts towards an 'eight-octave' ideal.

From the practical 'workouts' on the voice, it is obvious that all possible means are sought to help unblock tension and assist the different 'voices' to be released.[61] There is a great deal of physical involvement accompanying the vocal exploration, from bouncing, hopping, swaying, knee-bending, shaking the body out, pelvis-tilting, spine-stretching and collapsing, much of which is accredited to the Alexander technique,[62] where compatible physical movements are incorporated to encourage particular sounds. The need to work on the voice becomes a need to get to know oneself, as this following explanation by one of its members bears witness:

> Not working on my voice means not being in touch with myself – singing is a part of my life. There is a release of emotion. Energies go up to my head, however by working on my voice and taking these energies down into my centre, this brings me back to a more real feeling about life.[63]

Working with a text in the Roy Hart Theatre is often an exploration of a collage taken from different sources, where very little importance is placed on logical deductive events or the language of words. Parallels are seen here with the Artaudian approach. They do not attempt to entertain in the sense of inviting an audience to lose itself in the story – rather they seek to 'liberate' the audience's tensions along with their own, through sound. As Enrique Pardo explained:

The main purpose of our productions is the liberating and creative energy of the voice. Through it you get in touch with your own humanity, with your weaknesses and everything ultimately that creates character and strength, because the voice creates human beings.[64]

A good example of their work in the theatre was *Hymn to Pan*, which was performed as part of the Scensommar Festival in Stockholm in 1982, where the audience was confronted with the eight-octave voice/personality of the solo performer, Enrique Pardo, who explored his voice and body in such a way that the sudden changes from animal to human led the audience into believing that the two elements were one. This was enhanced by a technique of speaking in two tones simultaneously, which fully realized Pardo's intentions 'to investigate a sort of hiding place, where the body is instinctive and animalistic, then suddenly reverse the process and become spiritual and idealistic'.[65] Pardo attempted to investigate the psychological parallels between the figure of Pan and human behaviour. Often this took the form of screaming and expressing raw emotions through sound, to the disapproval of some people in the audience.[66] The success of this performance can be gauged by one of the reviews:

> With his *Hymn to Pan*, Enrique Pardo has shown how one can discover an artistic form with an unbelievably enriched and enlivened character, within this extended vocal range, which not only finds its own corporal, bodily expressions, but which also lives in symbiosis with them. Enrique Pardo has created a mythological and poetic language.[67]

The unique nature of the Roy Hart Theatre's vocal instruments has attracted a number of modern composers such as Henze, Stockhausen and Peter Maxwell Davies, who composed his *Songs of a Mad King* for them. Another production, which exceeded the boundaries of normally accepted opera and questioned the very nature of opera as an art form was *Pagliacci*, also part of the Scensommar Festival in Stockholm in 1982. In their exploration of reality and unreality they demonstrated the liberating and creative power of the voice.

A later piece, entitled *Poesis* (1985), was a concert for saxophone and six voices, which was the result of much research into the dramatic relationship between voice and movement at the crossroads of theatre, contemporary opera and dance. There was no text other than the poems of Wallace Stevens, recited in turn by the actors, which was the only time words appeared. Otherwise the voice was the star, and the saxophone played the protagonist, giving tone and colouring to the voices of the actor-singers in the way it offered:

> a continuous flow of images moving from the violent ones of a nightmare to a context of an amalgam between dance, gesture and sonority of the voice and the music . . . even used orchestrally to the point of being able to stand on its own in terms of the structure of the piece as a whole. It succeeds in this way in understanding the significance of the images in perfect fusion with the percussion, a synchronicity of rhythms and of everything which contributes to the conjunction and continuous disassociation of the choral movement. A collective lamentation, rhythmic guttural sounds, brushing against the onomatopeic, following a tonal crescendo which climbs always higher – one exalts this musicalisation, which is the objective of the vocal research of the 'Roy Hart'.[68]

It would seem that the more recent work of the Roy Hart Theatre has taken it into the domain of mythology and psychology. Their research activities into the human voice's possibilities have resulted in performers being able to use their voices however they wish, as one French reviewer commented following *Poesis*: 'The women can growl like polar bears, the men sing like divas. And all of them together form mystical, shadowy, bewitching choirs cut across by cries, howls, macabre or diabolic screechings.'[69]

The Roy Hart Theatre comprises a group of over forty members who are now working freely in many parts of Europe. Although originally Anglo-Saxon, they have never felt at home in Britain, where their vocal experimentation and liberated screaming has generally met with scepticism, except by Peter Brook, who was greatly excited by their work in the sixties. Since then, one can see how many of their ideas have been incorporated into Brook's own theatrical experimentation. Similarly, their discoveries about vocal resonating areas inspired Jerzy Grotowski to experiment further with other possible resonating centres by means of which the voice could exceed the boundaries of traditionally accepted vocal delivery.

In its search for self-confrontation, the Roy Hart Theatre has become the voice of the Third Theatre with its demand for the liberated voice, where a vocal delivery is not 'text-bound' but rather the result of a deep exploration into the mysterious but fascinating relationship between the human voice and emotion. Even the ideology of the Roy Hart Theatre is open-ended these days: some of its members have moved into areas of social awareness and others into more mystical ones. The umbrella is as wide as the untrammelled possibilities of the human voice.

Its effects have been felt not just in the Group Theatre Movement, but also in the whole approach to the voice as means of communication. Parallels can be drawn between this approach – using free vocal imagery – and modern dance, which found a new theatrical impetus in its use of association and irrational, fragmentary visual imagery. In this non-definitive theatre, the theatrical message has a thousand possibilities and awakens a highly personal response – nevertheless a response which, in the best Artaudian sense, is intended to awaken strong feelings.

A 'POOR LANGUAGE' APPROACH: JERZY GROTOWSKI

Grotowski's ideas about vocal delivery in the theatre can best be seen in the light of his evolving ethics for a 'poor theatre'. In his early years as director of the Theatre of Thirteen Rows (1959–61) his work demonstrated a total rejection of the 'artistic kleptomania' which post-war Polish theatre exhibited at the expense of the actor.[70] Believing that the core of theatre art was the 'personal and scenic technique of the actor', Grotowski set about exploring ways of bringing back something of this lost tradition by experimenting with the actor–audience relationship and by reintroducing a disciplined actor-training programme.

Although his early training in Stanislavski acting technique had made a lasting impression on him, Grotowski turned away from the realistic school of acting in his search for a theatre which would speak to modern audiences here and now through its images and which was not content to illustrate dramatic texts.[71] It is not surprising that Artaud's ideology became so pertinent to him.

His approach to vocal training was a rejection of the noble tones and perfect diction which were being taught at drama schools in Poland at that time. Instead Grotowski insisted on the voice being able to 'penetrate the spectator as if it were stereophonic', so that even the walls would resound with the actor's voice.[72]

This insistence on carrying power necessitated mastering total respiration so that the column of air could escape with total force. In order to achieve this, Grotowski devised exercises from a variety of sources, including Hatha yoga and classical Chinese theatre. His realization of the importance of the physiological resonators which modify the voice and its carrying power led him to further experimentation and the location of twenty-two resonators.[73] Influenced by the work of the Roy Hart Theatre, Grotowski came to realize that the function of the body as a resonator was purely a convention and one not based on any scientific facts. This led him to develop organic exercises based on images to assist in the opening of the vocal apparatus. Nevertheless his vocal work at this time was highly disciplined.

The Theatre of Thirteen Rows endeavoured to rectify the decayed relationship between theatre and text. Grotowski believed that theatre had to go beyond literature in order to discover its own language, which was not a language of words but 'the score of human impulses and reactions. The psychic process, revealed through the bodily and vocal reactions of a living, human organism'.[74] This principle guided his productions, where, in the vein of Artaud, he endeavoured to address the audience through feelings and not the spoken word. The text for him was not the core of the theatre – rather the 'encounter' was: 'For me, a creator of theatre, the important thing is not the words but what we do with these words, what gives life to the inanimate words of the text, what transforms them into "the Word"'.[75]

This approach was demonstrated in his productions at the Theatre of Thirteen Rows. In his first production, *Orpheus* (1960), Grotowski showed his intention of entering into a polemic relationship with the written text. In the words of one contemporary critic:

> The director wished to transmit the philosophical contents through purely theatrical means. Therefore the literary aspect becomes a scaffolding, on which theatre can build its own construction. Each sentence, almost each word has its own internal rhythm. The action is formulated like a musical score.[76]

In his next production, *Cain* (1960), Byron's dramatic poem,

Grotowski pursued this approach to the written text even further, which is characteristic of all his work at this time. There were elaborate effects it would seem, such as the text being used as orchestrated sound played through loudspeakers, to which the actors moved in rhythm. One critic summed it up as follows:

> There are continual changes in the acting and a thousand ideas, insistent deafening music, a loudspeaker talking (none too distinctly) in place of the actor on the stage, an actor amongst the audience, actors addressing the public, actors improvising during scene changes. A general tower of Babel and confusion of tongues.[77]

Byron's verse was given a free interpretation: it was sometimes treated seriously and at other times parodied, or delivered as an operatic aria, or with the rhythm totally obliterated, making it sound like prose and everyday speech. The dialogue was supplemented by action in the form of metaphors taken from sport.[78]

In his production of *Mystery-Bouffe* after Mayakovsky (1960) Grotowski took the playwright's instructions regarding treating his texts simply as scenario quite literally. Although he did not change the text so much, he combined this play with another play by the same author, *The Bath-House*, and even included some medieval Polish mystery plays as a prologue and an epilogue. With this production, Grotowski took up the question of director/author autonomy.

The choice of *Shakuntala* (1960) was a determined attempt to explore the possibility of creating signs in the European theatre in order to find the sources of ritual play such as existed in the Peking Opera and the Oriental theatre.[79] This search for gestural and vocal signals was important for the company, as it emphasized their need for special vocal exercises and established the style in which the theatre was to continue – a ritual theatre as opposed to a theatre of illusion. A particular quality of the performance was the artificial manner of speaking adopted by the actors as an allusion to conventional liturgical incantations thrown into juxtaposition with the everyday meaning of words. The audience was also delegated a special role in this production. Further experiments with the theatrical space and actor–audience relationship were conducted in the Theatre of Thirteen Rows' last performance, *Dziady* (Forefathers Eve), in 1961.

The second phase of the Laboratory Theatre (1962–8) was marked by a gradual departure from theatrical elements and the practice of consciously manipulating the audience, in favour of research into the art of acting together with a crystallization of the creative concept of 'poor theatre'.[80]

The training particularly characteristic of this period was concerned with discovering the 'laws of man's expression', so that the actor's body would not resist the actor.[81] The training was not a kind of preparation for each production, an activity which Grotowski dismissed as an impossibility, but a way of ridding the body of fear and preparing it for the 'total act'. The daily training session consisted of two to three hours of vocal and physical exercises.

The voice work was primarily concerned with acquiring breathing techniques and discovering extra resonators as used in the Oriental theatre. The playing style which Grotowski was trying to build up at this time was also Oriental in the way it endeavoured to use vocal and physical 'compositions' to communicate by association and allusion.

However, during their preparations for *Dr Faustus* (1963), *The Hamlet Study* (1964) and *The Constant Prince* (1965), a change took place in Grotowski's attitude towards the training, which became more orientated towards the individual. The purpose of the exercises was to eradicate obstacles – blockages which hampered the creative flow. As Eugenio Barba explained: 'The exercises represent neither a formula nor a system, they are merely an approach, a way of leading one to find one's biological impulses'.[82]

In time, Grotowski came to realize that work on the resonators was becoming too conscious, which only created further blockages. As a result he devised a method of working on the voice's echoes instead of the mechanism itself. In this way the process became more organic and spontaneous instead of consciously manipulated, which supported Grotowski's principle of 'via-negativa', or non-interference, whereby the actor was encouraged to confront the character within himself and offer the result of that encounter to an audience. This was the most important aspect of Grotowski's discoveries about training the voice: learning to release psycho-physiological blocks rather than trying to force the 'natural' voice to learn unnatural techniques, and the key principle underlying them was: 'Bodily activity comes first, and then vocal expression.'[83]

This second phase of the Laboratory Theatre's work took the experiments with text and language further away from the language of words and more towards the language of orchestrated sound and images. In *Kordian* (1962) both tragedy and the grotesque were explored by means of a device of using incantation counterpointed by physical action of quite another character, as Kordian fell into a coma and delivered his monologue as if he were in a state of delirium, while a doctor performed a medical operation. Much of the original text had been cut or manipulated, while other effects were gained by experimenting with the actor–audience relationship.

In *Akropolis* (1962) Grotowski had refashioned Wyspianski's drama into a montage 'with fragments, scenes and with a concentration camp', combined with inspiration from another source – from the stories of Borowski. The greater part of the performance action was the result of improvisations around the verbal score, which the group had constructed. In this production, no attempt was made to manipulate the audience. Rather, all attempts at a non-emotive form of expression were employed – including use of face as mask and use of language to bring spontaneous associations to the spectator's mind. Flaszen described the vocal score as follows:

> starting from the confused babbling of the very small child and including the most sophisticated oratorical recitation. Inarticulate groans, animal roars, tender folksongs, liturgical chants, dialects, declamation of poetry: everything is there. The sounds are interwoven in a complex score which brings back fleetingly the memory of all the forms of language.[84]

With *Dr Faustus* (1963) the structure of Marlowe's text was rearranged. The production began with the final hour of Faustus's life on earth and took the form of the last supper. Again Grotowski adopted a polemical attitude to the original text and made of Faustus a saint – a lay martyr. In a production which was heavily religious, there was a development towards a 'poor theatre' in the total absence of props. However, once more physiological sound was used to create atmosphere and this gave an impetus to the daily exercising which the group was undertaking at this time with Eugenio Barba. As one observer noted: 'Their voices reached from the smallest whisper to an astonishing, almost cavernous tone, an intoned declaiming of a resonance and power I have not heard from actors before.'[85] This production realized for the first time Grotowski's concept of the actor in the 'total act' of sacrifice, which was made manifest in the piercing scream emanating from the mouth of Faustus, who as a trapped animal is carried off by Mephisto.

The production of *The Constant Prince* (1965), which took almost a year to prepare, has been acknowledged by many as best demonstrating Grotowski's acting method. It was the last production by the Laboratory Theatre that had a conventional text as its base, although as with other productions this was a collage from many different sources, where again the theme was brutality and the human sacrifice of the individual pitted against the group. Eric Bentley dismissed the group's attempts to capture the text's 'inner meaning' of the play by disregarding Calderon's three-act structure, while at the same time praising the spatial arrangements.[86] Other critics saw Grotowski's rejection of the language of words and intellectualism in favour of the poetic concept of the text as highly successful. One of them, Peter Feldman, even maintained: 'The effect of this theatre's unique use of vocal rhythm, pitch, dynamics, tonality and careful orchestration is to enhance the *word*, to restore it from idea to image.'[87]

The acting of Ryszard Cieslak in the title role realized Grotowski's idea of the actor being 'penetrated', having 'transcended the state of his inner dichotomy'.[88] His vocal and physical technique, which was described as 'acrobatic', also received great praise. This bore out Grotowski's theories that body and voice were one: 'The voice is the summit of the reaction of the body (to a cycle of associations) ... I have a contact with you and therefore I have a voice. The contact does not exist if it does not exist in the body.'[89]

With *Apocalypsis Cum Figuris* (1969), which was three years in the making, the Laboratory Theatre departed from literature altogether. This production was not a montage of texts but something arrived at through improvisation in rehearsal and, in Grotowski's words: 'It was only then that we turned to the text, to speech.'[90]

During the twelve years it was presented to the public it underwent continual transformation. A description of it can be gleaned from the following:

> as an art form it was possibly closer to poetry than anything else. There was a poetry of body complementing a poetry of

sound, in which the reverberations of each action or word were inexhaustible. Associations were condensed into rich metaphors or naked imagery, and a response from actor or audience did not necessarily operate on the conscious level.[91]

It was not only the text which was relinquished: the acting area was devoid of staging devices; eventually costumes were abandoned; only the very basic properties were retained and the key word was 'transformation'. It became an obvious external manifestation for the 'poor theatre' concept, with the actor's art in the centre and the spectator able to abandon the role of observer.

The performance, which was conceived as a Second Coming, has become a classic of modern theatre. Its evolution over the years reflected changes within the group, which finally resulted in their rejection of theatre as an artistic form and eventual involvement in post-theatrical experimentation in para-theatre projects, where the emphasis was shifted from theatre to psychotherapy.

Grotowski's approach has had considerable influence on leading avant-garde directors such as Jean-Louis Barrault, Peter Brook, Joe Chaikin and Luca Ronconi. He instigated the rash of 'theatre laboratories' which sprang up in the early seventies. Perhaps the most significant of these groups has been Odin Teatret under Eugenio Barba's leadership in Denmark, The Performance Group under Richard Schechner and the Living Theatre under Julian Beck and Judith Malina. These groups share a common rejection of discursive speech for the 'poor language' approach - the cry, the shout, the litany or the chant and 'text-less' plays. As well as exploring modes of non-verbal communication, the groups have sought to recreate ritual drama as a primitive ceremony and seen their role as prophesying, with the actor as priest or shaman.

IN SEARCH OF THE METAPHYSICAL MOMENT OF CREATION: PETER BROOK

Like Grotowski, Brook is concerned with creating theatre which is important now – an 'immediate theatre' – and like Grotowski his concept of theatre is a pragmatic one, in which he is able to appreciate different dramatic forms while at the same time rejecting the theatrical status quo as 'a cultural garbage heap'.[92] This is reflected in the changing approaches to the theatrical event which he has experimented with. Nevertheless there has been one guiding line in all Brook's work, which he himself sees as being a consistent point of view to which he has been totally committed.[93] This has been his fight against 'deadly theatre' – 'a theatre which exists on politeness, where people do not respond directly to one another and where the audience also reacts politely'.[94]

His changing directions reveal a search for the essence of a theatrical event which is simple but compelling. This explains why he has abandoned artificial theatricality in set, costume and lighting and concentrated upon the performer. Brook maintains that, apart from the space, the actor is the only instrument without whom a performance cannot exist because he fills the 'empty space' with his voice and body and ability to tell a story. Consequently he advocates a theatre which combines elements of the 'holy' and the 'rough' because he sees society as having lost all sense of ritual and ceremony and yet craving an experience that is beyond the humdrum. At the same time he acknowledges that people need a vital theatre which is close to them, which deals with their actions, and sees an immediate theatre as the only way to feed their spiritual and social needs.

Brook's concept of the creative actor is one who is constantly searching. He does not believe that a character is 'built', but that the actor should explore aspects of the character which are always partial, maintaining that if he is searching honestly, he sheds and starts again and again by constantly destroying and abandoning, so that a character is born and reborn.[95] In fact, Brook's ideas about acting can be seen as a synthesis of all the aforementioned theoreticians in this chapter: from Stanislavski he has learned that an actor must practise how to be insincere with sincerity – how to lie truthfully; from Brecht he has learned the value of distancing oneself from the work by stepping back and looking at the results; from Artaud he has learned that by abandoning the text and working through improvisation one can return to the roots of physical expression; from the Roy Hart Theatre he has learned that there is a language of tones and sounds that have no conceptual meaning; and from Grotowski he has learned that actors are mediumistic.

Brook has always been concerned with the role which language plays in performance, but has grown more and more dissatisfied with the language of words in his search for another language as agile and penetrating as that the Elizabethans created, full of intensity, immediacy and density of expression.[96] He became a devotee of the Artaudian approach in which the play, the event itself, stands in place of the text. Believing that communication on a deeper, more universal level was hindered by cultural and linguistic contexts after his tour of *King Lear* to Eastern Europe, Brook has sought the non-verbal. This has encouraged him to experiment with the ritual properties of language – breathing, rhythm and chanting – and even to search for an 'international' language, which could communicate by using the associative, connotative aspects of language instead of the conceptual ones. In this way he feels he will be able to work on the audience's feelings rather than their intellects.

His interest in the voice is intrinsically wound up in his belief about acting: 'The body must be ready and sensitive, but that isn't all. The voice has to be open and ready. The emotions have to be open and free.'[97] In this way, Brook feels that the actor will be open and ready for any new demands which changes in the text may make. He is critical of declamation and the manner in which old classical actors seemed to sing their lines, because this tradition perpetuates an acceptance of artificiality.[98] He prefers the actor whose voice and creative abilities are open to nature and the instincts of the moment, believing that the actor needs precise exercises to 'liberate the voice, not so that one learns how to do, but how to permit – how to set the voice free'.[99]

This maxim was carried over into his work on Shakespeare's texts in rehearsal, where he advised what a liberating force the rigidity of the rhythm and the use of vowels and consonants could be for bringing out the meaning of the words,[100] although he maintained that Shakespeare was trying to explain something beyond words altogether and that the actor should seek and sound out the word's impulses. This approach was reflected in his rehearsal techniques in *A Midsummer Night's Dream* in 1970, where he had set up obstacles against which actors with monologues had to fight in order to face the text afresh. In this way he was constantly searching for a 'necessary theatre' and broke with the prevailing approaches to speaking verse at the Royal Shakespeare Company in the sixties, which had been operatic on the one hand or naturalistic on the other.[101] He is adamant that an actor should not approach a speech or monologue by looking for its music or only for its meaning, but that 'verse is more like a formula where within the crackling consonants a meaning writhes that's ever on the change – carried by meaning's bearers – images'.[102] Because of its esoteric nature, this directive is hard for an actor to understand; nevertheless Brook holds fast to the belief that this is a fundamental part of an actor's technique. His belief in the magic power of words has encouraged him to acknowledge that Shakespeare is trying to explain something beyond words altogether and that rehearsing a play is like going into the woods, where, by continually destroying and abandoning, the actor should sense the life of the words as he speaks them.

His productions verify and clarify his commitment to continual experimentation with vocal delivery. It was obvious in his Theatre of Cruelty Season (1964) with some of the members of the Royal Shakespeare Company, where, together with Charles Marowitz and Grotowski, he explored the meaning of language in the 'holy' theatre. In an effort to rediscover ways of communicating which would correspond to the 'broken and fragmentary way in which most people experience reality', the traditionally trained actors set about exploring theatre language designed to demolish conventional dramatic value. Their research activities entailed exploring ways of communicating an internal state by thought transfer, then adding vocal sounds and physical rhythms, in order to discover the least amount of information needed before one could reach an understanding.[103] Grotowski was to take these principles further in his Theatre Laboratory. Another important similarity with Grotowski can be seen in Brook's attempts at environmental theatre.

In his production of *Oedipus* (1965) Brook furthered his experiments with language when he came upon the realization that whereas audiences have always shown an interest in the myth and the formally shaped work, they refuse to listen to contemporary events. Therefore he engaged Ted Hughes to rewrite Seneca's tragedy so that parallels could be drawn between the bloodshed of Rome and Vietnam. According to the director's notes, the speeches were patterned on Maori chants delivered in depersonalized monotones, and stylized emotional effects were to be achieved by strong and irregular rhythms of breathing derived from recordings of a witchdoctor in a trance.[104] All of this was intended to engender excitement.

According to Innes, Gielgud set the tone by delivering a four-page impassioned speech accompanied by one restrictive movement, while vocal effects came from the chorus placed around the spectators, repeating the words to create echoing chants and accompanying the description of the plague with rapid rhythmic panting and chest-beating.[105] In the best Artaudian tradition, the non-comprehensible language and shock-tactics for the audience at the end of the play were meant to force them out of a state of dazed applauding pity.

Audience confrontation was explored further in the 1966 experimental work *US*, where the use of a contemporary, highly perishable fun language and a multiplicity of contradictory techniques were intended both to woo and annoy the spectator. The aim of the production was 'to articulate world-wide political tragedy in all its aspects, searching beyond documentary "theatre of fact" to the deeper currents of thought and feeling which a theatre performance can provide'.[106]

The theme of Brook's first year of research at the International Centre for Theatre Research in Paris (1968) was, in his own words, 'to be a study of structure of sounds. Our aim was to discover more fully what constitutes living expression.'[107] The group of actors from different countries was without 'shared words, shared signs, shared references, shared languages, shared slang, shared cultural or subcultural imagery'.[108]

After returning to London, the group's experiments with *The Tempest* in the same year marked the beginning of a recurring method of work. This started with improvisation and reduced the text to a couple of words, often delivered in a dehumanized chant, explored by the group in mass action and choric speech. At this stage of 'work in progress', Brook relinquished the surface plot and 'pretty writing' of the original, in favour of exploring the buried themes which would foster a more universal statement on the condition of man. The film of the production shows the breaking down of traditional actor–audience zones, the primitive nature of man beneath the veneer of civilization and language as an 'instrument of oppression and exploitation'.[109] The results of this questioning and experimentation crystallized in *The Empty Space*, which was published at this time.

Brook's continuing search for an immediate theatre resulted in the RSC production of *A Midsummer Night's Dream* (1970), where, in his own words, they were always 'at the beginning of something' –

experimenting and discarding what was not useful. This openness applied not only to set and costumes, but to the words as well: 'You must act as a medium for the words. If you consciously colour them you're wasting your time. The words must be able to colour you.'[110] As one of the actors explained, Brook wanted the text to play them, rather than they the text. By employing these means, he felt they would be forced to experience the metaphysical moment when the author first created the words.

The most remarkable linguistic experiment was without doubt *Orghast*, at the 1971 festival in Persepolis, Persia, for which Ted Hughes created a special mode of speech, whose aim was to underline the 'organic' unity of content and form. This language was not only designed to reflect 'the sensation of a half-barbaric world', but to affect 'magically' the mental state of a listener on an instinctive level in the same way that sound can affect the growth of plants. Richard Peaslee, the American composer who worked with Peter Brook on *Orghast* in 1971, said that the production was a big leap forward for the theatre, from representational to abstract, abandoning the meaning of words for their sound; a similar leap happened in art fifty years ago, when the form of an object was abandoned in favour of studying its colour and its shape.[111] Sounds were given specific emotive values and where words were created the aim was to give the listener the experience of the moment. The resulting 2,000 odd words all had semantic meanings – many of the roots being an 'onomatopoeic rendering of physiological states'.[112] In spite of its 'organic' intentions, the production was a bewildering event for many members of the audience who did not have a feeling for the esoteric language and who needed some intellectual clarification.

A change in approach to the language used in performance was evident in Brook's work on subsequent productions, where the group began to move away from the practice of fragmenting the text. Their next work was taken from the book *The Conference of the Birds* by John Heilpern. It toured extensively in Africa, where the group experienced the possibility of creating a universality of sound when they managed to communicate with a group of villagers by pouring all the intensity of their life's experience into one single sound.

Besides improvising directly on Colin Turnbull's *The Mountain People*, they made a script which gave them a broad outline, then discarded the script and improvised page after page for weeks.[113]

Finally this was formally welded into dramatic form and renamed *The Ik* (1975). In both these works, Brook was again exploring man and his relation to his environment. His intentions were to combine the 'ceremonial' with the 'everyday' and this seems to underline the direction which his work in the eighties has taken. He has shown a desire to renew contact with the near-forgotten oral tradition of folk-tales and popular theatre. This was particularly true of his reworking of *Carmen* (1981), which was taken 'off its pedestal' and in which the singers were encouraged to act by singing 'to' each other as in normal dialogue and to synchronize gesture and voice.[114]

The production of the Hindu epic *Mahabharata* marks the culmination of this approach to working on a text: the narrative of everyday life is interspersed with improvised scenes, which add dimension and highlight certain ritualistic moments in an almost inexplicable way. In the logic of the East, this is according to Brook the essence of *dharma* – the essential motor. Whatever opposes it or is ignorant of it is not evil in the Christian sense – but negative.[115] One cannot say this has ever applied to Brook's theatrical contribution – particularly in relation to vocal delivery. In all his experiments with language and communication, Brook has been searching for a theatre, albeit 'necessary', 'immediate', 'rough' or 'holy', but nevertheless a theatre where the actor was to resume centre stage. This has been revealed time and again in his work with Shakespeare, where he has challenged the actor, in his handling of the verse and prose, to try to understand how to combine emotionality with intellect, literariness with the commonplace, in order to arrive at a form which gives the meanings life.[116]

Although he admits to disliking the term 'style' Brook's research activities indicate his fascination for it, where by mixing the naturalistic with the absurd and the epic in classics as well as modern dramas, he urges the actor to transcend the commonplace and engage an audience to appreciate the deepest reality of its present existence. That Brook's interest in combining doctrines and styles has played an important part in shaping his own theories is reflected in the following statement: 'For Artaud theatre is fire; for Brecht, theatre is clear vision; for Stanislavski, theatre is humanity. Why must we choose among them?'[117] The success of his many experiments with theatrical form speak loudly in support of this interculturalistic approach.

4

DIRECTORIAL VISIONS

In the modern theatre as opposed to the theatre of the nineteenth century, one cannot overestimate the part played by the director. It is the director and not the playwright who assumes responsibility for the play initially and it is his interpretation which shapes its realization. Everything in the final production must comply with his vision. It is usually his conception of time, place and behaviour which he expects the actors to be able to recreate rather than the actors themselves being free to create their own characterizations. His treatment of the play's language is also part of this interpretation together with all the other elements which combine to make the performance: scenography, costume, lighting, sound, music and so on.

The search for a new theatrical language, which the aforementioned theoreticians experimented with in their reanalysis of the basic elements of the theatre, has influenced many directors in the twentieth century, particularly in their approach to Shakespeare. Others have taken different directions, adopted new approaches to the text, incorporated the playwright into the rehearsal situation, followed particular political points of view or sought new performance places. Some have come to rehearsals with very precisely calculated notes and *mise-en-scène*, allowing very little room for actor-intervention or ensemble playing. While others, wishing to remain open and flexible, have created everything as they have proceeded. One element has nevertheless been common to all of them – a re-evaluation of the Word.

INGMAR BERGMAN: THROUGH SHAKESPEARE DARKLY

One of the most innovative directors of the modern theatre, not to mention a film-maker of international reknown, is Ingmar

Bergman, whose seventy major stage productions extend over a period of four decades. Although most of these productions have been seen in Sweden only, more recently they have been performed internationally as well. Bergman refers to himself as much more a man of the theatre than a man of the film because he regards working in the theatre as a way of life: 'To go to the theatre in the morning, to go to the rehearsal room, to come together with the actors and sit down, and to work with them . . . learning to listen to the playwright's words and to his heart together with the actors . . . that is a way of living; that is the best of all'.[1]

Bergman has stated that the director's role is one of communicating the author's text to the audience via the medium of the actors, as straightforwardly and effectively as possible, maintaining: 'I cannot and will not play a piece against the writer's point of view and I have never done that.'[2] He prefers the play to live inside him during the pre-planning stages and then 'infects' the actors with his intentions during the rehearsals. For this reason, Bergman is adamant that he has directed only plays which have interested him, and that he has not imposed a particular line or dogma on them. This is reflected in his fascination with *Macbeth* and *Twelfth Night*. In his analyses, he does, however, try to discover the reason why the author has written the play, in the belief that in this way he can inspire and stimulate the actors.

Bergman dislikes the kind of directing which tends to do everything else but the play itself and is sceptical about the kind of approach in which everything about the play is explored in an open ensemble fashion, working from an open book and improvising, as is the case with Brook. He admits that even prior to rehearsals he knows where the actors are going to be and whether they will have contact with each other. This has earned him the unsavoury title of 'puppet-master' over the years, a criticism which he unflinchingly refutes, asserting that someone must set the 'march-tempo' and that the actor has an intense need for a correcting and controlling ear and eye.

This attitude is reflected not only in his work with actors in rehearsal, where, according to Sjögren: 'Every gesture, every pause, every movement is established with the utmost care. The precision is created often by physically manipulating the actors – tried and fixed.'[3] It is also revealed in his longing for precision in the treatment of a text. Bergman believes that whereas the reading of a musical score provides enormous freedom and security in its strictest forms, people put themselves too much into the reading of a text in the theatre instead of reflecting the text's obvious reality. Consequently, the lack of precision in the theatrical *partitur/score*, in everything which is not noted – key, pitch, rhythm, intensity and dynamics – is what Bergman tries to give in his stage directions, just as a conductor does, often reminding the actors to look at the notes and not the words.

On the question of text fidelity, Bergman fully supports his readiness to cut and change by referring to himself as an 'interpreter and a re-creator' who interprets in the same way a conductor interprets a score:

> In my case it has always been a matter of reading closely. . .
> If the text is a hidden path into the writer's consciousness, the director ultimately must translate the explicit or implicit choices and values he discovers there into his own theatre language – which is, in the final analysis, the only language in which a playwright can be heard by a living, contemporary audience. The act of producing a play on the stage creates a new organism, an integral work of art responsive, by definition, to a whole set of circumstances.[4]

In this way, Bergman fully hopes to make the plays live in the hearts of the audience, naming repeatedly the following four items as the only important ones for a production's success: the play, the words, the actors and the audience.

Although his repertoire is wide, Bergman's productions of the classics indicate best his treatment of the text and his approach to vocal delivery. He has repeatedly professed his particular preference for classical plays, maintaining that they often express the problems of our own time better than does contemporary drama.[5] This has been demonstrated in his productions of Molière's plays, and in brilliant new interpretations of Strindberg and Ibsen, as well as in his handling of Shakespeare.

Bergman's Shakespeare productions can be divided into three different periods, the forties, the seventies and the eighties, and consequently indicate the particular direction his attitude to the vocal delivery of verse has taken in the complicated production matrix, where he has also tried to accommodate his fascination with rhythm and timing. His reason for not doing any Shakespeare in the fifties and sixties was that another Swedish director, Alf Sjöberg, was doing such crystal clear productions that he had nothing to add.

In his early years as a director, Bergman attempted *Macbeth* no fewer than three times. His first production with a group of students attracted widespread interest when it coincided with the German invasion of Denmark in 1940. The second one was in the autumn of 1944, when he became the fourth artistic director of the Hälsingborg City Theatre. Again the theme of the production was Nazi totalitarianism, and programme notes refer to a ferocious confrontation with a murderer and a war criminal. In a simple setting, where the visual effects were projected against a background of red and black, Bergman revealed his predilection for bold suggestive compositions, winning for his production the title of chamber play, a trend which was to follow him throughout his career.

Another trend which was already in evidence in this *Macbeth* was textual modification – particularly in the interpretation of the heath, which was depicted as a battlefield where the bereaved wives of the fallen had gathered, and where the most talkative of the witches had been translated into a fortune-teller! According to one critic, they all appear in a ragged group at the foot of Macbeth's bed – obviously obsessing his mind – and the room is filled with the sound of disembodied voices.[6]

Bergman's next production of *Macbeth* was in 1948 at the Gothenburg City Theatre, in itself one of the most technically advanced and difficult theatre spaces in Sweden at that time. The simplicity of the former production was replaced by one of Wagnerian proportions, in which, according to most of the critics, the visual spectacle seemed to overwhelm both Shakespeare and the actors with what one of them called 'its numerous periphrastic flourishes around the heart of the drama. . . The sensations keep our attention alive, but they distract our gaze from the faces of the actors, which ought to be the true focus of our attention.'[7] Another critic, Grevenius, agreed, declaring that 'the ceaseless raising and lowering of stage machinery and the whole weight of the scenic apparatus served to dissipate the ability to listen with real attentiveness'.[8]

The stage setting was a massively elaborate split-level playing area connected by a perilously steep spiral staircase. This could be utilized as a drawbridge for some scenes by lowering it, and by raising it space could be allowed for the banquet scenes. The designer, Carl-Johan Ström, made great use of contrasting the dour Scottish court, with its reds and browns, with the lighter, more airy, Renaissance festivities of the English court, by a technique of foregrounding silhouettes. A gigantic oak tree on one side was used to suspend the bodies of hanged men from, 'like overripe fruit', during the more diabolic scenes, and carcasses of oxen during the banquet scenes. It even allowed the witches – transformed into seductive creatures – to writhe alluringly through its branches.

Later, Bergman admitted that he learnt from this unfortunate production to mistrust effects which are not organically integrated or motivated: 'Superimposed trappings always hang loosely and rattle. . . One hears and sees from them that they hang on the outside and are dead, no matter how unusual or tasteful they may otherwise be.'[9]

Another major factor which influenced this production was the fact that Bergman and the leading actor playing Macbeth, Anders Ek, were not in agreement about the interpretation of the central themes of the play. Ek saw the murdering tyrant as a product of society, while Bergman believed that it was inherent evil which destroyed him, and was more interested in the character's psychological behaviour. Nevertheless, it was while at Gothenburg City Theatre that Bergman was forced to see for the first time that 'compulsion won't work' and that a director is obliged to respect the playwright and his work. As part of his training, he was also forced to explain his motivation for productions to his mentor, Torsten Hammaren, from whom he learned the importance of meticulous preparation before commencing rehearsal.

In terms of style of vocal delivery, it is not surprising that neither Macbeth, Anders Ek, nor Lady Macbeth, Karin Kavli, pay much attention to the verse or the text in this production. Ek sounds as if he belongs to the previous century, performing in the old declamatory style, with a little tremble of passion in his voice.[10] Kavli and most of the supporting roles demonstrate a very natural vocal delivery style, more in keeping with post-war trends in vocal delivery in Sweden, which was following the new wave of psychological realism in playwriting at this time.[11]

The lessons learned in these early formative years shaped Bergman's approach to his next Shakespeare production, *Twelfth Night*, nearly thirty years later, at the Royal Dramatic Theatre (Dramaten) in Stockholm in 1975, and later revived in 1979. The staging for this production was kept to a bare minimum, suggesting an Elizabethan innyard or hall, with a musician's gallery across the back for musicians to accompany the action. The furnishings, which were minimal, were carried on and off the central platform playing area by stagehands as required. A special feature of this production was that the actors were in full view of the audience awaiting their entrances, a technique which had impressed Bergman at the Comédie Française and which he was to incorporate in further productions, believing that it kept the actors concentrated and involved in the play.

At this stage in his development, Bergman expressed his fascination with the human beings on the stage, rather than with the visual or auditory effects which had marked his earlier productions, believing that film and TV could show these things much better: 'The theatre calls for nothing. TV includes everything, film includes everything, there everything is shown. Theatre ought to be the encounter of human beings with human beings and nothing more. All else is distracting.'[12] This practice had been successful in his Strindberg productions from the seventies, where, by abolishing effects, he brilliantly activated the audience, and the end result was that the text was given primacy. Bergman's method of working on a key speech from *The Ghost Sonata* in 1973 was given the utmost praise by Egil Törnquist who, following the rehearsals, remarked on the similarity between conductor and choreographer:

> Frequently he demonstrates how a speech can be broken up into shorter movements, each one with its own particular tone, so that the speech as a whole is molded into a word-melody, rich in psychological nuances. And on the stage he demonstrates, usually by applying his hands in various ways, the positions, gestures and movement patterns of the actors.[13]

Such was not the case in the handling of text and vocal delivery style in this production of *Twelfth Night*. The verse was on the whole treated as prose, in a new translation by Allan Bergstrand. The spoken rhythm and tempo was slow and heavy in what can best be described as a natural delivery style and nothing was overdone or unbelievable.[14] This was not surprising to critic and Shakespeare expert Leif Zern, who maintained that the main problem of performing Shakespeare in Swedish is one of not understanding the text: 'Shakespeare's theatre begins and ends in the language and the text. It does not work to play him without a very exact knowledge of the text. And when "that" does not exist with the director then it does not exist either with the actors or with the audience.'[15] The other problem, according to this critic, is that most productions since the middle of the seventies have been content to settle for a traditional approach. He gave full praise to Bergman, however, for bringing out the darker, more pessimistic side of this comedy.

Most of the critics were very positive about the production, in particular the music and the simple Elizabethan stage setting by Gunilla Palmstierna-Weiss. The lack of over-impressive decoration drew attention to the text, according to Tord Baeckström, who found that: 'When all this is removed, one acts so to speak directly from inside the text completely prepared to listen to its fantastic music.'[16]

It was the season's great success and was given for the first time as part of a summer repertoire at the national theatre. Its renewal in 1979 met with equal praise, although Bengt Jahnsson felt it was equivocal – half following authentic Elizabethan traditions and half the Romantic Shakespeare traditions of the 1800s.[17]

In Bergman's next Shakespeare production, *King Lear*, again at Dramaten in 1984, many similarities could be seen with his *Twelfth Night*. Once more a preference was shown for simplicity in the acting area; however, this time there was no attempt at reconstructing an Elizabethan playhouse. Maximum empty space was the criterion for the stage setting, which comprised an enormous red semi-circle – with red carpet covering the entire stage floor and red cloth on the walls. Entrances and exits were seldom made, as most of the characters remained on stage throughout the entire performance, however a barely discernible place was allowed for these at the back centre stage behind a red screen, and further possibilities were through the wings. In this proscenium-arch theatre, the stageframe itself was outlined in black, thereby emphasizing the distance between the audience and the stage, which enhanced the idea of a 'world of illusion'. A bewildering effect was created by Cordelia, who upon being banished sat on stage throughout, observing the action, while a ramp extending out to the first row offered the possibility for making contact with the audience at times.

The setting remained the same throughout the performance –

abstract in character – with no particular reference to either time or place. Neither was there any difference between the interior and exterior scenes. The only significant change was the last effect in the production, where after a deafening noise, the red walls collapsed, revealing the naked black walls of the theatre itself. Properties were barely used at all, but where this was the case, they were carried on and off – otherwise they were created by the physical bodies of the extras on stage, who represented thrones, stocks and so on. A special feature of the scenography was that many extras were choreographed back and forth and in special groups depending on their size and the colour of their costumes. The costumes suggested the 1600s, with Lear, his daughters and the court in splendid Renaissance court attire of warm pink and orange tones, while every attempt was made to suggest typical everyday wear for the other characters. The only group whose costumes took on more semiotic significance was the group of two-metre-high soldiers whose padded black uniforms and helmets were more reminiscent of the film *Star Wars* than the Renaissance.

Many and varied are the possibilities for interpreting what Bergman and his scenographer, Gunilla Palmstierna-Weiss, meant this setting to represent. One could be led to believe that its abstract nature would throw all the concentration on to the text, which, in accordance with Granville-Barker's theories, is the only way to play Shakespeare.[18] This was not the case, however, in this production, where the text was a greatly simplified new translation by Britt Hallquist in answer to Bergman's request for a 'playable, speakable and above all understandable version'.[19] The problems of translating Shakespeare into Swedish are many, but it was not only the language itself which in this translation underwent a great deal of up-dating and simplifying. Approximately 34 per cent of the text was cut, many of the lines were given to other characters or were shared, while many of the scenes were rearranged.[20] Most of the poetic imagery was eliminated, as were all specific references to time or place. In addition, most of the titles were removed or replaced with names, thereby eliminating the possibility of showing the degree of respect for power or social hierarchy which their costumes would otherwise seem to indicate. As a result of this, the character of Lear was given less importance, while the daughters and the characters who stand for evil gained in importance.

In realizing this text in performance, it was almost inevitable that Bergman should be forced to emphasize the visual aspects more than the auditive ones. They did not, however, appear to strengthen or support any particular directorial line. Nevertheless the foregrounding of the stage setting – this pulsating, red, womb-like world unrelated to time or place – forced itself in on the audience in a relentless and frustrating fashion. The references to the 1600s in costuming and in the music and dance which served as a prelude – a lively presentation by jesters and acrobats similar to a group of wandering players – were contradicted by the ever-presence of a threatening row of modern tall soldiers carrying long spears and wearing padded black costumes with helmets over their faces and by the use of such modern language. Even further confusion arose over the meta-theatrical effect in the last instant of the production, the collapse of this theatrical 'no-man's land'. Was this an attempt to underline a theme such as 'All the world's a stage, and all the men and women merely players'?

Further consequences which this particular textual reading had on the production were of a more essential character, and this involved the whole question of the main theme of the tragedy of *King Lear*. Without doubt, this play centres on the question of what the consequences are which can befall a vain and self-satisfied man of power. Central to this motif is the main character, Lear, and the drama's *peripeteia* is structured around the changes which he undergoes. The reduction of textual content for Lear in this translation greatly affected his possible realization on stage. He was a weak character at the beginning of the performance, and had not undergone any catharsis at the end, therefore his character was rendered uninteresting. Not even the fates which befell him were of interest in this production. Of much greater interest were the perverse sexual activities of Goneril and Regan, to which their diabolical struggling for power incited them, although even here their characters remained on one level.

Most of the actors maintained high levels of emotion in their role-presentations, as illustrated by the frequency of shouting in their vocal deliveries. Very little use was made of the verse form or of the structure of the text. The text was not simply overshadowed but rather replaced by an emotional and physical kind of theatre, where what the audience saw and experienced through its senses was given priority. The single exception was the actor playing Lear, who revealed that prior to the première he had memorized all his text and even practised aloud with all the emphasis and pauses in place. He delivered his lines in a mannered way reminiscent of the style of one of the older romantic actors of the last century, while the rest of the characters employed an emotion-filled vocal delivery style.[21] The audience's attention was not engaged by this production on any deeper level other than that of interest and admiration for the effects which the colourful groupings and choreographic configurations could render. The constant visual reorganization even succeeded in breaking the audience's concentration, preventing them from listening to what was being said. The emphasis on grouping also managed to divert attention from the individual characters – or to interpret their kinetic significance in a particular group formation.

The reactions to this production were varied, although as was usually the case with a Bergman production, the expectations were high and much praise was given. Most of the enthusiasm was directed to the visual magic of this production, although one critic, who was critical of the declamatory vocal delivery style of Lear and of the directorial line taken, dared to question: 'Lear is a senile old man who gets what he deserves – is that *King Lear?*'[22] Another referred to the desperate 'Beckett-effect' in the final scene as being an anti-climax. Leif Zern seemed to get to the heart of the problem when he wrote:

> The problem with Bergman's *King Lear* is that it is so definite in its form, and it is curious that a play which to a great extent is about chaos and destruction – and which takes place in rain and nasty weather, tempest and hail – is played on a red velvet mat and with a choreography which is pure *Swan Lake*.[23]

Perhaps it is only just to allow the director himself the last word, taken from the preface to the newly printed text of this production:

> *King Lear* is a panorama over our human lives . . . it has succeeded in getting brilliant commentators such as Kenneth Muir and others to pour out interpretations which exceed all limits. In the storm scene, moreover, the language accelerates to a Beethoven-like frenzy which for us with our modest and somewhat watered-down speech habits becomes mainly comical.[24]

In his production of *Hamlet* at the Royal Dramatic Theatre, Stockholm in 1986, Bergman showed many similarities of approach. Britt G. Hallquist was once more responsible for a new translation – a collaborative effort with Bergman which they tried to make 'understandable and believable' while approaching the familiar lines with a certain care.[25] Again the stage setting was an empty space with little other than the actors and extras who were used choreographically to create certain effects, such as a row of judges all wearing long court-room wigs, or a group of umbrella-twirling mourners at Ophelia's funeral. There was no direct indication of time or place, although this production, more than the previous Shakespeare productions, emphasized timelessness – or games with times and styles. This was particularly evident in the costumes, which ranged across many different epochs: with Hamlet in modern dress, wearing a black polo-necked jumper and grey trousers and hiding behind black sunglasses, Claudius and Gertrude in reconstructed Renaissance red, Polonius and Horatio in sober grey modern-day business suits, Rosencrantz and Guildenstern in sporty golfing attire and Ophelia in what looked like a simple blue nightdress.

As in *King Lear*, the main colour scheme was red (for the Danish court) and black (for the other characters). Already in the opening scene, Bergman established a mood of distanced theatricality through his use of three curtains (the last one black) to the accompaniment of the popular *Merry Widow* waltz. Even the soldiers in this Danish court appeared clad in the style of Hungarian soldiers from an operetta. The acting space was empty and black, within this proscenium-arch opening, except for a red circle carefully marked out on the stage floor. As in *King Lear*, characters remained on stage observing the events – mainly Ophelia, who even witnessed her own funeral and was often seen stalking distractedly around this area, always on the perimeter. The final scene also came as a complete surprise, as Fortinbras and his army virtually exploded through what turned out to be an imitation back wall, tearing it to shreds. Again the same *Star Wars* effect was created by the futuristic costuming in this scene, accompanied by thundering rock music, as in *King Lear*.

In this translation of *Hamlet*, Bergman had cut and trimmed away almost a third of the original, but in spite of this, the performance time was almost four hours long. As in *King Lear*, the consequences of this were seen in the role portrayals, where there was less freedom for character development along emotional lines. It would seem that Bergman did not want to distract the audience's attention from the political power game which was being played out. This was supported by a statement from the director prior to the première: 'This is a game, a game with illusions, where the result is what we have read out of the text.'[26] The character of Reynaldo was cut, and together with it Polonius's text, which indicates much of his deviousness and meddling – even where his own children were concerned. Similarly, the characters of Voltimand and Cornelius were cut and with them attempts to do business with the Norwegians. Rosencrantz and Guildenstern's scene with Claudius and Gertrude, where they are questioned about Hamlet's activities at Wittenberg, are also cut and with it the opportunity to show the double-faced aspect of their characters.

Perhaps the most significant change in the original order of scenes was to Hamlet's 'To be or not to be' monologue. Bergman moved this further on in the play to act III, scene ii, where it becomes part of Hamlet's advice to the players. Instead of expressing his own fears about life and death, it is a lesson in bringing rhetoric down to some psychologically believable level.

In realizing this adapted text in performance and marrying it with such a strong directorial line, Bergman shifted the emphasis. Rather than being a play about a young man fighting against all odds in order to avenge the murder of his beloved father by his evil uncle whom his mother has remarried, it became a war between the sexes, where the overthrown Ophelia was the central witness – rather than Hamlet, who has cut himself off and gone into hiding behind his sunglasses. This Hamlet has become impotent, physically and perhaps emotionally. He trusts no one except Horatio, whom he kisses passionately, implying a homosexual relationship between them. This is given support by the role portrayals of Rosencrantz and Guildenstern, who snigger insinuatingly at them while chanting their lines simultaneously, like Tweedledum and Tweedledee in *Alice Through the Looking-Glass*.

Perhaps it was a directive from Bergman that the characters' external appearance and behaviour should mirror their internal motivations. This certainly was the case in Claudius's and Gertrude's role portrayals. Claudius was an overweight and sexually fixated upstart, who alternated between drinking and giving vent to his seemingly uncontrollable desire to 'take' Gertrude from behind to the politely applauding amusement of the Danish courtiers present. Gertrude, also attired in passionate red, was portrayed as equally lust-filled. Polonius, in his mourning suit, the epitome of a discreet member of parliament, matched this in his unemotional and mannered role portrayal. Finally, Ophelia, dressed in simple blue, was the essence of innocence even when following Hamlet's command: 'Get thee to a nunnery', as she distractedly smeared her lips with harsh red lipstick, at the same time donning bright red high-heeled shoes in an effort to become the prostitute he insinuates that she is. Nowhere was Bergman's idea more clearly stated than in the final scene when Fortinbras burst on to the stage, dressed in a black futuristic *Star Wars* uniform, signalling the way for the future.

The vocal deliveries in this production followed these role portrayals: Hamlet, the misunderstood youth, alternated between shouting passionately and mumbling incoherently; Horatio delivered his lines rather colourlessly; Claudius ranted and spat out his lines with an over-abundance of passion, while Gertrude was all heavy breathing. Polonius adopted a rhetorical and mannered delivery stlye, while Ophelia's was earnest naturalism until she lost her mind, when her delivery became distracted. On the whole, however, the visual dominated over the auditory in this production, and in spite of the very much shorter text used, the rhythm and timing was slow as the play was often interrupted for special choreographic effects.

Reactions to the production by both public and press were mixed, but most of them agreed that Bergman had once more come up with a visually fantastic dramatization, while at the same time his interpretation was confusing. Ingmar Björkstén remarked that at times the audience laughed in completely the wrong places.[27] Many of the critics were in agreement that Bergman had gone his own way through Shakespeare's drama, leading us into his own world far too much, with his trendy modernizing and overtly sexual overtones. Tove Ellefsen was highly critical of the production, which 'had got stuck in external action and which felt jerky and unrhythmical, at best unready'.[28] Finally, Leif Zern summed it up as follows:

> It is possible that the production with its black landscape, its desolate lighting and its metallic rock sound in the final scene wishes to reflect the world which is ours just now. In any case it does this with the help of assertions which refuse to be changed to the play's flesh and blood. These signs and images do not convince us of their necessity.[29]

He also remarked on the similarity between the actor playing

Hamlet and Bergman himself, which was used as an intra-theatrical technique extending to imitation of speech rhythms at times, physical mannerisms and even clothing, and wondered if this was the director's intended interpretation of Hamlet – a self-portrait. Many critics referred to the lack of coherent speech in the production as a whole, so that as a result the audience got nothing. One of them stated:

> Diction is neglected once more by far too many so that it would not be laboured in this production by Ingmar Bergman, who is visually in high form, but too coldly-ironically distanced to the subject for his bewitchingly beautiful interpretation with its varying, strong sexual undertones.[30]

In conclusion, one can see that although Bergman demonstrated a change in approach to Shakespeare from his early attempts at *Macbeth* in the forties, slowly a formula has been making itself clear: the repeated use of red and black in stage setting and costuming; a preference for an empty, almost naked, playing area; actors witnessing the events which transpire, suggesting that these are only illusions, which, as in *The Dream Play*, take place in their minds; the game with time and place which hints at the eternal struggle which these issues have had; the sexual innuendoes; the stripping-down of the text to allow for his interpretation; and finally the devaluation of the word in performance. These radical postmodern traits, which his Shakespeare productions of the eighties demonstrate, suggest that Bergman has attempted to deconstruct the plays as if he fears that otherwise they will not work for modern audiences today.

ARIANE MNOUCHKINE: SHAKESPEARE EASTERN STYLE

One of the most prodigious directors of the modern theatre, who has succeeded in creating theatre performances which have constantly challenged the status quo and who has managed to keep her group of actors together for over twenty years, is Ariane Mnouchkine, founder of the Théâtre du Soleil in Paris. During the sixties, when they were without a permanent theatre location, they performed mostly scripted plays, such as Wesker's *The Kitchen* and Shakespeare's *A Midsummer Night's Dream*. However, in 1969 they developed their first collective piece, *The Clowns*, which Mnouchkine also directed. Their move out to Bois de Vincennes on the outskirts of Paris and to a permanent home, La Cartoucherie, in 1970 was part of the mass movement towards the end of the sixties shared by many other Parisian theatre groups, who had strong political and ideological views, and who challenged their audiences to seek them out. Although initially they attracted a young audience, over the years the Théâtre du Soleil's more established position has also attracted a middle-aged public.[31]

Their first production in the Cartoucherie, *1789*, was seen by more than a quarter of a million Parisians. It was written by one of the members of the group, and suggested many parallels between the French revolution and the political climate in France in 1968. A sequel to this was *1793*, a collective work which explored the problem of how power should be handled. The text was created by the actors in rehearsal and was interspersed with songs and historical facts in an epic manner. The ensuing years witnessed a return to scripted plays, such as Molière's *Don Juan* and Klaus Mann's *Mephisto*.

The problem which most concerns Ariane Mnouchkine is the relationship between the artist and power, and her productions reflect her untiring search for a way of making this actual.[32] In 1981 she confided to her ensemble the difficulties she was having in writing on a contemporary theme with the view to the creation of a play around the following essential question: how to resolve the confrontation between the world around us today and the theatre, where one can transform existing conditions to poetic metaphor. Coupled with this, and of vital importance for her theatre, was how to avoid the dangers of realism, of psychology, of the everyday, or of public opinion, and she began to search for a kind of narrative which could be inspired by the history of our own times.[33]

Faced with this problem, Mnouchkine re-read Shakespeare's histories: *Richard II*, *Henry IV*, *Henry V*, *Henry VI*, *Richard III*; the Roman plays: *Coriolanus*, *Julius Caesar*; and certain of the comedies: *Twelfth Night*, *Cymbeline* and *Love's Labour's Lost*. She proposed that the group should place themselves for a time in Shakespeare's school, and plunge themselves into the world which he describes, thereby coming to an understanding about how he created the chronicles of his day and how the people in his plays acted. The cycle of plays which she suggested was to be selected from the histories of the kings – an exclusively masculine world – and the comedies which describe the ups and downs of amorous desire. The three plays chosen were *Richard II*, which premièred at La Cartoucherie on 10 December 1981, *La Nuit des Rois* (*Twelfth Night*), which had its première at the Festival of Avignon, 10 July 1982, and *Henry IV*, at La Cartoucherie, 18 January 1984.

The first two months of rehearsals were a time of exploration and experimentation, providing a chance to see which new actors should be taken into the group, and to discover an acting style which would be suitable for the Théâtre du Soleil's interpretation of the Shakespeare cycle. Fifty new actors were admitted, and Ariane Mnouchkine translated the plays (not always completely in advance of the rehearsals, but in instalments) after working on improvisations with the group members. Their initial approach to the text was not a formal round-table analysis, but an informal reading aloud of the plays, with the actors listening to their initial sounds. These early days gave the impulse for working through improvisations in a search for an acting style.

Mnouchkine believed that the Elizabethan period was a superb era with Shakespeare in the centre as its chronicler, journalist and poet; however, she also feared that the Elizabethan theatre did not produce a great form of acting, such as the *commedia dell'arte* or the forms of Oriental theatre – Japanese, Balinese and Indian. Nevertheless she was aware that audiences came to the theatre in those days in order to learn, to listen to the histories and to extract from them their lessons, moreover that the public was part of the production and the action, which the architectural shape and central location of the Elizabethan premises bear witness to.

On the question of a particular style of acting, Ariane Mnouchkine is most emphatically against the school of psychological realism. Her impulses have come from Meyerhold, Brecht and the theatre of the East, where physical Gestalt and theatrical distance play such an important role in the performance. This has encouraged the Théâtre du Soleil to experiment with different styles of acting: at times playing both with and without masks in the same performance, experimenting with the text and vocal delivery and blending together styles from different epochs and countries.

Mnouchkine believes that the actors are the authors of their texts, which they create in rehearsals from ideas and improvisations and in the way they use their feelings and their bodies.[34] Often this results in a collage consisting of snippets of an original text interspersed with song and historical facts on current events. On the whole she has a greater belief in acting than the text, and in this respect shows quite an opposite point of view concerning Shakespeare to Brook, who believes that Shakespeare is a very intimate writer, that in every line of his plays there is some element which belongs to the intimate life of the characters, and that every production where the epic style is overemphasized risks as a result losing the real nerve in the text.[35]

In their approach to the Shakespeare cycle, the Théâtre du Soleil adopted the Eastern theatre forms: Japanese Noh and Kabuki, the Balinese theatre as well as Kathakali. Mnouchkine explained the reasons for this as follows: 'We searched for a point of departure for our work in the theatre of the east because in it lies the origin to all theatre form . . . everything exists there, music, dance religious art, theatre.'[36]

In their preparations for *Richard II*, the Théâtre du Soleil worked from one strong central image taken from John of Gaunt's famous speech prior to the murder of Richard: 'This royal throne of kings, this sceptred isle,/This earth of majesty, this seat of Mars'.[37] This was decisive for their interpretation of the play as a whole, where the island, England, was regarded as 'a hard-won shore, isolated, battered by the winds and the savage sea, stunted and small'.[38] Mnouchkine believed that parallels could be drawn between a Utopian kind of society and the inhabitants of this island:

A happy breed of men is at the dawning of the world, discovering, constructing, creating a society which is archaic and enormously primitive and which is peopled by dragons and day-dreams; the rivers are full of scalps and the scars of the bloody battles of men; the earth is a woman, a mistress, a mother – self-contained. The characters test themselves, just as primitive men do, hiding nothing and harbouring no secrets. They are visionaries, who discover the unknown and on the way describe their own internal journeys by observing and scrutinizing themselves without the help of psychology. On their island (which is a metaphor for the universe) they are in the infancy of the world – and each one behaves just as children do – in the centre of the world.[39]

In order to work with these warlike heroes, it was necessary for Mnouchkine to find a grand epic form, which explains the adoption of the Japanese forms of theatre and in particular its use of masks. This forced the actor to rediscover in a simple fashion the truth of an emotional state before executing it via signals from the body, the voice and the expression. She was aware that this could not be done too quickly, without finding the truthful expression of the internal emotion and then allowing this to transform the actor's exterior, otherwise he would end up with artificial acting and not art – a showing of form without content. The purpose of the mask was to lead the actor towards a simple passion and towards his character; to give him his physical expressions and a voice. By listening carefully to the mask, the actor could create a distance from his character. In a similar way, by adopting Japan it was possible to create a distanced world which could stand as the England of Richard II – a savage, lawless society, peopled by fighting-cocks in a confined, blood-stained place, with only their rules of warfare and primitive violence. Adopting Japan enabled the Théâtre du Soleil to explore in breadth in order to arrive at some profound truths concerning the spirit of each of the two central characters: on the one hand a king, Richard, who is the representative of God on earth, and on the other, the person who was able to plot against him using violence and scandal, before finally succeeding in forcing him to abdicate before the entire court.

In rehearsal they endeavoured to arrive at the crux of the problem, that is, 'the spiritual state of the characters of which the words are only one of the symptoms', believing that initially the actor receives the text inside and creates the physical signs, thereby embodying the poetry created by Shakespeare. In their staging, they were mainly influenced by the Japanese Kabuki. Initial efforts to recreate an island and a sea were dismissed in favour of a large square playing area defined in clear geometrical lines with tatami mats outlining particular areas. From the stage, two bridges stretched out towards the audience into two striped tents, through which the actors, running, made their entrances and exits; marking the ends of scenes by swinging around the enormous stage area. By using their imaginations, the actors conjured up the colour of the shore of England as well as the length and terror of their journeys.

The baroque flamboyance of the Kabuki was reflected in wide skirts of beautiful lines and patterns, although this was combined with a hint of Elizabethanness in terms of ruffs and some of the hairstyles. The predominating colours were red, white, grey and black, with an adequate sprinkling of gold. The warlike nature of the samurai heroes was given emphasis in the use of swords stuck through wide sashes, and the actors' movements and combat-like posturing were choreographed along the lines of traditional Noh theatre – arms akimbo and the body always shown towards the audience – while their make-up was mask-like white.

The actors shouted out their lines, with their faces always turned towards the audience, never towards their fellow actors. In short, every step towards intimacy or a removed fourth wall was avoided, because Mnouckhine believed it was completely wrong for Shakespeare:

> Not just inadequate but killing. Every time during rehearsals the actors discovered that they began to speak with each other it went wrong. I told them to tell the audience. It was the secret and we never forgot it ... I am convinced that Shakespeare's text is created in order to be said in the way we do. As soon as one begins to modulate, polish, make subtle – one makes the text too mild.[40]

The anti-realistic, anti-naturalistic style was a conscious choice for Mnouchkine, who acknowledged that although Shakespeare knew everything about life and people, about love and power, there was no similarity with reality in the formal expression of his plays.

In order to enhance this epic style, music and percussion were used to accompany the spoken text. This was the result of a process of experiment and research during the rehearsal period, when the musical director, Lemêtre, discovered the importance of working on the metre of the language necessary for Shakespearean verse, where the

> internal line of verse of each word and phrase is an integral part of the acting – of the searching of the emotions and of the expression which carries us beyond the dangerous paths of realism. For *Richard II*, the problem with the music was that Ariane immediately thought of it in relationship to what she was looking for concerning diction and declamation. The work with the music, the rhythm and the voices grew together. It was from the text itself that everything took its form: we were forced to find a metre for the language in some way, and furnish this speech with a high-placed pitch. . . It was important that the music not only supported the text, but

that it also surrendered itself to it. What remains is the most important in every respect – the actor – his voice, the way he articulates and presents the text. In *Richard* the music emphasizes as well the entrances and exits. It musn't be pathetic: it should be like a path written in space. The music is not to suggest anything. It doesn't have themes. In *Richard*, we work with the beat, the text and the actors who move the tragedy forward... When I speak about 'the beat' it is not something which tears a hole in the story-telling (the play's story line – its action) and expresses something by this means; the beat is quite simply in the text.[41]

He later revealed that when the performance found its stability, the kettle drums and the voice became absolutely inseparable because their relationship had been harmoniously thought out.

Reactions from the critics to the production were both positive and negative. The visual aspects were highly praised, in particular the directorial concept and its highly theatrical artistic presenta-tion, but the vocal delivery style received much criticism. According to theatre critic Gilles Sandier, Mnouchkine's attempts to match the symbolic physical expression with an epic delivery style did not work:

The text is presented without intonation *recto tono*, each syllable is articulated: the words as a result are spelt out in large letters – like the school alphabet... In this way, the text is presented throughout the performance, for five hours – five very long hours, and above all it conceals the play and the heady politics which are at stake, and in addition, the specific aspects of the characters are obliterated. By endeavouring to efface all psychology, one renders the characters scarcely discernible or comprehensible. In the Japanese theatre, the precision and exactness of their code system allows room for this individualizing of the characters; here it is not the case: everything becomes slightly indistinct.[42]

Another critic who found the delivery style in *Richard II* to be on the whole somewhat 'forced' was Göran Wirén.[43] In their next Shakespearean piece, *La Nuit des Rois* (*Twelfth Night*), the orien-talism was somewhat freer than in *Richard II* and directed more towards South-East Asia, to a country:

far away, which has the colours, the smells and the femininity

of India: images of carnival impregnated with fragrant
perfumes and heady sonorousness, which form the walls of
Olivia's house, like the sea which has sent Viola to the
legendary shores of Illyria . . . a far-away country, housed in
the depths of our unconscious, where everything is possible,
where every dream, desire, fear, presentiment is voiced in
man's search for happy fulfilment – a land where the gods
descend and take the form of flesh and blood in order to
manipulate the hearts of men with compassion.[44]

In this production, the Théâtre du Soleil attempted to explore the
ups and downs of amorous passion. Ariane Mnouchkine was not at
all worried about doing a fairy-tale piece as she explained: 'I have
given myself the opportunity to talk about love and only about
love. . . For three hours the public can laugh and cry over love, I
think one has the right to do that in the theatre today.'[45] The early
stages of rehearsals were fraught with problems for the women,
who worked from an early image of being enclosed in a harem,
where they dreamed their desires of fulfilment; this idea was
abandoned. Ultimately it was sufficient to approach the play
without superimposing any particular idea. Viola's disguise was
interpreted as the simple poetic sign of her travels to the country of
Illyria and did not need to be acted – it was simply there, the
essential thing was the adventure into which her spirit was
plunged. This applied in fact to all the characters, and the actors
had to find a way of executing their passions without restraint or
concern for contemporary values.

Early improvisations with the costumes reveal the stages of this
exploration. Each actor attempted to find a costume from
spectacles of the past which would best express his character's
possible fetish. Little by little a civilization of shapes and colours
emerged, signifying a hierarchic world of passion, and these ideas
were outlined for the scenographers who then composed an
imaginary and coherent world for these characters to live in. Again
the preference for geometric lines and space predominated;
however, the colour range for *Twelfth Night* was warm, soft pastels,
lyrical gold and silver, which were used to great effect in enormous
silk curtains suggesting the colour of a scene. In this way the
imagination was free to create all the space possible – both interior
passion and exterior countryside. According to Sörenson, the

intimate tone which is demanded in *Twelfth Night* was not so easily executed in this enormous playing area; however, Mnouchkine succeeded in creating uniformity in an interesting way by having the servants hold different-coloured umbrellas over Orsino and Olivia, thereby creating a feeling of a particular place on stage – a picture in a picture. Her ability to create quick-moving pictures was illustrated in the way she allowed thin silken curtains to fall from the ceiling, like quick takes in a film.[46]

Music was also used in a special way. This took the form of traditional instruments from India, Bali and Africa, which were used for their particular evocative qualities. In rehearsal, work progressed in a different fashion from that on *Richard II* because of the nature of the comedy, the directional concept with smoother entrances and exits, and the fact that the actors moved a great deal while they spoke. Something resembling a *leitmotif* was developed for each of the characters, which established his mood in each scene as well as helping to create the scenic environment. The musical director explained the approach as follows: 'Together with me, the actors chose a tonal colour and an instrument for their characters, then we worked on the theme. The music announced and followed every entrance.'[47] Nevertheless the music was not intended to dictate to the actor but to follow the language. It was created by combining the verse with the internal rhythm of each character. As Sophie Moscoso related:

> The punctuation creates emotional resonances in the air. In this way one could say that the space is created by the music. It traces and exteriorizes the magnetic space around each of the actors, whose bodies and headgear quiver like enormous colourful birds at the height of an emotion before the tension is released. It forms each actor's aura by the magical, imaginary circle which it traces around him in order to relate each of his adventures and it moves about with him in each of his movements, following the course of the narration.[48]

Because the rhythms were created freely by the actors' bodies, the musicians did not impose anything. This explains the eventual broad range including cha-cha, reggae, Gregorian chant and rock, without settling on any particular one of them. Each of the characters gave the colour to the instrument, even though the same instrument was utilized for different characters at different moments, and in this way sounded different.

However, it was also the approach to the text that was particular in this production. The word came late in the rehearsal process, because Mnouchkine translated the text bit by bit. This enabled the actors to work their way through gestures and body movements towards their characters, so that when they came to the text it gave them something new, 'like a shot of energy or a blood transfusion', as one of the actors explained.[49] The vocal delivery style in this production was more successful than in *Richard II*, according to Wirén, because it was less bound and restricted.[50]

In *Henry IV*, the next production in their Shakespeare cycle, the stage setting was also kept open and based on geometrical lines, whilst again the tatami mats were used to mark off particular areas. Curtains and umbrellas were also incorporated again to suggest particular scenes: the rebels' scene had a backdrop in different shades of red, while Henry IV's scene had a broken golden glazed backdrop with splashes of red seeping through like blood. Again the central concept was Eastern, but in this production, the costumes and use of head-gear referred to India – to the mountain regions of the Himalayan foothills – a perfect setting for telling this tale of a king's love for his son.[51]

Red and black predominated in the costuming of the rebels, whereas Prince Hal's costume was pale blue with a heavy brocade sash and outer garment on top. The king's costume was light gold, with heavy gilt brocade in the linings, and he wore a mask. All the characters were equipped with swords and the make-up was mask-like white with much free use of red for shadowing eyes and cheek bones and to symbolize blood flowing. This contributed to the stylized nature of the production and even movements and gestures were in keeping with this epic style. Again music was used throughout, but whereas it was rhythmic in *Richard II* and melodic in *Twelfth Night*, in *Henry IV* it was both, as the music director explained:

> In *Henry IV* the music is a support for the narrative, but in a specific place: it places the character in the desert and it advances the play in time (this is the role of the hollow drums in the distance) like a caravan in a desert.[52]

As in the other Shakespeares, music was used to communicate the emotive construction in the subtext clearly. The variety of instruments from so many different countries and the extensive use of rhythm and melodic line rendered a 'sort of universalization of that which is in Shakespeare', according to one of their musicians.[53] This practice was utilized again in their production about India and colonialization in 1988, *L'Indiade ou L'Inde de leurs rêves.*

The whole approach to vocal delivery in the Shakespeare cycle was an enormously rewarding experience for Georges Bigot, who played the leading role in all three, and who acknowledged that the Shakespeares made his voice comprehensible for the first time and strengthened it – qualities which he considered absolutely necessary for the actor – and maintained that 'there are times when the actor is only eyes and voice on stage which necessitates putting all of himself into his voice'.[54]

These sentiments had been anticipated by Ariane Mnouchkine, who enthused that Shakespeare was an excellent teacher for the actors – particularly in the area of their speech, which was not on the whole very good – and lamented over the length of time it took to improve it.[55] Unlike the previous Shakespeares, the vocal delivery was apparently much more related to the text in this production, which Wirén praised as 'dazzling and sensually sparkling, where acting styles are mixed freely, and intimate and wildly burlesque scenes are added'.[56]

In conclusion, the Théâtre du Soleil's choice of vocal delivery style in their Shakespeare cycle was dependent upon an extremely heightened epic style of acting. The balance between voice, text and emotion was also greatly influenced by the predominance of a continuous musical undercurrent, which, although springing from the character and his intentions, nevertheless also attempted to create mood, show time passing and define place as well as work as an adjunct to the dramaturgy by heightening conflicts and indicating exits and entrances.

PETER STEIN: SHAKESPEARE BY DRAMATURGICAL DISSECTION

Peter Stein has been the artistic director of the much-acclaimed Schaübuhne in West Berlin for the past twenty-seven years. He admits to having been greatly influenced in the post-war period by Fritz Kortner at the Kammerspiele, one of the major theatres in Munich with a long history of experimentation, where he was employed as dramaturge and assistant director in 1964. Kortner, whose expressionistic style had made him one of the leading actors in Germany in the early years of the twentieth century, had gone on to the Kammerspiele where he was numbered as one of its leading directors. They hold each other in high esteem: Kortner is quoted as referring to Stein as 'the greatest hope for the German theatre', and Stein admits to 'adopting Kortner's recipe of mistrust and respect while at the same time learning from him precision, clarity, the importance of the word, close observation and untiring concern for detail'.[57]

In his first production at this theatre in 1967, Edward Bond's *Saved*, Stein revealed himself as a voice of the times when he rejected the usual High German translation for one which reflected the language of the proletariat, and shifted the working-class setting from South London to a working-class area of Munich. In performance he insisted on the actors using dialects instead of the usual stage German. This production was acknowledged as 'production of the year' by *Theater Heute*.

The repercussions of this approach were seen in the acting style, which, owing to the discipline which the dialect imposed, prevented the actors from falling back on emotional clichés. As a result the acting of the younger players was not the usual exaggerated expressionistic style of most German performances, but was described as so natural that the acting of the older actors playing the parents seemed 'stagey' by comparison.

This approach is significant in that it reveals how Stein's primary concern has always been for the dramatic text, not for any specific theatrical dogma. According to Patterson, 'instead of working from preconceived images, he has consistently begun with the word, developing his theatrical treatment from a thoughtful analysis of the author's text'.[58] His usual practices are long, intensive rehearsal periods where the text is thoroughly dissected and analysed. Therese Giehse, who first met Stein in Munich, called him Brecht's true successor: 'He tries to get to know a play completely. He clarifies the piece, peels off its different layers with all his curiosity and imagination, but he does not change it. The play is there, one has only to bring it alive.'[59] This meticulous working method was the result of the hard lessons learned with Kortner and was to become Stein's trademark.

During the rehearsals for *Saved*, Stein also discovered something very important about acting style. By challenging every expression and gesture to assess whether it was convincing or not, he helped his actors reach a point which went beyond naturalism by encouraging them to pass through this stage to a stage of more reality, where they could create specific effects. Stein called this style of acting, *plakativ*, which means having the size and clarity of a poster. Although this style owes much to Brecht, Stein rejects the alienation theory, believing that the audience does not experience anything in that kind of theatre. He described his approach to acting in a programme note as:

> the loosening up of speech and body patterns through minimalization, the scrutinizing of every expression and gesture for the basis of its believability and justification of its function – a process we later called 'beginning from zero'. . . The prerequisite for such a method of continuous examination was an especially long and intense rehearsal period. . . A consistent unyielding sureness and naturalness in the social atmosphere of the play was our goal. We didn't want to allow the audience to be able to differentiate between the personality of the actor and that of his created character.[60]

Stein's next production was Brecht's *In the Jungle of the Cities* (1968) and this confirmed his importance as an emerging director of note. Again the same strong style of acting and staging were in evidence, and here again Stein indicated his concern for important political and social questions. His subsequent production of the fiercely topical *Vietnam-Discourse* by Peter Weiss in 1968 brought his time at the Munich Kammerspiele to an abrupt close. However, the piece was invited to Berlin by the Schaubühne am Halleschen Ufer, and thus began Stein's new career, in what was to become his permanent home.

In his approach to the classics, Stein adopts a method of appropriation in which the preoccupations of a work of the past are not wrenched from their social and political environment but are examined in that context to discover what points of relevance can be found for today. He happily explores the tension between historical context and modern relevance.

In his production of Goethe's *Torquato Tasso* in Bremen (1969) Stein demonstrated his ability to read the text with clarity. He cut and reordered the text, so that it was finally more epic than the original and thereby demystified the very character of Tasso, making the issues clearer than any other contemporary staging of the piece. Each actor shared an awareness of the intentions of the production, which informed the delivery of their lines. Once again,

Stein worked with precision on the text. Ivan Nagel described Stein's method in the *Tasso–Regiebuch* as follows:

> Having revealed language in its most general function as the self-protective cocoon of the ruling class, having determined from this the specific dramatic value it has for each of the five characters, he undertakes a line by line examination of the actual content of this sententious blank verse . . . He takes Goethe at his word who maintains that all his characters preserve the elevated form in every one of their sentences – that for them the uncommon is commonplace. This idealistic conversation (the magically protected homogeneity of elevated speech and response) must now be put to the test, must be confronted with the intonation which its actual content would demand in everyday conversation.[61]

Edith Clever, as Leonore, apparently created a critical distance to the elevated tone of Goethe's verse by speaking the lines in a manner entirely appropriate to the content but at such odds with the form that it had a grotesque and blasphemous shock-effect. All the characters adopted a particular manner of speaking their lines, which evidently enhanced character and situation rather than simply pointing up the poetic effects. Stein believes that the text must be approached sceptically and not with the blind respect usually given to the classics. This does not mean changing the written words, but freeing the text from its performance tradition, and examining each word for its actual, not its literary, meaning. He is also interested in showing how the author himself is caught in certain values prevalent in his period of history – values that must be examined critically for the influence they bring to bear upon our modern time.

The acting style in the classics is also an attempt to base the expression in reality and to re-examine theatricality. Stein himself explains this in an interview with Bernard Dort in *Travail Théâtral* (1972) as follows:

> This style of playing is based on an active use of the theories of Brecht and principles of Kortner. The result is a manner of presentation that is simultaneously descriptive and narrative – that recounts, shows, presents, but that does not renounce communicating psychic and theatrical events through the means of identification, nor renounce psychic tension or

suspense. This is very important for us – but one must do this while still remaining capable of showing that one is showing something – revealing the working process itself, the fact that it is an actor who is presenting a gesture, an intonation, a reflex – and all of this without falling into abstraction or diminishing the value of the real events happening on the stage.[62]

Stein's *Torquato Tasso* is a striking example of this complementary function of objectivity and involvement – through employing 'classical' acting gesture to an extreme, but at the same time finding a realistic basis in the language and situation. Stein reveals the discrepancy between Goethe's conservative desire to glorify the characters of the court, who believe they are absolutely justified in their social situation, and the actual torture of their predicament. In other words, grand gesture becomes a parody of itself. A period of socially conscious productions followed, and when the New Schaubühne opened in 1970, its main aim was to express the socialistic convictions of the company. They experimented with a very democratic system, whereby all the members shared not only the artistic work, but the administrative work as well. When Stein eventually realized that it was no longer viable to simply offer socialistic plays to a non-existent working-class audience, he began exploring a bourgeois repertoire in order 'to rescue the master-pieces of the bourgeois theatre from an erroneous tradition of thought and concepts'.[63]

In their approach to the text of *Peer Gynt*, Stein and dramaturge Botho Strauss cut a great deal with the full consensus of the ensemble, in order to attain a particular political/economic analysis of the play. In production, each scene was preceded by captions which emphasized the adventurous nature of the piece more than attempting to make it a Brechtian epic one. It was therefore more in line with a Victorian theatre playbill. All the properties which Stein used were false, or 'quoted', as he would say, because what reality they achieved existed in the minds of the spectators, not within the artificial confines of a theatre. The acting style was a blending of the epic and realistic schools – where, according to Volker Canaris:

> there is no distancing, no difference established between what is said and what is meant, between character and actor. . .
> Peter Stein has developed this style with his actors with

staggering precision. They act the role *and* criticize it. The bourgeois aesthetic of 'embodying' a role has here been so perfected that it becomes a new style in itself, a critical dialectic, an aesthetic means to knowledge.[64]

In their text analysis, the ensemble saw Peer as a *petit bourgeois*, whose opportunism leads him into all his adventures. The troll kingdom was seen as representing the *petite bourgeoisie* which Peer struggles to avoid. In order to drive this theme even further, Stein made the trolls into a society of pigs – complete with snouts and hairy bodies – dressed in human clothing and having human feelings. This practice of taking the ideas in the play further than the playwright conceived them and turning them into very strong visual images has become characteristic of Stein's text analysis. The gigantic production in 1971 was a great success for the Schaubühne and for Stein although it made him realize the shortcomings of working in a collective.

Attempting to deal with the problems of bourgeois society in the 1970s Stein directed Peter Handke's *They Are Dying Out* in 1974. In his approach to the text, he was unusually reverent – not making cuts, as he customarily did, but working on the text in rehearsal in his usual fashion: 'from sentence to sentence – clarifying, rendering more plausible, not necessarily on a psychological level, but in terms of certain representative figures within a given situation'.[65] For technical reasons he abandoned his original plan to amplify the voices of the actors by the use of microphones; nevertheless he was intent on preserving the theatrical distance of the action. Gerd Jäger praised Stein's production because he clarified, did not offer a particular interpretation, but simply endeavoured to transfer Handke's text to the stage.[66] Later, after much adulation from both critics and Handke alike, Stein turned his attention to a more psychological realistic style.

In Gorky's *Summerfolk* (1974), Stein attempted a naturalistic acting style for the first time since *Saved*. The programme note stated that the realism of the play 'arises more from debate than from the psychology of the individual character'. He thereby allowed his actors to break with illusion when they needed to. Edith Clever spoke her central speech in act 1 beginning 'I don't know . . . I can't express myself very well . . . but I feel strongly that people must change', with her face turned towards the audience, positioning herself exactly in the middle of the stage to deliver her lines. At other times Stein broke with reality by allowing the characters to enter a dream-world. He also made use of the technique of 'freezing' the action when he wished to draw attention to specific moments or particular lines spoken. Here one can see a move away from the *plakativ* didacticism of his earlier productions – although now an alienation effect was achieved through ultra-naturalism. In rehearsals, Stein worked for the fullest possible development of every character and balanced the revelation of their lives in such a way that the audience could not choose any one figure as protagonist or as the 'good' or 'evil' one. The illusionistic world created by the picture-frame stage, with real birch trees and real soil, was enhanced by scenes being played simultaneously in various parts of the setting – thereby forcing the audience to consider the proxemic factors of the actors within the pictorial composition as much as the verbal communication. This production was hailed as a great success, and regarded as Stein's best production since *Peer Gynt*. It had 135 performances and toured extensively in Europe and to the National Theatre in London.

Stein's approach to Shakespeare was cautious. His ensemble was not so much concerned with how Shakespeare could best make an impact on a modern audience as to rediscover the world which Shakespeare inhabited and thereby understand the social and cultural forces that shaped his writing. After an initial preparatory period under the guidance of Botho Strauss (1971–3) where the ensemble met regularly for seminars on Shakespeare, Stein joined the group and they began to read the plays in earnest looking for a suitable play with an even distribution of parts. At the same time each actor chose a subject which interested him and set about researching this in earnest. These were concerned with the following: Elizabethan theatre; sources of the theatre and the related arts; natural sciences and philosophy; political practice and theory; Elizabethan patterns of thought. Realizing the enormity of the task, Stein rejected most of the plays before deciding to present the results of all this work as a 'kind of living museum of the Elizabethan age'. It was given the title *Shakespeare's Memory – Pictures and Texts*, and was presented over two evenings to packed houses in the CCC Film Studios in Spandau, several miles from the centre of Berlin.

Although it was not a production in the accepted sense of the word, it was a theatre event which not only attracted a lot of interest, but laid the grounds for the next production, Shakespeare's *As You Like It*. As a working method, Stein was to utilize it again in what he called his *Antikenprojekt*, which developed also over two evenings – the first one *Exercises for Actors*, serving as a preparation for a production of *The Bacchae*.

From the full description in English by Peter Lackner in the *Drama Review* (1977), one can see the extent of the work and the fruits of their research and special skills. In a fluid performance situation, the audience were able to experience at first hand the feeling of being in an Elizabethan crowd.

Evening one incorporated mummers placed in the audience; Morris dancing; fencing with reconstructed Elizabethan weapons whilst delivering some of the text from *Romeo and Juliet*; tumbling, juggling and acrobatics; English ballads played on old wooden instruments and madrigals sung; an enactment of the *Second Shepherd's Pageant*; tableaux of allegorical presentations of the triumvirate – Grammar, Rhetoric and Dialectic; selected texts recited without characterization, such as Elizabeth I before the battle of the Spanish Armada, *Henry V* and *Richard II*; a cage of fools from different plays delivering speeches quite naturally without characterization; an excerpt from Fritz Kortner's radio production of *King Lear* played over loudspeakers; a 'Museum' of Elizabethan thought – where actors speaking directly to the audience communicated theories about evolution, infinity, man and the humours. Many of these acts were performed simultaneously from different vantage-points or galleries around the enormous space in which the audience wandered at will. During the second item, the audience was invited to eat and drink at long banquet tables which had been rolled out.

The second evening began where the previous evening had left off: in the same Museum, where a number of specific locations took up the following Renaissance issues: the newly discovered concept of perspective in the form of sketches by da Vinci; hand gestures as developed from classical rhetoric and adopted in the theatre. The Museum was replaced by a Pageant Wagon bearing two Queen Elizabeths – the young and the ageing – where in the main, the question of the nature of kingship was raised. This gave way to the emergence of a huge cross-section of a ship which provided the setting for relating the story of the voyages into the New World and the effects of colonization. Finally a gigantic island was constructed from all these moveable pageants, wagons and platforms and from here a collage of speeches and scenes was enacted simultaneously by the twenty actors in the ensemble, while the audience was invited to wander around it. Peter Lackner described this part of the programme as follows:

> In partially Elizabethan dress with few props and only the contour of the 'island' as a set, the actors interpret all scenes simply, but with psychologically motivated emotional action, rather than merely reading the words. Although the characters have few external idiosyncrasies, an intensely portrayed characterization arises out of the actor's immersion in the text situation alone.[67]

Not all the reviews were as positive; Patterson found 'the delivery of the speeches singularly unexciting',[68] and German critic, Benjamin Hinrichs agreed:

> What made a mockery of the idea was the communal attempt in the last of the 7 hours to attempt to play Shakespeare properly – it ended in an exhibition of outmoded theatre styles, in Christmas-card schmaltz, repertory theatre emotionalism, and mannered intensity.[69]

On the whole *Shakespeare's Memory* was a valuable experience for Stein and his ensemble. On the one hand, Stein succeeded in mastering promenade staging, to which he had previously objected violently as a poor excuse for audience participation, and on the other hand, his ensemble was forced out of its introverted playing style and made to mingle directly with the audience.

The choice of Shakespeare play was a difficult one; however, after rejecting *Richard II* and *Twelfth Night*, it fell to *As You Like It* and the location was again the vast film studios where *Shakespeare's Memory* had been staged. Only there, Stein felt, could the magical world of the Forest of Arden be realized for a Berlin audience for whom any forest or green-belt area was an unattainable Utopia. This was to be the point of departure of the play.

In his approach to the text, Stein re-edited the court scenes, reshuffling them so that they were all together at the beginning. This necessitated many cuts and redistributed dialogue. As the playing style at the beginning was simultaneous, speeches overlapped, and lines of dialogue normally giving a leisurely exposure of the plot were suddenly grouped together as a montage. The result was that all the information-giving took on new connotations, as representing a general air of discontent at the court. The characters would often freeze in various poses in a long powder-blue-coloured court room, where the scenes were performed on raised platforms lit from underneath. This gave an eerie and cold effect and the audience, standing throughout at the foot of the actors, reminiscent of the Elizabethan groundlings, also experienced these scenes as somewhat of an endurance test. This was assisted by the vocal delivery style, which, according to one eye-witness, took the form of slowly paced lines, rhetorical gesturing and an altogether pedantic delivery in stage German.

Further changes in the text were necessary for the wrestling scene, which was performed by a professional wrestler, thereby necessitating a reallocating of his lines to Le Beau, who spoke of Charles in the third person. By 'framing' this scene Stein drew attention to Orlando's sudden mighty strength in overthrowing such a skilled wrestler – a point which he was later to underline when Orlando struggles for his life with a wild beast in the forest.

The banishment to the Forest of Arden to the accompaniment of dogs barking was experienced as physical relief by the audience, who were encouraged to pass through an underground labyrinth before emerging into an enormous forest, where the threat of barking dogs was transformed by the introduction of hunting-horns.

This forest was a full pastoral paradise with real trees, shrubbery, a pond, and woodsmen's huts, all spread around the enormous architectural structure. There was always some kind of activity in this space, a simultaneity of woodland life, even when the text did not particularly refer to it. The action took place above, below, behind and in the midst of the audience, which was now seated for the remainder of the evening. According to David Zane Mairowitz, 'in this manner, the concept of "scene change" is abandoned and the play simply travels from tension to tension or from tension to relief, without significant pause'.[70]

The costumes in the court scene were authentic copies of Elizabethan court dress, whereas in the Forest of Arden this historical accuracy was replaced by costumes which vaguely suggested the late nineteenth century, thereby giving a timeless concept to the characters and the setting. Rosalind wore a loose-fitting shirt and trousers, complete with floppy hat, while Celia wore a sailor-suit dress, and carried a butterfly net – reminiscent of

Edwardian summers. Orlando was dressed in an elegant beige suit and wide-brimmed hat, while Jaques wore a travelling coat and tartan shawl.

Further indications of timelessness and rootlessness were present in the sudden appearance of Robinson Crusoe calling for his Man Friday, while the actor playing Jaques broke out of German and delivered the 'seven ages of man' speech in English. Further magical or uncanny events in the Forest of Arden were presented in a dream-like fashion, which was inspired by Jan Kott's 'Bitter Arcadia' essay, to which Stein made reference in the programme.

Similarly the style of acting was never allowed to become simply that of psychological realism, as the rehearsal protocol revealed: in a note to the actress playing Rosalind, Stein had remonstrated that 'it is impossible to approach these events in a psychological manner, because they cannot be played that way'.[71] Instead the actors performed more in a Brechtian sense – from situation rather than psychology – often utilizing some physical object to create a distance from the emotion. In this way, the otherwise genuine emotional relationships became staged displays of feeling. The actors contributed to this externalization often by playing games with their vocal deliveries. Touchstone delivered his lines in a squeaky voice befitting a childish clown, while the mock-wedding between Orlando and Rosalind was performed as a children's game with Celia officiating with priest-like voice. Jaques' rhetorical delivery in English was intended as a 'party-piece', and received a round of applause. A high point in the ritualizing was attained in act V, scene ii, when Stein had the hymn to love delivered as a litany, with Rosalind turning to face the audience to deliver her lines 'And I for no woman'. This moment was 'framed' by an accompanying crash, as a number of soldiers tore through the forest intending to invade Arden, but were overcome by its magical powers, and either collapsed on to the ground or fled.

When the wedding wagon rolled in, the lovers reassumed their court costumes of Elizabethan nobles before being wheeled off back to their 'artificial' world, while Corin moved around cleaning up the mess left by this onslaught of people from the so-called 'civilized' world. The point which Stein attempted to make – that the freedom of nature is an illusion – was given further support by the inclusion of a new epilogue to replace the one usually delivered by Rosalind. This took the form of a poem about the cycle of the seasons. Its intent was to suggest that although it is important to experience Utopia, one cannot really ever achieve anything by escaping from life, one has rather to re-evaluate and restructure it.

The innovative manner in which he uses the theatrical space has become one of Stein's most interesting trademarks, not only in terms of scenography, but also in terms of movement within the acting space. This was paramount in his seven-hour-long production of Aeschylus' *The Oresteia* (1980), where he not only experimented with the placement of the chorus – seating them out in the audience at a long wooden table, reminiscent of the twelve disciples at the last supper – but also experimented with breaking up the usual actor–audience domains, by having the chorus build up tracks through the auditorium upon which Agamemnon ceremoniously returns from the war after an absence of ten years. The same masterly hand was present in the production of Kroetz's *Nicht Fisch Nicht Fleisch* (Neither Fish nor Fowl) which had a guest appearance in Stockholm in 1982. Stein allowed Edgar's longings to return to nature to be externalized in a brilliant way, as the drab office environment seemed to undergo metamorphosis before the audience's eyes when a gigantic fish balloon materialized (slowly filling with air) and the stage was transformed into a natural wonderland. This Utopia was the joyful choice of escape for Edgar, who, tearing off his clothes, rapturously cast himself into the water and swam off.

O'Neill's *The Hairy Ape*, premièred in 1986, was given a monumental expressionistic setting which one reviewer described as including everything from:

> towering riveted sides of the great liner which opened to reveal the cramped stoker's quarters and the hell-hole of the stokers, to downtown Manhattan . . . and the final stylized zoo with its cages filled with every kind of ape, silhouetted most beautifully against the night sky, as Yank, physically crushed and spiritually shattered, breathed his last.[72]

In contrast to this, the purity and strictness of Stein's production of Racine's *Phedra* (1987) reflects the narrowness of French classicism on the one hand, and the extreme harshness of Phedra's situation on the other. Hers is a world of no escape, where the action is captured within a formal, octagonal playing area. From a cupola in the centre, a merciless light, symbolizing the 'all-seeing' eye, streams down on the action, driving it to its final resolve.

However, it is not only the visual images which Stein provides for his productions which make them so memorable; it is also his understanding of the potentiality for the auditive factors of communication which deserve mentioning. Commenting on *The Oresteia*, one reviewer remarked that she had never heard speech and voice used with such versatility; that the production was like a musical instrument which was fully mastered; that the strength of the word and the voice was tried out; that other voices tuned in or played against it and that the famous chorus carried the audience's thoughts to improvised music without ever once losing the seriousness or believability in the text.[73]

It was not only the choral *partitur* which excelled in *The Oresteia*, but also the vocal delivery of single characters. Edith Clever's Clytemnestra seemed to dredge her voice up from the depths of her soul – yet it throbbed with fire and the words were spat out with a diction as clear as the image which she created on her first entrance, standing dwarfed within the framework of a gigantic door, a diminutive figure of a waiting wife, who was also a force to be reckoned with. This was confirmed later in the production as she took her revenge by mutilating the bodies of Agamemnon and Cassandra.

In *Phedra* the normally difficult alexandrines of Racine's verse were delivered with similar clarity, 'every syllable is heard, nothing spoken is lost', according to Roland Lysell,[74] in spite of the fact that Stein broke with the declamatory tradition of speaking out to the audience and had his actors speak the verse to each other. While in *Nicht Fisch Nicht Fleisch*, Stein insisted on the play being performed in dialect following the indications of the author, Franz Xaver Kroetz.[75]

It is perhaps not so difficult to see what has made Peter Stein one of Europe's most important theatre directors of today. He has shown that he has the ability in reading classical texts to protect the dialectic between the past and the present so that the dramatic tension is always present. In the words of Leif Zern: 'He doesn't add things to the plays he directs so much as finds the most in what is already written in them; he reads the texts with the utmost care and weighs different possible interpretations against each other – he always goes from the structures to concrete details.'[76]

It is ultimately Stein's respect for the actor's creative ability and not his own – he often refers to himself as unimaginative – coupled with his ability to find the essence of the drama's theme, which helps his actors to find characters which can also give full meaning to this theme. Taken together with his attempts at democratizing the bureaucracy of institutionalized theatre, Stein has nurtured his humility and the success of his productions demonstrates how worthwhile this has been.

1 An allegorical representation of rhetoric depicting its two symbolic attributes – the lily (*ornatus* or flowering speech) and the sword (*persuasio* or the ability to convince).

2 Manual rhetoric recommended specific hand gestures for the speaker to demonstrate particular attitudes and emotions.

3 (left) John Gielgud demonstrated an ability to compromise between the music in the verse and a natural vocal delivery.

4 (below) Laurence Olivier. A quest for a truthful vocal delivery based upon vocal virtuosity.

5 (right) Paul Scofield. Communicating by thinking and feeling rather than verse speaking.

6 Stanislavski discovered that the text was part of the creative process – that it was verbal action.

7 Brecht, *Mother Courage and her Children*. Shown here instructing (left to right) Helene Weigel (Mother Courage), Angelika Hurwicz (Kattrin), and Erwin Geschonnek (the Chaplain), in the principles of gestic acting.

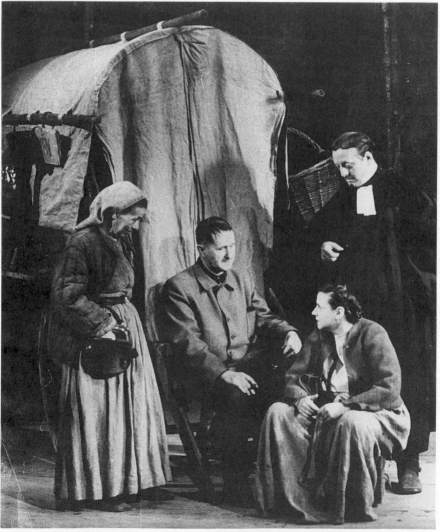

8 Artaud, *Les Cenci*. Language orchestrated as 'expression in space' was intended to capture the audience as in a dream. Note the stylized costume showing the internal features of the body.

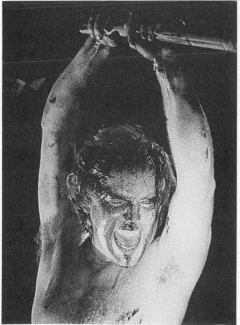

9 Enrique Pardo, *Hymn to Pan*. The Roy Hart Theatre uses language to liberate the audience's inhibitions along with their own through sound.

10 (left) Grotowski. *Apocalypsis cum Figuris*. Poetry of body was complemented by poetry of sound intended to work on the audience by its powers of association.

11 (below) Peter Brook, *Mahabharata*. By combining ritual with the narrative of everyday, the performers found the essence of 'dharma'.

12 (right) Ingmar Bergman, *Hamlet*. Games with time and place accentuated the visual aspects of the production and the shift of thematic emphasis.

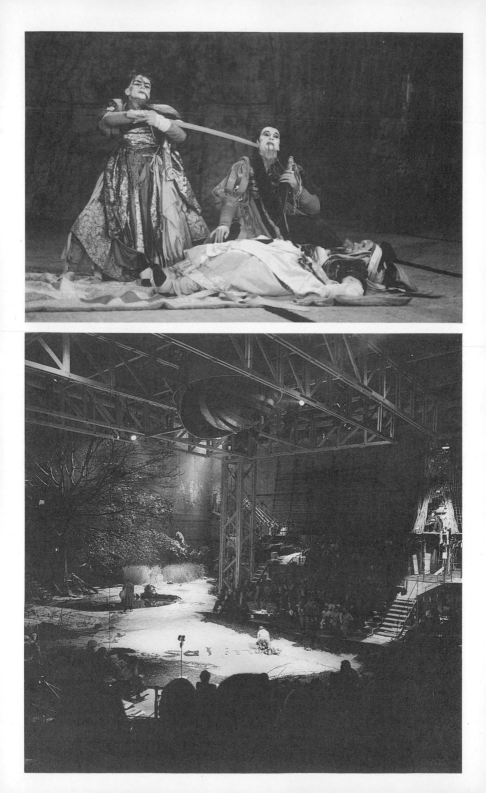

13 (top left) Ariane Mnouchkine, *Henry IV*. Music and percussions communicated the emotive aspects of the subtext rather than the actors' own vocal deliveries.

14 (left) Peter Stein, *As You Like It*. A false utopia created the perfect setting for experimenting with different styles of acting and vocal delivery.

15 (above) Joseph Chaikin, *The Serpent*. A new kind of gestural vocabulary used to retell the biblical myth in contemporary language.

16 (right) Richard Schechner, *Makbeth*. A vocal score replaced the dramatic linear text – offered in an environmental theatre arrangement.

17 Richard Foreman, *Kärlek/Vetenskap*. Polyphonic theatre where pre-recorded text fragments and sound-effects were replayed as the 'auteur' dictated.

18 Robert Wilson, *Einstein on the Beach*. Nonsense language accompanied the jury's arithmetical chorale in 'The Courtroom' scene.

19   Cicely Berry, *The King Lear Project*. Exploring the play through the movement of the language with Richard Haddon-Haines and Patrick Miller.

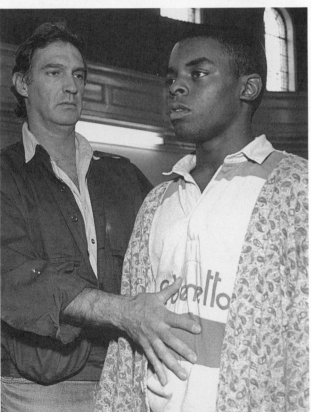

20   Gregory de Polnay (Drama Centre London) instructing a student how to gain freedom and flexibility through breath control.

5

THE POSTMODERN
APPROACH

Without doubt the approach to vocal delivery in the theatre has
been greatly influenced by the contribution of certain directors,
who in their productions have experimented with the balance
between voice, text and emotion. These directors have been largely
concerned with maintaining some vestige of the literary so-called
'verbal' theatre, where communication via the spoken word has
played an important part in the production. However a counter-
approach has been equally paramount in the past twenty years,
which has taken its impulses from Artaud and Grotowski, and has
chosen the 'non-verbal' style as most suitable for the postmodern
theatre. The leading characteristics of the postmodern theatre are
as follows: form dominates over content; fragmentation seems to be
the aim; there is no linear narrative; time and place are indefinite
as in a dream; there is an 'irrational' attitude to the series of
events; it is a polyphonic theatre; there is a breakdown in stage–
audience communication; there is a lack of communication
between the characters; heavy use is made of visual images,
stylized movements and groupings; many of the characters seem
'action-paralysed'; it is an archetypal theatre of myth and ritual
rather than a socio-political one; it presents a society which accepts
suffering and aggression; it appeals to an elitist audience who are
habitual theatregoers. In this theatre, language is not used to
communicate in the normal way, rather words are freed from the
tyranny of the text and give place to sounds, chants and broken
pieces of dialogue in an attempt to arouse connotative responses in
the individual members of the audience. Its stance is definitely a
deconstructionist one.

Many of these elements which reveal an irrational theatre were
in evidence in the early years of the twentieth century in the avant-
garde movements such as symbolism, expressionism and dadaism,

with such leading theatre-makers as Lugné-Poë, Reinhardt, Meyerhold, Copeau and others, as Martin and Sauter have shown.[1] They were enriched during the following years by Artaud's Theatre of Cruelty, rapid developments in modern dance, absurdism in the period following the Second World War, the happenings of the fifties and the Group Theatre Movement of the sixties, particularly in the work of Joseph Chaikin and Richard Schechner. This paved the way for the further experimentation of theatre-makers such as Richard Foreman and Robert Wilson in their search for a theatrical form which would better describe the frustrations and demands of living in the postmodern world.

THE GROUP APPROACH

During the sixties, a world-wide theatre movement sprang up in an attempt to redefine and reshape a theatrical form more in line with a society which had become riddled with violence, turmoil, foolish wars, assassinations and visible injustice on many fronts. In some countries this unrest had little or no impact, whereas in others it heralded the dawning of a new social-consciousness in the theatre. In America the answers had of necessity to be found Off-Broadway. As a result theatre was given a surge of new life by the enthusiasm of young idealists who founded groups such as La Mamma and the Living Theatre, and who were dedicated to putting the balance right in a world which they found had become debased on many levels. Conventions and traditional values were questioned on every level and many groups demanded the right to live by their anarchistic standards. The yearnings of these groups took visible external form in a rash of protest songs and an obsession with drug taking and consequently provoked a great deal of ridicule. Nevertheless, their search for a new aesthetic which would have a direct social and political bearing on society and their experiments in theatrical form, particularly in attitudes to the dramatic text, were to have a lasting effect on theatre on both sides of the Atlantic in the years to come.

Joseph Chaikin

Joseph Chaikin founded the Open Theatre in 1963 after a period of time with the Living Theatre, where he claims to have had his social and political conscience awakened, particularly regarding the practice of working together as an ensemble. Initially the Open Theatre was formed as a workshop for actors – to give them back more power – where behind closed doors and without the strain of having to continually stage a performance before a public night after night, they might be able to concentrate on exploring and studying theatre in the manner of a laboratory performing unfinished work. Chaikin championed an 'open' approach to the theatre where actors would not shut themselves off into exclusive groups, but rather would dare to expose themselves to all kinds of people outside their usual range of experience, from all levels of society, in an effort to create a more humanizing kind of theatre:

> We have to shake off the sophistication of our time, by which we close ourselves up and to become vulnerable again. We realize that life hasn't been too generous with us, and we've retreated. We've closed off a great deal of our total human response. But as actors we must open up again, become naive again, innocent, and cultivate our deeper climates – our dread, for example.[2]

Initially Chaikin was concerned with exploring another kind of theatre form than the naturalistic one with which the American theatre of the fifties and early sixties was so preoccupied. For him, this had become a 'deadly theatre' where naturalistic mannerisms and realistic stage productions presented audiences with stereotypes and perpetuated the myths with which social convention had saturated the privileged upper crust of society. For Chaikin, acting meant taking risks, not simply fitting into typical roles which contributed to what he called the 'moronization' of Americans.

It is not surprising that a new technique of acting based on sound and movement became characteristic of the Open Theatre. In developing his new techniques, which aimed at violating the psychological approach, Chaikin devised a variation of the method taught by Nola Chilton. In short this was a technique of physical adjustment, whereby the actor could find a way into character through the use of weapons and colours in approaching the plays of the Absurd.

This led to the Open Theatre's 'sound and movement' technique, which can be described as follows: working with partners, the actors share an action; then one of the actors 'transforms' the sound and action into something of his own. The 'action' leads the way into an emotional experience and thus the actor must open himself up to the emotional experience to which his action leads him. In this way the actor is made vulnerable to emotions which are difficult for him. Through the method of seeking the physical expression of an emotion or attitude and expressing it in sound and movement rather than simply selecting it, Chaikin revealed his belief in art as a process of investigation.

His main interest was always his workshop experiments and group dynamics. Although his strong personality controlled everything, at the same time he was able to give the group the impression that it was learning self-control. He was a philosopher and moralist, driven by the need to probe the confusions and anxieties of his living experience outside the theatre. In rehearsal, although discussion was minimal, the emphasis was laid on improvising and structuring an improvisation to shape the inquiry at hand. The overriding aim of all his work was a concern with making things visible in action – so that, by using sound and movement, the actor would be able to give visible shape to the emotional shape.

In Chaikin's theatre there was no room for character acting, rather the work of the ensemble came first and foremost. By sharing the dynamics, or form, of an action, and in transformations where they found ways of coming together over and over in the rapidly altering circumstances, they fully explored the kinetic impulses of the ensemble and thereby avoided character aesthetics. Chaikin explained it in the following way:

> Ensemble asserts the way that people are alike. We live and die separate. But there is a point where we are completely interlocked, a point where we are brought together, all of us, by our participation in nature, where we are brought together two by two, or in threes and fours, by our participation in something larger than each of us.[3]

Chaikin borrowed freely from the techniques of Viola Spolin, Grotowski and Joseph Schlichter. From Spolin he adopted many ideas for improvisational games to recapture the inventiveness and suppleness of the actor. At a later date he borrowed from Grotowski a number of disciplined movement exercises, and from Schlichter, who was a psychotherapist as well as movement expert, many of the dynamics which shaped future performances. For Chaikin, the workshop was always the focal point for his artistic energies and not the performance. Nevertheless the 1964–5 season marked the beginning of public performance for the Open Theatre, which at that time consisted of sixteen actors, four writers and four directors, whose repertoire consisted mainly of 'bright-spirited parody pop and pure performance'.[4]

In the Open Theatre, the writer participated in the workshop before writing anything down. This was very important to Chaikin, who defined a writer not as one who had written a script on which a work was based, as in the case of traditional production, but as one who would write a script related to the work which the troupe was improvising. In the early days of the Open Theatre the relationship between workshop and writer was very close, with writers being invited either to write for the troupe, or to tailor some writing to the specific matters of concern in the workshops.

Chaikin involved playwrights in the process of working out a new theatrical language that was not to depend primarily on words. The reason for this was that he despaired of conversation and conversational language, which he felt was unable to carry meaning any more. He preferred to see:

> each play have its own code in the use of words. Each play is only involved in its special poetry. It would become a kind of language, with the syntax carrying a special kind of meaning. The words have special meaning to the audience and the actor. That's what the playwright, finally, has to do.[5]

This was the technique with which *Viet Rock* (1965–6 season) came into being. It was organized around a subject which was being explored in the Saturday workshops and was finally written by one of the Open Theatre's writers. The narrative was that of birth to death and rebirth with a subtitle which read: 'a folk war movie'.

In order to underline only the high points of the action – either because the story-line was familiar or because the events had a thematic or conceptual relationship rather than a narrative one – Chaikin developed a device to structure such a group-created play, called 'stop-and-start'. Actors sat on the sidelines, assumed instant characters, and began the action. In this way they emphasized dramatic event and de-emphasized character. There was a dead break between the actions of the 'stop-and-start' and in this way the approach is related to Brecht's, with its concern for the actor's commitment to the ideology of the drama he is helping to unfold. Further similarities with Brechtian aesthetics can be seen in Chaikin's attitude to the actor–audience relationship, through a technique called 'expecting'. By having the actor 'expect' that the audience would react in a particular way, Chaikin realized that he had more chance of reaching them intellectually or ideologically.

The Open Theatre's ideology was not a political one in the radical sense, although one can easily discern the serious nature of the issues which have been the subject of inquiry. Chaikin purposely steered away from this kind of theatre, finding it too limiting both in subject-matter and theatricality. His concerns were of a more universal nature, where social issues were explored in order to question man's behaviour.

The techniques which were developed in the workshops were devised to assist this kind of epic theatre. Games such as 'inside-outside', 'worlds' and 'the phrase' were intended to break with the linear narrative and were related to Brecht's 'gestus' as well as to the ideograms of the classical Chinese theatre. This was the particular case for the technique called 'the phrase', where the actor repeated a phrase in identical form a specific number of times or for a specified period of time as the paradigm of a character. It constituted the entire characterization; thus, although it was naturalistic in form, it was emblematic in function and became ritualistic – inevitably suggesting automata and types, either social types or archetypes.[6]

Although *Viet Rock* was not well received by the critics, another project from this season – a collection of three plays written by van Itallie and collectively entitled *America Hurrah* – received very favourable reviews when it opened at the Pocket Theatre, and became a hit. The first play, *Interview*, is an oratorio for eight actors, with an opening chorus; eight arias are supported by a chorus and linked by short choral passages, and a closing chorale recapitulates the aria motifs. It deals with the so-called 'ice age' in which we live – surrounded by people, yet isolated and alienated. To underline this theme, Chaikin directed the actors to speak intimately to and focus directly on the audience as if they were speaking to themselves. This emphasized the characters' alienation from one another. According to one eye-witness, the peformance was 'rich in Open Theatre techniques, some of which were indicated by the author in writing the play, the others evoked by Chaikin in producing it'.[7] The second play, *TV*, is more conventional. It presents a split scene, where real people, sitting in their own living-room, are invaded by the unreal people from the television screen and finally, without being aware of it, they become completely consumed by the fake world. The third play, *Motel*, was inspired by Artaud's *The Theatre and its Double*. It was a short play of ten minutes' duration, which explored the violent destructive level of contemporary American life. There are only three characters: a motel-keeper and two visitors. The verbal score of the play is a disembodied recording of the motel-keeper's voice enumerating the contents and merits of her rooms, which forms the background accompaniment to an act of total destruction, when two travellers arrive and set about defacing the room and, as tension mounts, even destroying her as well, before departing.

Chaikin's involvement as consultant in Peter Brook's *US* workshop at the Royal Shakespeare Theatre, where he also encountered Grotowski, led him to the realization that the Open Theatre's actors had no real formal training. When he returned to America, he adopted Grotowski's 'Cat' exercise as well as many other exercises from Eugenio Barba, and even brought Grotowski to the troupe the following autumn (1966–7) to impart the spirit of the psycho-physical work.

In preparation for his next project, which he alluded to as 'the impossible study', Chaikin built a new company, rented a loft on Bleeker Street and with a grant from the National Endowment on the Arts, set about giving his new company some of the 'techniques' which he felt it needed for the coming project. The visits of Grotowski and Cieslak helped them shift the focus away from the old self-conscious emphasis on physical prowess towards investigation and process, with Grotowski insisting that the actor should 'commit a total act, one for which he mobilizes his entire outer being (body and voice) in order to exteriorize his deepest inner being (psyche)'.[8]

The topic for inquiry was to be the Bible. The method of rehearsal was familiar. Although there was some discussion, major importance was attached to visualizing the inquiry through improvisation. Some matters were, of course, textual ones, as Lahr has indicated; for example, the Bible says that God cursed his creatures through their own tongues and the workshop had to find a way to make that happen theatrically. Further issues, such as Adam's shame over his nakedness after eating the apple, were worked on in the nude under Schlichter's guidance. In this way, the actors were 'sacrificially' present, in the Artaudian sense. Chaikin's delight with the workings of the new group encouraged him to make a performance piece out of some of the images discovered. He engaged van Itallie's assistance and, after an eight-month period of experimentation, this resulted in a scripted piece entitled *The Serpent* (1969).

The Serpent doesn't tell a story so much as project kinetic images related to the story's monumental events. The serpent tempts Eve, Eve succumbs; Eve tempts Adam, Adam succumbs; God casts them out; Eden is erased on every level – physical, psychic, spiritual; Paradise is lost. In performance, there were six episodes. Each episode was a unit compounded of visual and aural images created by the actors with their bodies alone. There were some percussion instruments and a bag of apples. The scenes were interrelated through the repetition of sensory motifs, mostly aural and visual.

As Pasolli has commented: 'The play's "kinetic" vocabulary, which the verbal text serves as a score, rather than the usual reverse, endows the biblical events with the character of mental pictures in motion like dim imaginings, which will not go away, in some deep recess of the mind.'[9] The new kind of gestural vocabulary in *The Serpent* was assisted by a new kind of language which was both concrete and economical, allowing it the generalizing power of mythic speech. The author described it as follows:

> In *The Serpent* there is a great deal of incantation, because there is no confrontation between one human being and another in a direct way. The problem with Adam and Eve was how do you get them to speak. The moment you have actors and actresses open their mouths in a naturalistic fashion, you've lost their myth's potential. How do godlike figures speak? How do images which are larger than life speak? The sound has to carry a lot of grandeur or extend a stage image. . . I'm trying to do with words what Chaikin is trying to do with the actors – get to the very essence of things. It's the only extent to which you can reach the archetype.[10]

Van Itallie has a chorus of three women who stand apart from the biblical events. They were contemporary figures, the accursed descendants of Eve, who witness the events and meditate on their present difficulties. Another crucial scene is also contemporary – the assassinations of John Kennedy, Martin Luther King and Robert Kennedy, in ritualized form. On this scene, which occurs early in the play, the rest of the action depends. The biblical portions of *The Serpent* are an investigation of the psychic climate out of which the Kennedy–King–Kennedy violence sprang, and as Pasolli has observed:

> The alienation, disintegration, and importance inherent in the violent acts of modern America are *described* by the contemporary episode, and *defined* by the biblical scenes. In *The Serpent* the story of Adam prefigures the very real acts of our contemporary public life. It is in the relationships of the play's parts that I see its unique character and a recognizable synthesis of the inner and the outer strains of the Open Theatre's work.[11]

The task which confronted van Itallie was that of trying to create in each moment a size and a resonance beyond particular space and time. In interviews he spoke of trying to show 'vertical time' instead of 'linear time' where the pull of mythology could draw one back to imaginative first sources. He was greatly influenced by Chaikin's technique of externalizing internal states of being – the ability to make life transparent, to confront its complexity with the clarity of living symbols.

The Open Theatre called *The Serpent* a 'ceremony' – a ceremony of mourning – where the actors became priests at the offering. They examined the myth of Eden for its personal relevance to themselves and ceremonialized what they discovered. As Chaikin explained:

> When we explored Adam and Eve, we found ourselves much more involved with these stories, these myths, than we imagined. It became clear that although we had rejected these stories as being true in any way, they still claimed us. We were absolutely surprised how personal the discussion and the improvisations were for us. That's what made me continue to work on it. There was a visceral energy and it seemed important to follow and let it have its own autonomy.[12]

One eye-witness who saw the performance at the loft observed that it seemed to touch the spectators in some secret place where they had not known sensation before. They seemed to be experiencing wonder and sometimes awe. This was due not merely to the awesome themes with which the play dealt, but primarily to the uncommon control, fed by an unusual degree of personal conviction, which the troupe brought to its performing.[13]

In 1973, after nine years of experimentation and at times enormous frustration, Joseph Chaikin decided to close the Open Theatre, fearing there was a danger of their becoming institutionalized. The time was right in his opinion because: 'People were doing master's degrees on the work of the Open Theatre, and more and more Foundations were willing to give grants.'[14] Nevertheless, they had made their contribution – the break away from the traditional linear narrative was made, and a new form of sound and movement presentation had been realized successfully. In 1974 the Open Theatre presented a 'work-in-progress' performance of *Electra*, drastically reduced to a one-hour version, where a change was clearly obvious in Chaikin's approach. The most important element in this production was a renewed interest in speech and not sound and movement, as in their previous works.

Richard Schechner

Another American director who has had a great influence on the non-verbal aspects of vocal delivery in the modern theatre is Richard Schechner. A proclaimed disciple of Grotowski and Artaud, Schechner founded the Performance Group in New York in 1967 and set about exploring ritual drama, the connections between human and animal behaviour patterns in play and ritualized activity and the types of religious performance surviving in primitive cultures.[15] Schechner's belief that the avant-garde theatre does not differ from primitive ceremony has led him to emphasize the performance as 'process' and not product.[16] However, he redefined 'tribal culture' to mean 'community' and regarded it as imperative to persuade the spectators to participate in his productions by discarding their social and political conventions – even by using nakedness as a further means of rejecting the 'system'. With this anthropological approach he endeavoured to transform the audience into a community.

Schechner saw ritual as replacing narrative in the postmodern theatre,[17] and therefore his experiments with the dividing up and reallocation of the theatrical space, so that the audience became the 'environment' for the actors, became significant for the Performance Group's continued way of working. One can agree with Innes that environmental theatre is only a short step away from the rejection of scripts and verbal communication in the best Artaudian fashion, where theatre is used as corrective therapy for a sick society and where his search for 'scenic rhythms' makes us forget the necessity of speech.[18]

As with many of the groups which sprang up in the sixties, The Performance Group did not consist of trained actors with performance techniques which set them apart from the man in the street; rather it was a group aiming at self-expression and liberty. In accordance with Grotowski's theories of *via negativa*, where the actor becomes self-penetrated, Schechner encouraged his actors to try to attain full emotional potential and thereby exercise a shamanistic power over the audience. The way to these 'character-less' performances was to be attained through psychoanalysis and group therapy.

Schechner supports Grotowski's belief in Artaud's proclamation that actors should be 'like martyrs burnt alive, still signalling through the flames' because this contains the whole problem of spontaneity and discipline which gives birth to the total act. In his opinion this is the very crux of the actor's art:

> The kind of performance I am talking about . . . discards the buffer of 'character'. . . . During rehearsals the performer searches his personal experiences and associations, selects those elements which reveal him and also make an autonomous narrative and/or action structure . . . What results is a double structure – the first is the narrative and/or action structure. The second is the vulnerability and openness of the performer.[19]

Schechner was specifically against the notion of 'building a character' and all the systematic elements which Stanislavski advocated. He believed that not playing a character was playing the actions, regardless of their consistency. He maintained that the performer did not play himself, nor did he play a character, rather he played the actions; he believed that these actions were objective, or part of the *mise-en-scène*, and that their function was to bring to the audience's attention what the director and performers decided upon. He contended that the actions did not vary from performance to performance, that improvisation was a tool to be used in finding and making this *mise-en-scène* and ultimately a score, and that what happened for the first time each performance were the feelings stimulated by the score.[20] This procedure influenced the way The Performance Group worked on a text in rehearsal before finally evolving a performance score. Schechner views the practice of regarding a performance as a 'realization of a text' to be very old-fashioned, believing that everything determines everything else in a production and that there is no way of knowing in advance what the dominating element will be. He supports Gordon Craig's beliefs about action, scene and voice being the material for the theatre of the future: 'When I say "voice" I mean the spoken word which is sung, in contradiction to the word which is read, for the word written to be spoken and the word written to be read are two entirely different things.'[21] One can understand the criticism which was directed at The Performance Group's textual analysis in approaching their first theatre piece *Dionysus in 69*, where Schechner's interpretation of Dionysus as an irrational, ungovernable, ecstatic life-force was somewhat contradicted by Euripides' presentation of the god as ironic, self-controlled and intellectualizing – a death-force. This 'ambivalence' of the god formed the basis of *Dionysus in 69* and was intended to represent the tendency towards fascism inherent in the retreat of the 'new left' from political revolution to the introverted sexual liberation of the drug culture.[22] However, the ritualistic action, emphasis on nudity, orgy and dancing seemed to change the focus, according to public opinion, to one reflecting the contemporary clash between the 'establishment' and 'hippy' freedom, sexual fulfilment and the student revolution.

The dialogue in *Dionysus* was entirely written by the members of the group, who candidly admitted in retrospect that they were acting out their own neuroses. Nevertheless, the emphasis in this production was on the physical aspects, as John Lahr observed:

> *Dionysus in 69* is the first American theatre event to take as its theme the new self-consciousness towards the body and the unshackling of the sexual instinct. The actors in *Dionysus* are trained to a heightened, acrobatic concept of performance. The males stripped to a jock strap; the females in brief body tunics (sometimes nude) move through a series of carefully disciplined images. . . [It] is best when it is vivid and simple. Men lie prone on the floor while the women straddle them, fixing their legs tight between groins. Bodies pass under legs and bare backs squirm in a tortuous rebirth.

At the conclusion of the event, the men are slaughtered, lying like flayed beef, in textures of flesh.[23]

The whole performance was restructured into an initiation rite; 'opening ceremonies' were designed to create contact between actors and audience when the audience was carried individually into the performing area. The entire cast formed the chorus, which became the dominant element of the play, with scenes and characters emerging from choral activity and dissolving back into it as 'initiation by example'. The spectators were invited to join the bacchanal as Dionysus repeatedly encouraged them with the words 'it's a celebration, a ritual, an ordeal, an ecstasy', allowing only those who had taken off their clothes into the central playing area or 'holy place'. In fact a degree of audience participation was necessary for the continuation of the production, and the audience was encouraged to join the 'community' by stripping and dancing with the performers.

In *Dionysus* the performers made biographical references to themselves, thus going in and out of their mythical and legendary characters. They often referred to one another by their own names and would move from formalized ritual action to ordinary 'non-theatrical' action, as if they had left the play. They would also move from a formal rhetoric (lines from Euripides) to an assumed spontaneity manifested through the colloquialisms of the contemporary hipster.[24] It appears that during rehearsals, Schechner had laid down specific rules – the Dionysus performer, a god, was allowed to improvise and to use hip language, but the Pentheus character, man, had to adhere to the script, to the formal language of his time. The script then evolved partly through what Euripides had to say, partly through what the performers and Schechner had to say about themselves, and partly through current social problems such as sexual liberation. It was generally thought that this treatment of the text was naive and rather too inbred, and ultimately the intense psychotherapeutic sessions even caused a final rift in the group. However, The Performance Group was concerned with the political scene as well as social mores, and attempted to make a contribution in this area also.

Schechner was very particular about how the audience should be seated in all of these performances; in how they participated in it, what their spatial relationships were to each other and to the action; whether the performance was localized in one or several places or if it was generally distributed; whether the performers were very near the audience or at a medium or very far range. For each of the productions named, the 50 × 40 × 20-foot space was entirely redesigned and each of the spaces used had its own 'feel'.

The overall tendency was to keep much of the action in the centre so that the audience could see most of what was going on. The walls were painted white for *Dionysus* and *Makbeth*, but for *Commune* they were a light earth colour and the ceiling sky blue. Schechner's reason for this was so as not to blacken out the audience: 'Putting everyone together in one space is the architectural version of sunlight. It makes people share in the event; it makes them responsible for the event.'[25]

In *Makbeth* (1969) Schechner invited the audience to remove their shoes and move around during the performance from one carpeted area to another, so that they could intensify their own and the performers' experience; to try to understand the action and go with it; to think of themselves as witnesses, or people in the street. Apparently there was a good response to this invitation – during the banquet scene, the empty table swiftly filled with people who became guests at Dunsinane, and the murder of Banquo, which took place under a platform, had a few witnesses.[26]

Although the final text arrived at in Schechner's *Makbeth* was based on Shakespeare's text, it was the end result of a number of 'association exercises' where again the personal fantasies of the performers were interwoven with fragments of the original text. The emphasis on audience involvement was designed to activate a similar response in them, and narrative and character were replaced by spatial and sonic structures. The performance area, which encompassed the audience, was divided into distinct territories for each group of archetypal characters as follows: Doers, Macbeth and Lady Macbeth; Victims/Founders, Duncan and Banquo; Avengers, Malcolm and Macduff; and Dark Powers. A table in the centre was the 'no-man's land' which each group struggled to control. The vocal score was composed by Paul Epstein to replace dramatic (linear) text with choral (simultaneous) textures, distorting the form of words to tonal patterns, and layering speeches by dividing them between different voices or having them spoken as rounds, in which themes were repeated and varied as descants. The audience had to force their way through a 'maze' before entering the performance area, struggling through

life-size photographs from previous traditional *Macbeth*s, placards
bearing well-known lines from the play and walls of mirrors against
which they were continually being thrown in the dimly lit
passageways, as they came face to face with the fragments of the
Macbeth legend.

Commune, their next production, was finally staged in December
1970 after ten months of painstaking composition. Unlike the two
previous productions, the text was assembled from a variety of
sources: newspaper clippings, old American writings, Melville,
Thoreau, Shakespeare, Marlowe, the King James version of the
Bible and group improvisation. Schechner outlined the method of
rehearsal as follows:

> First at the end of and blending from 30 to 45 minutes of
> psychophysical exercises (taken from Grotowski, Yoga and
> The New Orleans Group) I would lead some or all of the
> Group into improvisations that used or needed the invention
> of texts. Sometimes these would be free verbal associations
> closely related to a specific psychophysical exercise. That's
> how we got the 'Songs of First Encounter' and the 'Death
> Raps'.[27]

Many of the scenes finally used were incorporated because they
were being worked on at the time. Three of them were from
Shakespeare and one was from Marlowe; they embraced love, rage,
death and rebirth and were of an archetypal nature, according to
Schechner, who outlined the Group's approach in the spring of
1970, as follows:

> They sank into *Commune* until they were embedded at the
> very base of its Structure, its foundation. Along with slow
> motion running, an exercise in hearing sounds and moving
> 'singing' to the sounds heard, elements of the Manson–Tate
> murder case, and our relationships to each other, these four
> scenes are the données of *Commune*.[28]

The text evolved at the same time as they were developing the *mise-
en-scène* and beginning to work on individual scores. In other words
the text was focused on action and the relationships between the
actions. None of the text/performance was based on feelings – as
Schechner was not interested in this kind of theatre – rather it was
based on facts. He likened The Performance Group's way of

working on a text to Stanislavski's method of working from beat to beat:

> We have shifted from building characters and coaxing feelings to planning actions and letting whatever feelings there may be flow freely. We move toward the extremes, a strong autonomous *mise-en-scène*, precise and detailed actions through which the performer cannot help but express himself.[29]

Schechner has very definite opinions about the importance of the text to a production, maintaining that up to 1950 the playwright and his ideologies dominated; that the text was untouchable and the function of director and performers was simply to interpret the text; that the nature of criticism had been to analyse playtexts and that even the underlying politics of the theatre historians had come from playwrights. At this time characterization was all-important, which supported the myth of the identity between humanism and individualism and the flourishing bourgeois theatre.[30]

Furthermore, Schechner believes that although mimetic theatre has given great opportunities to acting and the theatre, young people today are 'whole-seeking', and he calls for a new approach, maintaining that directors and performers are more creative today in the post-industrial world, where there is no longer room for a playwright to dominate. His formula for this theatre is that texts are taken apart and put back together with meaning for modern-day living – in other words, that they are 'deconstructed'. He has developed this theory further in dividing up drama, script, theatre and performance.[31] The contemporary sources for *Commune* and the personalization of the text by the actors rendered it too external according to one critic, who found that 'its brusque rhetoric rarely reaches a plateau of inner necessity'.[32]

A closer examination of the text reveals very few stage directions. Much of the play is sung and the imagery is iconographic. Apparently the rehearsal time was endless and the group's exploration of the theme 'commune' exasperating, as no shape appeared in the narrative. It was only following the Sharon Tate murder, when Schechner suggested that the group should relate the text to themselves – their own private murders, the Tate–Manson syndrome, America and the world – that the performance began to take some shape. *Commune* opened eventually after a very long rehearsal period, in New York in December 1970, with a cast of nine characters, and met generally with poor reviews. It was later changed a good deal with a cast finally pared down to six.

Similar experiments with environmental theatre characterized the 1975 production of *Mother Courage*, where the whole of The Performance Garage was incorporated into the scenography: the interior represented Mother Courage's wagon, while ropes and pulleys were suspended from the ceiling and the walls to represent harnesses or tents of a military camp. In this way the audience was set inside the environment of the play. Further attempts towards breaking down the barriers between illusion and reality could be seen in the scene acted out on the pavement outside, where Mother Courage actually haggled over her prices.

All of this, together with the additional inclusion of personal anecdotes and comments by the performers, tended to make the work of The Performance Group rather undramatic. It was generally felt that in spite of efforts to incorporate the audience, the event became something like psychotherapy for the members of the group itself. The rejection of characterization, and the attempts at recreating a shamanistic performance, which could exorcise the 'disease' of the community by rejecting texts in favour of hypnotic structures of sound, became in themselves clichés, and in Schechner's own critical appraisal even narcissistic, where 'the locus of the essential theatre shifted from the page to somewhere between the navel and the genitals of the performer'.[33]

Schechner's later experiments, such as *The Marilyn Project*, have moved somewhat away from the ritualistic and towards a more structurally experimental approach, in which the action has been 'consciously made multivocal and ambivalent', with two sets of actors playing the same scenes simultaneously on a split stage.[34] In this regard he can be seen as typifying trends of the postmodern theatre, where the audience is offered bits of information and strips of fragmented behaviour without the assistance of the narrative or discursive speech, and where the text is predominantly 'deconstructed'.

THE ART-PERFORMANCE APPROACH

Another approach which has become representative of the postmodern theatre is the 'art-performance' one. Characteristic of this theatre is a fascination with highly evocative visual imagery and athletic movement, and a very specific use of the 'canvas' of the theatrical space, where a scripted text is seen as an adjunct to the visual effects. Unlike Joseph Chaikin and Richard Schechner, whose successes can be attributed to the combined efforts of their groups, Richard Foreman and Robert Wilson have made their contribution to the postmodern theatre through this art-performance approach by their autonomy – controlling every moment of production. As a result they have won for themselves the title of 'auteurs',[35] the reason being that, although texts exist together with music and stage designs, the work is difficult to decipher and this quirkiness makes their work impossible to produce without the authors themselves being present.

Richard Foreman

During the late fifties and sixties Foreman became influenced by the 'underground film movement' as well as by Happenings, which had begun to appear in the avant-garde theatre in New York. This encouraged him to begin writing his own plays and to experiment with staging them. He founded his own group, the Ontological-Hysteric Theatre, in 1968 and acquired a small theatre with only seventy places but with a very large playing area, where he staged two plays a year for the following five years to a very enthusiastic, if somewhat 'closed', audience. When he sold it, he began to do productions in France, Italy, Holland and Sweden. In all he has staged fifty-two productions, and his 1987 production *Film is Evil: Radio is Good* earned him the New York critics award for best production.

Foreman's great interest in composition and structure in the theatrical event is clear from the following assertion:

> I am interested in creating a totally polyphonic theatre where all the elements work together to fragment each other, so that the audience, free from strong feelings and the need to identify, can enjoy the playfulness in the theatrical elements. This is despite the fact that the theme in the plays is fear and aggression in their most extreme forms. My goal has always been to go beyond the painful content with a dance of manic theatricality.[36]

Nevertheless, Foreman's stagecraft did not follow the trends which the group theatre movement had been investigating. In fact, as

Michael Kirby has observed, his Ontological-Hysteric Theatre seemed to be quite opposed to them:

> It uses the traditional viewing arrangement; it extremely reduces and limits the activity of the actor; it does not attempt didactic socio-political statements; and it is quite clear that Foreman is both the playwright and the director of his theatre.[37]

All of Foreman's settings follow the same pattern: the audience looks into a box as they would into a proscenium stage. Nevertheless, the content of the stage image does not follow traditional lines. Up to the mid-seventies, as Roose-Evans has stated, Foreman's attention was mainly concerned with presenting 'the object' in theatrical terms: 'putting it on stage and finding different ways of looking at it'.[38] The nature of the 'object' varied from performance to performance, but the object itself was significant for Foreman's 'deconstruction' theories, where by isolating the individual items in a production and fragmenting the usual narrational line, he would keep the audience concentrating and on their toes as none of the meanings would be obvious: 'If a work of art has a MESSAGE it means putting the spectator to sleep. The minute man "knows" he sleeps. . . Art can only keep man consciously rooted . . . if no conclusions are drawn.'[39]

In later years, Foreman has been chiefly concerned with the realization of fragmented texts in his productions. When he came to realize that unfinished sentences and fragmented language were an indication of his own times, he began to concentrate on this very breakdown in communication. In my view, his productions have an effect on the audience similar to that of switching from one television channel to another, that is to say, they appear confusing and unrelated.[40]

'All Foreman's plays are made to the same formula,' according to Roose-Evans, 'they avoid central themes and depict a sequence of static and unrelated "pictures"'.[41] Nevertheless, Foreman admits that his manner of writing his texts has undergone changes, that he no longer simply goes through his notebooks and decides 'Hum . . . go from here to here and I have a play'.[42] This was the way he began to write, or in his own words 'dewrite' plays:

> I made a rule of not changing anything, but simply chose a page as the start for the play and decided how many pages

long the play should be. In this way, the text became a sort of revelation of what I had been going through for a period of six months.[43]

Later Foreman became more open in his attitude to the text during rehearsals, rewriting and adding things during the whole process. He admitted that he used different strategies in order to create the text fragments which he put together to make plays, but that he had been influenced by Gertrude Stein in his early days, particularly in terms of inviting the spectator to be 'in the moment' – to match the play's time – which made him see the importance of replacing narrative with process.

That Foreman is the 'auteur' of his productions is undeniable. His ultimate goal seems to be to please himself rather than any prospective audience: 'Most theatre is built on people trying very consciously to manipulate the audience's response. I'm certainly not trying to do that. Really, I'm just trying to make an object that I'll end up loving.'[44] Finally, when the rehearsal period is over and he has finished experimenting, Foreman 'fixes' his productions. This is reflected in the manner in which he works on the text in rehearsals. The words of the text are not meant to function as mere background for the visual placement of the performers, although this is 'nine-tenths' of Foreman's rehearsal technique; rather he attempts to stage the 'process' of writing – of visualizing how the mind operates when writing a play. He admits that while writing he is constantly aware of the 'kind of room' and the 'feel of the space' that the play exists in; that he sees the props and the 'activities of the body', but that he does not see the characters because 'I really think they are all me'.[45] Perhaps this explains why Foreman prefers using non-professional actors in his productions.

The self-referential nature of Foreman's texts affects the way they are realized in performance. In order to appreciate the place which the text has in the performance matrix, it is almost essential to regard Foreman as a sculptor, who is endeavouring to realize on stage his own process of creating art. He is always part of it, and like Polish director, Tadeusz Kantor, physically takes part in the performance. He sits in the front row of every performance, operating a tape recorder which often contains the entire text together with all the sound-effects, 'tape-loops', multi-vocal effects and music. He uses a buzzer in order to break both the actions and the words into fragments, which also acts as an abrupt intrusion into the play. As the conductor, he can then determine the pace of each production – by adjusting the speed, and even at times entering into the 'living sculpture', adjusting a body here, or commenting on something which is happening there. This tape recorder is most important in Foreman's productions, as he records all the dialogue into it as a rule, so that in performance the actors only say a word or two quietly or repeat words as they are heard on the tape, echoing them slightly. Unless there is an accompanying gesture by one of the characters, the words heard remain anonymous – they are not related to any one in particular.

In recording the text, the actors are instructed to speak slowly and clearly, reading their lines in a measured and uninflected manner. They do not have to project their voices, because their soft speech may be amplified. As a result, the sentences that are heard are loud but unemotional. This gives the speech that is heard from the loudspeakers an unusual quality – laconic and deliberately expressionless – which has become characteristic of the delivery style in most of Foreman's productions. However, additions are made to the recording during the rehearsals. As Foreman detects situations that need clarifying, he adds explanations and comments in his own voice. The result is a mechanical recording of the production, with much of Foreman's own voice dominating, and fragments of the characters' voices interspersed with 'tape-loops' and other interjections. It becomes the centre of the play around which he choreographs the rest of the production, and it can be stopped at any time by his buzzer to bring attention to a particular point as the mood takes him that night.

One could erroneously assume that all this depersonalization of speech should foreground the visual apects of Foreman's productions; however, this is not the case. Foreman believes that theatre is about the text and the performer relating to the given architectural space. He makes use of the traditional picture-frame stage where almost all the scenes are presented as sequences of static pictures, and even groups his actors in the same plane parallel to the proscenium, turning the performers so that their bodies present essentially two-dimensional images to the spectator. Even chairs and tables are consistently placed to face the audience directly.

The actors are often motionless, posed in positions like mannequins in a store window, their eyes also motionless, steadily gazing out into the audience. Often only one actor at a time adjusts his position or moves to alter the stage picture. His change of position is intended to imply a 'different structural extension of the preceding thought', as Foreman's recorded voice instructed the audience in the 1974 productions of *PAIN(T)* and *Vertical Mobility*.[46]

Foreman uses other 'framing devices' in order to emphasize or bring into the foreground a particular word, object, action or position. In *Vertical Mobility*, he instructed a crew person to attach a string to one wall about three feet from the floor and to draw it horizontally across the stage, parallel to the floor and attach it to the opposite wall. He then instructed Max, one of the principal characters, to raise his leg so that his toe touched the string. To this a 'frame' was added, as the crew person attached a rectangular piece of white material to the string directly behind the foot – thereby framing it.

Other devices are all manipulated and controlled by Foreman during the performance, such as the use of projection screens in *Sophia = (Wisdom)* Part 3: *The Cliffs* (1973), the use of slides upon which some lines are written, and the use of a long narrow blackboard on wheels, which stretches across the entire playing area, upon which the words 'think harder' are written in white chalk. Although he uses other 'framing devices', such as movement of a kinetic kind and even group dance, placement and movement of objects, nevertheless Foreman's primary vehicle for framing lines and activity seems to be the tape-recorded words, music and noises. Many of the latter are added during rehearsals and can range from foghorns, thuds, pings, boings, glass shattering, drum rolls, bell whistles and screams, as in *PAIN(T)* and *Vertical Mobility*, or the regularity of a metronome ticking, as in *Sophia*.[47] The noises punctuate the performance and allow him to address the spectators directly by calling their attention to particular things. Not that Foreman appears to encourage audience participation, rather he seems to distrust anything in the stage situation which might depend upon an audience. He hopes that these repeated interruptions will force the spectators into a more acute state of self-awareness, and that their consciousness will be heightened at the pleasure of discovering all the hidden patterns and connections.

It is easy to see how important the scenography is to Foreman, and why he always does this himself. Not that he has the habit of working on a thought-out scenography prior to working on the text. In his case, the scenography is always a reaction to the text.

For this reason, Foreman is insistent that he is first and foremost a writer, a dramatist, and explains that he directs his own plays because no one else knows how to do it.[48]

The rehearsal period is very stringent. Foreman instructs his actors to do everything without explaining the reason for so doing. There is no improvisation or invited interaction. In the rehearsal process for *PAIN(T)* they seldom asked questions and rarely suggested solutions. All Foreman expects of his actors is that they write down all their actions, positions and pauses, and memorize them to the utmost detail of precision. Often he demonstrates how a certain position should look or how an action should be done. He even instructs them to deliver the lines flatly and in normal speaking voices. No attempt is made to project or interpret the lines, except occasionally when he decides to inject a moment of colour: then he gives a performer a specific instruction about how to deliver a line.[49]

One wonders what effect these performances have on an audience, the work being so self-referential, a kind of journey into the psyche of Richard Foreman, where one is made aware of experiencing his concern for various topics and themes, although never really involved on an empathy/identification continuum. Given the surrealistic nature of the staging, 'frozen' picturization and disjunctive sound, where it is almost impossible to arrive at any logical meanings, one could assume that the audience is totally left out, that it voyeuristically witnesses the production. Is this not another form of alienation – purposefully emphasizing the theatricality of the event, not in order to force the audience to contemplate some polemic or political point of view, but in order to activate it to engage itself in sorting out the theatrical puzzle? Not according to Foreman, who fully believes that his plays have a profound effect on an audience because of this act of forcing them to remember and that as a result they experience an awakening of consciousness. He advises the spectator that in order to understand his plays, one needs to observe the momentary 'cells', and all their possibilities, which, like polyphonic music, should be heard vertically, so that one really experiences the extensiveness and excitement and above all the thematic modulations.

Given that these are the intentions of Richard Foreman, it is almost an admission of failure to reveal that, as a member of the audience, my own reactions and searchings for meanings in this polyphony were those of confusion and frustration during the

Stockholm production of *Kärlek och Vetenskap* in 1987. Many members of the youthful audience present were similarly confused. One of the critics believed that the fault lay in the fact that Foreman had too much text in this production:

> A great deal is unbelievably captivating and confusing on a directly conscious and subconscious level. But when Foreman expresses himself poetically, it is quite pathetic. In my opinion he was much more interesting when his productions had less text. It is his ecstasy in movement, his ontological/ hysterical body language which is fascinating.[50]

In this production, the same trends were in evidence in the staging devices as have already been mentioned, with one exception: Foreman himself was not present manipulating the machines; instead this was done by a technician. Perhaps this explains why the production did not meet with success: without the presence of the subject for whom the piece was staged, there was no apparent reason why it was staged at all. Or perhaps it justifies Foreman's own claim to being the 'auteur' of his theatre pieces – because no one else knows how to do them.

Robert Wilson

Like Foreman, Robert Wilson has moved away from a linear narrative approach to his theatre pieces in his search for a theatre of non-verbal communication. A self-proclaimed follower of Gertrude Stein, he was dubbed by Louis Aragon as the 'heir to the surrealists'. His position in the postmodern theatre gradually became clearer, both on the home front in America during the sixties, where the influence of John Cage was reflected in his rather minimalist productions, and in Europe in the seventies and eighties, where his novel approach has made him one of the most sought-after directors in the contemporary theatre.

Wilson's approach to communication is a very personal one, which has been determined by his own problems with language and his speech impediment as a child. This was radically cured by a dancer who taught him to relax the tension in his body and to trust his energies. Since then he has been inspired to try to teach brain-damaged and autistic children, who do not possess the normal skills of verbal communication, and even to work with them in the theatre.

These experiments have influenced Wilson's concept of a performance text, which he refers to as an 'audio score', whose prime function is to accompany his ideas as collected in a 'visual book' (Wilson is a trained architect and has worked as a painter). His work bears a great resemblance to Foreman's, in that he too uses unrelated sound-effects, many tapes running simultaneously and recurring isolated words and parts of words, which are intended to refer to motifs and images as if in a dream. There is no dramatic structure which links any of the actions, rather, as Roose-Evans has stated:

> Actions become simply activities performed in a vacuum bearing no relation to a coherent whole. Each element is viewed in isolation, and . . . it is up to the spectator to make sense out of what he sees and decide if it's chaos or order, formed or formless, or if that matters.[51]

Wilson's first 'performance piece' as he calls it, to distinguish it from a play, was performed in 1963 and was dance-orientated. This marked the beginning of his own manner of working in the theatre – its nature suggests the origin of his 'theatre of visions', a theatre as epiphany of the performer's individuality and a theatre dedicated to non-verbal communication. This performance piece dispensed with the usual 'plot' line and with 'actors'. There were three performers, but the audience apparently had a problem with the question of 'time' and the clarity of the movement, as Wilson recalls:

> The play had no literary structure and had at that time almost no symbols . . . I was trying to go back to the simplest thing I could do; how do I walk, how do I walk out on the stage, how do I sit in the chair and walk off, is it necessary to have a story, is it necessary to have characters, is it necessary to have symbolism . . . at that point I was just wondering if I could sit in front of an audience, or if we could be a room full of people, just sitting together, having an exchange.[52]

From 1967 onwards he began doing other performance pieces such as *Poles* – a giant outdoor environment/theatre/sculpture piece consisting of 600 telegraph poles in an open field in Ohio, and other theatre pieces such as *Baby* and *ByrdwoMAN*. At this time he founded the Byrd Hoffman School of Byrds at the Byrd loft, where, through his workshops, he began to develop his ideas for theatre further. At this time he conducted workshops in psychosomatic therapy with grown-ups, and these did not differ greatly from his theatre workshops, which were mostly concerned with showing performers as themselves. This awareness of the performer's individuality replaces the awareness of a personality or a character as represented by an actor, and seems to be the key to Wilson's theatre.[53]

The second element in Wilson's theatre that is indicative of his particular style is his use of stage imagery. The visual concept replaces the dramatic one and the 'individual' is seen in a number of changing images. What the individual does cannot be interpreted as a representation of an action by a character – nor can the view of the stage and its changing images be regarded as a representation of a setting. Rather the spectator views the whole as a spectacle, devoid of reality, where backdrops and stage-sets are isolated from each other, where costuming and lighting are 'somewhat abstract in the manner of the surrealist painters', and affect the spectator as does a painting.[54] For this reason, Wilson has indicated a preference for the proscenium-arch theatre and for traditional theatre architecture with large stages. He makes great use of curtains and other devices to separate the audience from the spectacle, which he wants to be appreciated at a distance without any possibility of self-identification.

It is not difficult to understand why Wilson prefers using performers who are not professional actors, as he also rejects any attempt at characterization. The basic requirement for a Wilson production is sensitivity to the group's energy-discharge, or the rate and volume of its flow into action. From the performer's point of view, the subsequent awareness of his movements is not so as to make deliberate effects with them, but rather to be alert to his body and to respond to its signals regarding how far to carry a gesture, or when to end or begin an action. It is an ordinary, simple awareness of the simple activities of everyday life when one is not doing anything very much, something akin to habitual daily movement.

As a result, a prominent characteristic of Wilson's theatre is slow motion. One participant recalls that the rate of discharge seems to relate not so much to the speed of speech and gestures as to how often the situation changes, which one has to sense from the wings.[55] From the audience's point of view, this slowing-down of the action effects a change in normal perception habits. According to Deák, Wilson creates a tension betweeen the speed of the audience's perception and the speed of the action, because the image is not grasped in continuity but contemplated as a continuous present.[56] The audience's attention is directed to the patterns of the performer's movements as a result.

Wilson's rehearsals are very closely associated with his workshop activities, which have been consistently concerned with helping participants discover their own unique ways of moving, 'to help them find their own vocabulary of movement'.[57] What interests him theatrically is people presenting themselves naturally on stage without self-consciousness, although one cannot deny its therapeutic aspects. Although each of the workshop sessions had its own structure, depending upon the particular needs of the individual members, some aspects remained consistent over long periods of time. Usually there was some movement in unison, such as running round the room, jumping up and down, sitting back-to-back in pairs rocking back and forth, or lying on the floor breathing with eyes closed. Often they tried to build and sustain higher levels of energy, which Wilson referred to as 'raising your energy and sitting on it'.[58] Sometimes they repeated a single action or activity over and over again or attempted things in slow motion.

Many of the other workshop activities were attempts to approach non-verbal methods of communication and perception similar to those of a young deaf-mute boy, Raymond Andrews, with whom Wilson began to work in 1968. In their workshops, Wilson and the Byrds attempted to learn his language by imitating him. They learned his gestures and the way he moved as well as the sounds he made, which the Byrds incorporated into many of their productions. This formed the basis for Wilson's theory about how people experience the sensations of the world on what he calls an 'exterior' screen, which records most of the visual and audial impressions of people and sensations; blind people see things only on an 'interior' visual screen and the deaf almost entirely on an 'interior' audial screen. As a result their interior screens are often much more developed than other people's. By imitating Andrews in the workshops and performing in the long, almost wordless plays, where the audience tended to blink more and more slowly and where the interior and exterior screens became intertwined, Wilson and the Byrds found that they were becoming more attuned to their own interior screens.

Much of the effort of trying to understand Andrews's perceptions was incorporated into *Deafman Glance* in 1971 and used again

145

as the prologue to act IV in *The Life and Times of Joseph Stalin*. Wilson explained their approach to the work as follows:

> I started thinking about the way he, as I said before, the way he perceived things and we a built a play (*Deafman Glance*) with a vocabulary like that. Mostly with images, because it seemed to me that he thought in terms of pictures or images. As far as I could understand, that was . . . a large part of what was going on, in terms of what he understood.[59]

Deafman Glance did not have many words; it dealt almost entirely in images and in deaf sounds, like the ones Andrews made, and was the result of movements, gestures and drawings which Andrews had given Wilson. The following description by Deák indicates the style:

> It is performed on a raised plexiglass platform covered by a white sheet. Behind it, at the curtain line, a grey wall drop is hanging. On the platform are the Byrdwoman, facing upstage, and two children: a little boy sits on a low stool reading a comic book and a little girl is lying down under a white sheet. Stage left of the platform is a table covered by a white sheet. On the table are a knife, black gloves, a bottle of milk and a glass. The Byrdwoman turns towards the table, puts black gloves over the red ones that she is wearing, pours milk into a glass, crosses to the boy, gives him some milk, and returns to the table. She takes the knife, wipes it with a cloth, and approaches the little boy. At this moment, the Boy enters. The Byrdwoman stabs the child; the Boy screams. When the little girl is stabbed, the Boy cries out again. The Byrdwoman approaches him, puts her hand on his forehead and when he is just about to cry out once more, silences him by dropping her hand over his mouth. It was performed in extreme slow motion, in a concentrated way with strict economy of movement, without expression or emotion and initially lasted one hour.[60]

In this production the absence of speech was paramount, just as it is in a deaf-mute's world. Instead, the auditory signs became rather like quotations: Wilson's reading, verbal utterances, voiced thoughts and experiments with syntax, spoken into microphones, electronically transformed and transmitted through amplifiers located away from the speakers, enhanced the quotation-like quality. The sounds seemed to enhance the mood evoked visually rather than deepen any auditory mood.

Deafman Glance is typical of Wilson's theatre of visions and the postmodern theatre in the fragmentary structure of its visual imagery, the lack of emotion, use of dreamlike quality, archetypal nature of the performance with its choreographed movements and repeated use of *tableaux vivants*, together with images not connected with time or space, its simple trance-like movement, lack of interaction between the performers, lack of facial and vocal gesturing and, most importantly, its apparent absence of meaning.

Wilson's production of *Overture* in 1972 was a kind of bridge between *Deafman Glance* and *KA MOUNTAIN AND GUARDenia TERRACE*, which was performed later the same year in Persia. It marked the end of his theatre of visions and the beginning of his endeavours to use language.[61] The staging consisted of a varnished, pegged wooden pyramid about eight feet high, cut off at the top, and in the cabinet at the bottom Wilson spoke, chanted and declaimed as if 'his voice were coming out of the house of the dead'. The first image, that of a dinosaur, appeared on a screen which was unrolled to the floor, and accompanied Wilson's voice tussling with the thought associations emerging from a word – as if reason were trying to fight its way through layers and layers of language. The text, while semantically incoherent, was associative, in that phonemes and phrases grew out of each other in a frenzy of bodily registered sounds. In the words of one onlooker, 'it was a play of the vocal organs – a sound picture of terrible effort'.[62]

Language was again incorporated into the production of *KA MOUNTAIN AND GUARDenia TERRACE*, a marathon production with thirty members of the Byrds and twenty Iranians, which lasted 168 hours. Like Brook's *Orghast* it was staged on the side of a mountain and combined salient features of improvisation, action-painting and a planned 'happening' which included an audience.[63] The vocal delivery incorporated a frequency of high-pitched screams, contributed by Wilson, which he alternated with odd phrases in a deep bass voice, particularly at the mention of the word 'mountain'. Other deviations from the norm of discursive speech were uses of falsetto voice, slowed-down pronunciation, lapses into chanting in gibberish, disjointed phrasing and experiments with staccato rhythm, whispering and speaking 'past' each other. Many members of the audience were confused by the event, but for some it was a very rewarding experience, as one enthusiastic person remarked: 'For the first time, I experienced what I had always wanted to do myself: I experienced a work of theatre that was a genuine extension of all modern art. Without in any way being self-conscious about it, it was a modern work of art.'[64]

In spite of these experiments with language, Wilson's theatre work up to 1973 was mainly concerned with a theatre of visions – a theatre based on images rather than texts or stories – a 'left-brain' theatre, where the development of images governed the structure, but above all a theatre which exposed the individual as performer. Since 1974 his productions have been concerned with verbal, right-brain theatre, where he has incorporated language into his theatre pieces, but not discursive speech based on denotative meaning and syntactical logic.

At this time, Wilson started working with a brain-damaged boy, Christopher Knowles, who had problems with speaking and reading, and invited him to join the Byrds. He became fascinated by the way the boy structured his thoughts, and, as with Andrews, he realized that Knowles dealt with the word on interior rather than exterior screens. The boy was invited to lead workshops with the Byrds, not so that he should learn their way of communicating, but rather so that they should learn his. It was the graphic pattern of the word which seemed to matter to Knowles rather than the meaning, and this formed the basis for much of the use of language in Wilson's *A Letter for Queen Victoria* and *The Value of Man*. Wilson compared Knowles's use of words to molecules breaking apart in every direction:

> This was the word Kathmandu. Later, it would be Cat; then Cat-man-ru. Later it would be fat-man-ru, and then it would be fat man, and then it would be fat, and then it would be man or something. He would be breaking off parts. And every time he used it, he was not afraid to destroy the word. The language was really alive, the words were really alive. They were always growing and changing.[65]

In both *A Letter for Queen Victoria* and *The Value of Man*, Wilson tried to use language in the same way, while Knowles actually wrote much of the dialogue himself, as well as taking an active part in devising many of the physical exercises which formed the basis for the structure of the first play. Wilson did not have any specific image in mind for this play, but wanted settings in which people were to talk. One recurring theme seemed to be war and holocaust. In rehearsals, he instructed the cast of fourteen (as opposed to forty in previous productions) to learn from Christopher Knowles mainly by imitating him, believing that imitation would make communication possible. One of the participants, Stefan Brecht, recalled Wilson's intentions:

> This would within us hollow out/fill out what was to be the show piece of the piece, the form of rational verbal intercourse, would make it vibrate and would put it in counterpose to a non-verbal, arrational communication taking place (so Wilson seemed to suggest) by harmonious sensed reverberation. We would learn to relate, – communicate, – vocally without relying on or without concern for the meaning of what we said or of what was said to us. It would help impart to the conversation an ineffable formality, . . . but at the same time would no less discretely offer the public an example of true intercourse.[66]

The play turned out to be a comment on verbal communication. It was to be all about people talking with, to or at one another. A continuous accompaniment of music would assimilate speech to sound in the form of vocal gesture. In this piece, Queen Victoria is read a long and totally incomprehensible letter, while couples in white sit at café tables gesticulating frenetically and all speaking the same lines – 'chitter-chatter, chitter-chatter' – simultaneously. Two ballet dancers slowly spin on either side of the stage throughout the performance, and somnambulistic characters talk in nonsense language. A sniper shoots the couples who collapse one by one across their tables, and the performance ends with a long-drawn-out scream.[67]

Unlike his previous rehearsal methods, where he worked so painstakingly on the performers' movements, Wilson did not have the same attitude to vocal delivery in this production, although the emphasis was transferred to speech. One of the performers recalled that although Wilson experimented with delivery, centring on the distinction between 'skin, meat and bone', this was quickly abandoned. There was no other work done on the delivery: 'We were left to our own modes of delivery, it having been stressed that the meaning of the lines didn't matter, and it being understood that detachment from the content was *de rigueur*.'[68] Wilson had instructed his performers to 'get past the lines', maintaining that the most important thing was their awareness of where they were in space, whereas the dialogue was merely supportive and should be delivered as something secondary, as if they were doing something else. The result was very varied in terms of delivery styles, oscillating between two extremes, a great deal of expression on the one hand and a mechanical, inexpressive speaking of the lines on the other.

As the rehearsals progressed, Wilson kept demanding speed and fluidity, and later volume. There was to be no time allowed for the performers to pause before a line as if to make it their own, rather each speaker was to connect with the others by maintaining sensitivity to their sound and responding to it. The timing was split-second, and compared to previous productions: 'An aural microstructure had replaced a visual-kinetic macrostructure.'[69] However, it was not the aural aspects of the production which Wilson concentrated upon, rather he worked on it as a choreographer would.

The result was a visual performance, with the strongest image being conversation, or different ways of talking together. The tight choreographic structure foregrounded the image of vocal interchange. The lack of denotative speech and proper verbal meaning enhanced this abstract image of conversation. As a result, speech in *A Letter for Queen Victoria* assumed the role that movement had enjoyed in previous Wilson productions. The swing from movement to speech was obviously a determined effort on Wilson's part to show the emptiness of speech.

The aural effect of this production on the audience must have been confusing. The fact that the performers addressed and responded to one another's tone most probably created an impression of sociability, normally associated with discursive discourse, but this was only on the surface, as there was no literal meaning in any of the conversations. Nothing that was said was meant, neither was anything spoken in anyone's mind, since the manner of speaking did not relate to the meaning of the words. The voices had sounds, cadences, accents of expressiveness, suggesting specific attitudes, intentions and feelings, but all this expressiveness was merely formal. Neither was there any connection between what was said and what appeared to be the action. The only thing that was there was the form of expression. Although speech gave the impression of sounded thought, it lacked purpose.

All of this seems to support Wilson's negative attitude to language as being the bearer of discursive reason. He believes that there is a dichotomy between thought and language and as a result dislikes – even distrusts – language. One observer summed the production up as follows:

> In as much as *Letter* conveys a variety of relationships, attitudes, feelings, independent of what the characters say, but conveyed by their way of saying it, it demonstrates that communication is independent of verbal meaning, and suggests that what people say is not the content of communication. *Letter* is a gesture of contempt toward verbal meaning.[70]

A similar fascination with tight structure was evident in Wilson's *Einstein on the Beach* in 1976. This was a collaborative work with composer Philip Glass, and is indicative of the way in which Wilson approaches a theatre piece, starting with a form or structure and then filling it in. As he explained, he decided on the length of time, the number of acts (four) and upon three themes – A,B,C, which would be combined as follows: A/B, C/A, B/C, ABC. He also decided that each of the scenes would be about twenty minutes long. His next step was the compilation of a 'visual book' – where he had three definite images which he wanted to explore: Theme A 'Train', Theme B 'Trial' and Theme C 'Field'. Philip Glass took this formula and filled in the music. He did not know what the people would be doing in these settings, but admitted that light and space and the structure were all important.[71]

The musical structure which connected these themes was the so-called 'Knee Plays', five in all, which established musical themes and arranged them in such a way that the different movements for chorus, solo voice and instruments explored these themes and combinations of themes. The result was an integration of visual imagery, music, dance and song, which went over into speech at times. The formal structure of the music was followed in a vocal delivery which consisted mainly of counting or sol-fa, such as 'mi la mi la'. Changes of intention or emotion were connotatively injected into this limited vocal score by changing the rhythm, the pace or the volume. Other vocal elements included schizophrenic screaming, chattering nonsense language to the accompaniment of the jury's arithmetical chorale in the background in the courtroom scene, vivas, laughter, swearing and the use of cliché phrases.

Wilson's collaborative work on Heiner Müller's *Hamlet Machine*, which the playwright intended to be no longer than fifteen minutes, became two and a half hours long during its three-week rehearsal at the New York University. After two days of reading the text, Wilson and the group decided to dispense with it. He then began directing and after four to five days finished with the 'visual book' where he divided up the lines at random. As he explained, working from the 'visual book' first gave impetus to stage moves which one then found words for − a text.[72]

What disturbs him normally in the theatre is that what we see is only illustrating the 'audial book' whereas what is seen is as important as what is heard and should be structural. Wilson has persistently pursued a fascination for surface structure, as evidenced in his 1988 Paris production of *Le Martyre de Saint-Sébastien*, with text by D'Annunzio and orchestral and choral music by Debussy. He adopted the same approach to the text, which was reduced to half its original length. Lines were distributed at random: some were spoken by two narrators positioned on either side of the stage apron; many others were heard through the theatre's sound system together with orchestral pieces, odd sound-effects and a variety of ambient sounds. One reviewer observed:

> Wilson is faithful to the original in his fashion, respecting the structure and events but doing the telling in his own visual language. . . He (Wilson) has conceived a series of engrossing stage pictures, with an interplay of horizontal and vertical, of claustrophobic elements juxtaposed with distant vistas, all with a refined mastery of space and light, that intentionally or not, evokes and reinforces the pioneering theories and designs of Adolphe Appia.[73]

All this experimentation is intended to throw the onus back on to the audience. Rather than giving them explanations for things, Wilson wants them to come out of the theatre asking 'What have I seen?' He believes that the director's responsibility is to lead the audience on a journey of discovery, which will then inspire them, as was the case with John Cage's music in the fifties.[74]

For this reason Wilson has experimented with a theatre of therapy, by his working with autistic or deaf children. They symbolize the world condition where he believes:

> More and more people are turning into themselves. . . You

can see it in the subways, where everyone is bunched together, and nobody is looking at anybody. What they are doing is signing off. They have to because there's so much overload. . . It's actually a means of survival.[75]

Wilson's surrealistic audio-visual experiments have had varied effects upon audiences. The fact that many of his images are left undefined and unresolved, thereby creating many connotations, has often left the audience with a feeling of tedium or confusion instead of inspiration. This would seem to be the result of a too liberal experimentation with structure, where the form has dominated over the content, where themes are not explored in any depth, where the dreamlike nature of the action in slow motion and abstract stage imagery have often resulted in his work being dismissed as vacuous. In spite of the fact that Wilson has been adapting the spoken word and vocal delivery in his productions since 1974, it is obvious that his approach to language is one of negation rather than exploration, a trend which has become the trademark of many of the postmodern theatre pieces, seeming to indicate a total lack of belief in the spoken word for contemporary life.

6

ACTOR TRAINING

It is not difficult to appreciate that training an actor for such a diversified theatre, where the number of approaches has been so varied, is no mean task. The dilemma facing the actor, Basil Langton, when he realized that he had received absolutely no training for the kind of theatre which Robert Wilson created in his *KA MOUNTAIN* project (1976), where there was no place for the usual actor 'ego',[1] indicates the predicament which traditional drama schools find themselves in today. The majority of these schools structure their training around the individual actor and the creation of a role, and are text-oriented, whereas, as we have seen, there are a number of alternative forces at work in the modern theatre which are more concerned with an ensemble effort and group dynamics, and are interested in a non-verbal theatre which uses the text only as a point of departure. This chapter endeavours to explore the efforts made by a number of English drama schools in their search for a method of training suitable for the modern theatre and then to see how they have approached the question of voice and speech training. Finally a duality of approaches in modern voice training is examined, questions raised and international comparisons made, against which the Shakespearean 'ideal' in Britain can be seen more clearly.

BEFORE 1945

The situation in terms of the nature of drama schools in England at the turn of the century was as follows. Voice production and elocution could be studied in music academies, such as the London

Academy of Music (founded in 1861) or the Guildhall School of Music (founded in 1880), and there were so-called training companies, such as Sarah Thorn's at Margate and Frank Benson's Shakespeare Company (founded in 1883). No institution existed, however, which was devoted entirely to the art of acting. Sir Beerbohm Tree, recognizing the need for organized training, encouraged the establishing of a drama academy in the 1890s, but it was not until 1904 that he was able to found one in his own theatre, and consequently the first lessons took place in His Majesty's Theatre in the Haymarket, London. Despite initial derision from his fellow actors, Tree's academy soon proved so successful that in the same year it was moved to a house in Gower Street where it still resides. A board was formed of several of the great actor managers of the time, and so the Royal Academy of Dramatic Art was founded.

Elsie Fogerty, the founder of the Central School of Speech and Drama (1906), joined Sir Frank Benson in rooms at the Royal Albert Hall, which led to the founding of the country's first speech clinic at Saint Thomas's Hospital. She had been a close follower of the tradition of William Poel and the Shakespeare Revivalist Movement, where continuity of action and a lively pace of delivery were emphasized, so that a production should not be any longer than two hours, that it would have a minimum of scenery and thereby engage the audience's attention on an audial rather than visual level. She was succeeded by Gwynneth Thurburn, whose work in developing a natural voice based on scientific knowledge helped Sir Laurence Olivier to break with the former singing mode of Shakespearean vocal delivery. These principles were carried further by J. Clifford Turner (*Voice and Speech in the Theatre*). By 1935, the Guildhall School of Music had added Drama to its title. The London Academy of Music had been giving acting tuition since 1904, but it was not until 1938 that Wilfred Foulis introduced a one-year full-time acting course and changed its name to the London Academy of Music and Dramatic Art.

Because of the shortage of male trainees, these academies often had the air of ladies' finishing schools. One registrar recalled that in 1919, when Dame Flora Robson was a student, there were three male and seventeen female students in her class.[2] As all the schools relied almost exclusively on fees for their income, this often resulted in as many as 180–200 students being crammed into a space which eighty students use today. Needless to say, students were selected on their ability to pay the fees rather than on their exhibiting any special talent.

The training in those days was in keeping with the gentlemanly theatre of the time – straightforward and basic. In Flora Robson's class, they had two acting lessons a week: one in which they studied modern plays and the other for Shakespearean and Restoration works. Voice classes concentrated on correction to accent, diction and voice production, and there were elocution lessons once a week, in which the students worked on speeches from Shakespeare. Ballet, fencing and movement were also taught.

The French influence on the development of actor training in England and in many other countries is still very much in evidence today and stems from the work of Michel Saint-Denis, nephew of Jacques Copeau, the founder of one of the most legendary of all drama schools, L'École du Vieux-Colombier in 1921. The training at this school was unorthodox for the time because it included theatrical theory, dramatic instinct, history of ancient Greek civilization, grammar, singing, musicianship, sculpture, classical dance, acrobatics and mask work. One of the school's most important contributions was the emergence of modern mime as realized by Decroux, Barrault, Dasté, Marceau and Lecoq.

When Michel Saint-Denis took over from Copeau and became director of the Compagnie des Quinze (1929–34) they toured to Europe, notably Spain and London, performing at the Arts Theatre Club in 1931 with outstanding success. With their anti-naturalistic drama and insistence on non-illusionistic staging, they demonstrated that a new realism based on action and physical expression was possible. This created a shock in the West End theatre, then mostly devoted to solid, bourgeois comedy and drama. Their acting made an enormous impression on the classical actors of the day – John Gielgud, Laurence Olivier, Edith Evans, Michael Redgrave, Peggy Ashcroft, Alec Guinness and Charles Laughton – who were slowly to transform the English stage over the following thirty years.

Saint-Denis was also greatly influenced by the Moscow Art Theatre, which he first saw performing *The Cherry Orchard* in Paris in 1922, and particularly by their vocal delivery:

What struck me was the lightness of their acting: these performers seemed constantly to improvise their movements and their text. . . The words so clearly enunciated, expressed the mood musically; they soared from the actors' mouths. There were full-throated intonations as well as crystalline modulations, but their musical flexibility never became obvious.[3]

However, Saint-Denis was not without misgivings. He realized that although Stanislavski's work confirmed and complemented Copeau's in its rejection of theatrical artificiality, it would obviously have shortcomings in the performance of the classics, where the world is a poetic one. The Compagnie des Quinze set about developing a sort of invented mimed language which they called 'grummelotage', or the 'music of meaning', to help them in their epic-style productions, where many scenes were performed simultaneously. This means of expression, which attempted to transmit states of mind by cries, murmurs and chanting all related to the dramatic moment, but devoid of any apparent discursive logic, greatly impressed Artaud when he learned about it.

In 1935, Michel Saint-Denis formed the London Theatre Studio – the first school which aimed at training an all-round actor:

who could handle a sword as well as a cup of tea, an actor who would have expressive and imaginative, physical and vocal means, an actor whose voice would have the wide range necessary to carry classical and modern texts, rather than one capable of only the jerky, staccato delivery usual in the stock companies of the time.[4]

What he was aiming to do was to equip his actors with the ability to interpret the classics as well as modern plays in all their variety, but although the acquisition of a strongly developed technique of body and voice was of prime importance, technique was never to be allowed to dominate or supersede invention. His overriding desire was to serve the contemporary theatre in such a way that the actors could interpret all styles without letting the style deflect from truth. This meant, in effect, grafting the French tradition, started by Copeau, on to current English stage practice and blending it with the discoveries of Stanislavski. The training concentrated for the most part on improvisation, and on the technical side, on physical and vocal technique together with the study of a wide variety of texts. The Studio school acquired a chapel which was converted into a small theatre, and after two years performances were given before an invited audience. It was not long before the Studio began to make its presence felt in the theatre life of London. The London Theatre Studio was broken up by the war in 1939.

AFTER 1945

Together with George Devine and Glen Byam Shaw, Saint-Denis continued the work after the war with the Old Vic Theatre School and the Young Vic Company under the same organizing head: the Old Vic Theatre Centre. At the nucleus stood the Old Vic Theatre, one of the finest permanent professional acting companies in the English-speaking world at that time, which had built a great reputation as a result of its tours in Great Britain and elsewhere in the world under the joint directorship of Laurence Olivier, Ralph Richardson and John Burrell.

As General Director of the Old Vic Theatre Centre, Saint-Denis set about laying the foundations for training a group of actors who formed a liaison with a professional company, stimulating it and supplying it with fresh and exuberant young talent. Since the school was partially subsidized, there was no need to take in more than thirty-five students, and there were places available for students who came from a less middle-class background, since they were assisted by the educational authorities in many cities, who began giving grants to young people with a talent for acting. As a result, 'students with real talent, personality and presence were selected'.[5]

The length of the course was two years and its aims were to find an effective way of interpreting various theatre styles, particularly the classical theatre, and to widen the actor's range of expression so that he could sing, dance, mime and perform acrobatic feats as well as cope with the requirements of the 'normal' training. With the experience of the London Theatre Studio behind him, Saint-Denis was able to develop a new curriculum which he hoped would be able to bridge the gap between conventional and modern staging, particularly in rejuvenating Shakespearean acting. Integrated teaching was to be the key to this:

> The main line here was to be an approach to organic training, in all its branches, with constant attention to the interrelation between the various parts of the teaching. I

intended also to develop much further the teaching of voice–speech–language and adopt a far more imaginative approach to speech than we had time to develop in the short life of the L.T.S. As I was sure of the value of improvisation in the development of the actor's physical imagination, I felt that similarly we ought to find ways to train the vocal imagination of the actor.[6]

In all of the five drama schools which he planned, Saint-Denis did not advocate any one particular 'method', but placed the freedom of the actor at the forefront. He was, however, adamant that the following elements contributed to this freedom: a healthy artistic environment in which an ensemble-like professional training could flourish; encouragement; an open stage without a proscenium which should invite the actor to play physically; an interrelationship of the three disciplines – movement, voice and speech; the encouragement of dramatic instinct, invention and spontaneity; a first-year training in the non-verbal aspects of voice and speech training.

Believing in the balance between technique and imagination, Saint-Denis advocated first working on developing the actor's imagination, initially with improvisation then with mime and masks. Movement and outer physical expression was strongly emphasized, as was relaxation, flexibility and strength. The aim was to liberate the body, which was then to be used to serve dramatic expression and imagination in all other classes. Saint-Denis regarded movement as a more direct means of expression than speech, as it could increase the dramatic feeling, clarify the intention of a text and give a precise image of it.

The technique on which voice and speech were taught was based on singing in order to develop a vocal quality in the actor which would be strong, clear, rhythmic and musical:

> Our concern is to awaken in the actor a musical and a poetic sensitivity capable of being translated to the stage by the rhythmic quality of the voice and by modulated tones conditioned by the text. However well-trained the actor's pronunciation, it is the tone, the variety of tone in his speaking voice that has the strongest emotional and artistic impact on an audience. . . We want the actor to have at his disposal vocal resources that will permit him to work in all kinds of plays, whatever their form or style. It is therefore

159

necessary for him to have a wide range of tones, a powerful voice and a breathing system he can command; there must be a greater flexibility and complete control of his vocal faculties.[7]

The Old Vic Theatre School followed the methods of Jani Strasser, singing teacher for the Glyndebourne Opera, who had evolved a technique for actors, based on singing, which aimed at the production of sound that was meaningful and expressive. By singing phrases and verses with and without the accompaniment of the piano, the students gradually began to speak with resonance and in a variety of tones; their range increased and their breath control, so essential to good articulation, became more secure.[8] All these exercises were done with body movements, which Strasser believed contributed to the liberation of the voice. The same method was applied to singing in other languages, the aim of which was to increase the flexibility of the lips, tongue and other organs of speech as well as to improve the clarity of speech and placement of their voices.

Following the tradition of the Vieux Colombier, Saint-Denis advised a constant liaison between body and voice classes, as well as experimentation with speech. He advocated freeing speech training from its long servitude to elocution, by regarding diction, rhythm and modulation as servants of the text and the interpretation, not ends in themselves for a 'beautiful voice'. Although many of the voice and speech exercises were designed to open up vocal breadth, no exercises were to be done without relating thought and feeling to words and their real meaning. Real projection meant for Saint-Denis the two-way communication between the actor and the audience, when the audience is able to hear and see what he means and feels.

In interpreting a text, Saint-Denis advocated that the actor's sensitivity should be open to the text and not to his own subjective feelings or emotional reactions. The text was to serve as an inspiration to the actor, who should resist over-analysing it psychologically, in favour of allowing the author to speak in his own style. This would necessitate an understanding of the different experiments with form and meaning, which in Saint-Denis's opinion determined the 'style' of a piece of writing. The text was not to be interpreted in terms of contemporary language and styles, nor were translations to be treated too lightly.

Not that all the voice training was to be text-oriented. Saint-Denis recommended all manner of exercises which would make the student's voice expressive without the use of words, particularly during the first year: 'If we dispense at first with words, it is only to make clear that words are the result of an inner state, an inner, physical state, related to the senses, which conditions the spoken word.'[9] He suggested exercises of a non-verbal nature initially, which were then to be extended to one word and eventually to phrases.

Although the Old Vic Theatre Centre was forced to close in 1952 for monetary reasons, it provided a great stimulus to drama training by laying a foundation for a more comprehensive and integrated approach to acting. This has been carried on by many of its original students who have become leading actors (Olivier, Gielgud, Guinness and Plowright), directors (George Devine) and heads of other drama training schools (John Blatchley – Drama Centre London; Norman Ayrton – London Academy of Music and Dramatic Art; and George Hall – Central School of Speech and Drama). On the negative side, opinion had it that its methods worked only for plays of great depth and as a result: 'Many of the students were ill-prepared for the reality run-of-the-mill repertory work and drawing-room comedy of the West End.'[10]

Since the demise of the Old Vic School, new international influences have come from Rudolf Laban, Michael Chekhov, Lee Strassberg and Jerzy Grotowski. In spite of the fact that the major impulses in actor training in England have come from Europe, British acting enjoys a reputation as the most consistently excellent in the western world. The training has been designed to produce all-round actors, who can cope with the classics, musical, fringe, and West End theatre as well as radio and television.[11]

The training in most schools encompasses improvisation, voice production, play reading, verse speaking, dialects, singing, microphone technique, television technique, movement, modern dance, fencing, combat, acrobatics and stage make-up. Additional subjects not taught at all schools include the Alexander technique, T'ai Chi, history of world theatre, historic dance, classical ballet, tap dancing, encounter group sessions, mime, mask, *commedia dell'arte* and theatre-in-education. Most courses are of three years' duration, made possible by educational grants, and the competition is fierce, as most young people realize the necessity of having a comprehensive technique. Since the publication of *Going on Stage* –

the 1975 Gulbenkian inquiry into professional drama training – the National Council for Drama Training (NCDT) was set up in order to help raise the standard of training. After examining seventeen drama schools in 1981, it accredited only eleven of them. These schools can be examined from two quite different approaches: the orthodox approach, as taught at the Royal Academy of Dramatic Art, the Central School and the Guildhall, and the alternative approach, as taught at Rose Bruford College, East 15 and Drama Centre.

The orthodox approach

The Royal Academy of Dramatic Art (RADA)

Technical proficiency and professionalism are the aims of the Royal Academy of Dramatic Art's training programme. In 1981 its principal, Hugh Cruttwell, endeavoured to alter the stress and reinstate the actor as an artist in the creative process.[12] Entrance is by audition and the course lasts for seven terms, which can be increased in individual cases. Towards the end of the course, the number of classes diminishes and the number of rehearsals increases.[13] Classes in movement, voice and speech, fencing and make-up are offered, with the addition of the Alexander technique. Acting classes do not follow any particular method, but rather, according to Lubbock, 'there is a variety of approaches, and it is up to the student to find the one that works for him'.[14]

The early training in the Alexander technique is conducted by Anne Battye, who has spent many years teaching the technique at RADA. Students begin with three half-hour sessions a week, which is reduced to two and eventually one. This permeates the training and assists the voice work, in which the aim is to speak with a voice free from obstruction and with as much power as possible while maintaining a relaxed state. In order to assist in realigning the body, the Alexander teacher insists at times on the students speaking texts while she helps correct tension areas such as the back of the neck, believing that this greatly affects their voices.

The voice training is based on the organic and free approach, with much reference to 'centring'. As one voice teacher, Robert Palmer, put it, 'the main thing to learn is how to pass from Shock to Recovery as easily as possible . . . relax, renew and release'.[15] Another voice teacher advocates a different approach, where one imitates the teacher and works for beautiful vowel sounds. The area of speech training is greatly concerned with diction and terminal consonants, and even advocates Standard English as a model to be followed. In terms of text study, attention is mostly placed on the classics, mainly Shakespeare and Restoration comedy, around which the various departments endeavour to relate their teaching.

The Central School of Speech and Drama

As its name indicates, the Central School adopts a central position – an avoidance of extremism, while at the same time following a definite yet flexible body of principles. George Hall, principal in 1984, was also wary of systems. The acting course endeavours to prepare students for the widest possible range of work in every branch of the theatre and related media – television and films.[16] The basic aim of the course is the development of the student's imagination. The fact that Central also trains speech therapists and speech teachers as well as stage managers has a decided influence on the training.

Entrance is by audition and the course lasts three years. The school is an accredited member of the CDS (Conference of Drama Schools) which guarantees its financial stability.[17] The nucleus of the training is a penetrating study of texts of all sorts and the development of vocal and physical expressiveness and skills. It is constantly emphasized that acting, movement and voice are not separate subjects but different aspects of one activity. Singing, dancing and musical theatre are also important elements in the training.[18]

The influence of its founder, Elsie Fogerty, with her special concern for improved oral English, is still in evidence in the teaching of voice and speech, while George Hall's own training with Saint-Denis at the Old Vic Theatre School is reflected in the integration of classes – particularly voice and movement. This has influenced the approach to voice training which centres on an awareness of whole-body involvement whilst 'stretching throughout the body but maintaining relaxed vocal folds'.[19] In practice this involves much work being done on centring, widening the vocal register and learning how to exercise the folds by taking the volume down as low as possible whilst exercising the body at the same time. One observer was impressed by the simultaneous exercising of 'the body sliding down from high to low position and voice sliding down from high to low pitch'.[20]

Other organic muscular exercises are executed with the jaw, lips and tongue – where the emphasis appears to be placed on stretching and relaxing. A great deal of time is spent in individual tutorials as well as group lessons, where obvious faults can be corrected, diction worked on and texts analysed. Received pronunciation is upheld as a standard of speech. In order to develop a feeling for language and an ability to 'turn a phrase' with precision, a good deal of time is devoted to the reading aloud of various kinds of texts, mainly the classics.

The Guildhall School

The Guildhall School is unique in England because for the first time in the English-speaking world a major theatre company – the Royal Shakespeare Company – was made available to it as a teaching instrument. Facilities exist for the observation of this company at work in both modern and classical drama.[21] It is housed in the Barbican Centre together with a large music school and the London Symphony Orchestra. The drama course (started officially in 1935) is of nine terms' duration, and the school is an accredited member of the CDS. Entry is by audition.

The Guildhall School aims to teach actors how to work at being actors, but does not rigidly concentrate on a single system of acting; rather it has been influenced by all the great teachers of the twentieth century, according to Director of Drama Gillian Cadell.[22] She is primarily concerned with setting up a classical theatre training system but insists it has to be as flexible as possible.

In the first year there are classes in movement, voice, singing, make-up, stage management, mask work, tumbling, improvisation, period and modern dance as well as combat of all kinds. Consultants in the Alexander technique and speech therapy are available throughout the course. Students are encouraged to develop a musical discipline as an aid to the study of rhythm and phrasing, because this skill is much in demand in contemporary theatre. There are lectures and seminars on the history of drama and the visual arts as well as on current theatrical events. Work on texts gradually progresses towards work on scenes and projects involving Shakespeare, as well as other classic and modern authors (six hours a week). Throughout the year there is a constant emphasis on the imaginative response to language.

The following terms devote more time to performance on stage, television, film and radio, totalling fifteen hours a week. The final three terms are conducted as far as possible as a repertory company, together with professional directors and designers. As Guildhall believes strongly in using the *commedia dell'arte* techniques as a kind of stepping-stone to playing the classics with style, voice and movement continue throughout the training. Rea summarized this as follows:

> Its relevance is that it is an acting tradition and not a literary one – and that students must learn to play the intentions while moving on the lines. They must also make a choice of language – whether it be coarse, pompous, articulate or bizarre.[23]

This approach was brilliantly demonstrated in the acting of the Royal Shakespeare Company's *Nicholas Nickleby* in 1981, which can be seen as the fruit of the labours of Michel Saint-Denis and the skills and techniques which he had brought with him to the Stratford Studio of this company when he joined it in 1962.

The alternative approach

A number of experimental schools emerged in the fifties and sixties, which were mostly breakaways from the traditional schools and which based their work on specific philosophies: the Rose Bruford College, which propounded the theory that teaching and acting should be studied jointly; the East 15 Acting School, which built on Joan Littlewood's approach in Stratford East; the Drama Centre, with its European concept of methodological training.[24]

Rose Bruford College of Speech and Drama

The Rose Bruford College was founded in 1950 with the purpose of combining acting and teacher training within a single course. The regularization of teacher training in the mid-seventies forced the college to reform its curriculum and as it was no longer able to offer a teacher certificate, the course became split in three ways: theatre arts, community theatre arts and technical theatre arts.[25] It has been accredited by the National Council for Drama Training (NCDT) and is a recognized member of the CDS; however, it has been suffering financial cutbacks.

One of the courses at the college is three years long and leads to a BA honours degree in Theatre Arts. Entrance is by a combination of academic qualifications and audition. Its aims are 'to produce graduates who are able to work professionally in the modern theatre with a full understanding of how theatre in all its variety – word, gesture, movement, space, light, colour, sound – functions and how it may be used as a creative medium'.[26]

Believing that the informed and educated artist is more use both to himself and his art than the performer who works and thinks only within the limitations of any one skill, the Rose Bruford College attempts to combine an undergraduate drama course with actor training. This consists of two main areas: one in which students are able to develop their own performing skills, and another which puts performing skills into the context both of theatre language and of performance conditions, both contemporary and historic.

In practical terms, the training in the Foundation Course is for two years and offers the following areas of study: behaviour-based acting exercises, improvisation, modern naturalism, directing, nineteenth-century naturalism, Brecht, devised text work, Shakespeare, Greek theatre, experimental theatre. The Advanced Course, which is one year long, covers *commedia dell'arte*, Shakespeare, Restoration comedy, television and post-war theatre. In addition, technical classes are available in all aspects of voice and movement, theatre studies (seminars and lectures concerned with the history of theatre) and contemporary theatre studies (seminars and lectures devoted to an examination of theatre in its social context).[27]

An integrated approach is favoured in the teaching of voice, where the emphasis is placed on responding imaginatively to language and finding a way of expressing it in sound and movement. This is the point of departure for first-year students, who are kept away from texts and from performances.[28] Considerable emphasis is placed on interpreting texts further on in the course, where practical presentations form a significant part of the student's final assessment for his degree.[29]

The Diploma in Community Theatre Arts aims to produce actors who can devise the plays they appear in, especially in the context of theatre-in-education and community theatre. The emphasis is on audience contact and social awareness.[30] In this course the training encompasses the following areas: the community, devising, acting, performance and research. Voice training together with movement comes under the heading of 'acting' and constitutes one-fifth of the course.

The East 15 Acting School

The East 15 Acting School was founded in 1961 by Margaret Bury, who had worked extensively with Joan Littlewood at her theatre in Stratford East since 1947. She recalled: 'Initially it was intended to continue the kind of work which Littlewood had begun – of using improvisation as a means of finding the essence of character and social standing.'[31] There are two acting courses: a three-year acting course and a one-year postgraduate course. East 15 no longer has accreditation with the NCDT, so it is privately run. The student's position is, to say the least, most uncertain, since in spite of a very long audition process lasting six hours, approximately forty students are admitted, of whom only twenty are admitted to the second year and fifteen to the third.[32]

Margaret Bury intended the school to be as revolutionary as possible, hoping it would produce graduates who would create a more lively, more exciting and more relevant theatre than the one which had existed after the Second World War, and one where there was room for experimentation. Reflecting bitterly on the traditional training programme, she said:

> Judging from the comments of the N.C.D.T. assessors, there would seem to be a kind of establishment criterion that says how a drama student ought to be trained. I feel that the individual is of paramount importance and it is the individual we work with; we don't try to find a mold for people.[33]

Consequently training in technique has a minimal place of importance in the school's ideology, as Margaret Bury believes that the kinds of performances other drama schools offer are somewhat spiritless. Her approach to the teaching of acting was influenced by developments in British education in the late sixties, particularly the Plowden Report, which proposed that young children should come to learning not by rote methods but by the processes of feeling and of muscular experience. She believes that this kind of experience must precede any intellectual analysis or any learning of technique.[34]

Practically speaking, first-year acting students are taken back to very elementary child psychology of a pre-school nature in order to help them achieve a freshness and spontaneity of experience before they turn to text analysis. The acting course is fairly flexible in that it can be adapted to suit the needs of each year although an overall plan exists – guided by the teachings of Stanislavski and Laban, as one student tried to explain: 'The East 15 Method is strongly geared to living or experiencing the part so strongly that the characters should be able to live on – outside the confines of the text.'[35]

Although she quotes Stanislavski on the subject of a responsive vocal and physical apparatus, Margaret Bury does not include much formal training in this subject, because she is very critical of the restrictions which conforming to social patterns of behaviour has made on the individual and on the individual's voice: 'Once the child learns the English language, he begins to lose his vocal assets.'[36] The voice training aims instead to make the actor aware of how he is producing his voice and to what effect. Ample opportunity is given to him to practise the art of speaking and to measure the effect of his communication and emotional colour. The student is constantly reminded that he will finally have to speak with as many voices as the characters he has to create.[37]

The attitude to speech teaching and correction of deficiencies is also governed by the principal's philosophy that this kind of knowledge is detrimental and would make the student so conscious of his own particular faults that he would try to correct them by deliberate over-compensation. She believes that this process can be quite fatal to the realities of acting. It is perhaps not surprising that most of the criticism which has been directed against East 15 is that their technical standards are very weak.[38]

In terms of text work, ample opportunity seems to be provided for interpreting the classics including Shakespeare, Goldoni, Molière and the Restoration comedies as well as twentieth-century dramatists, such as Shaw, Wilde, Brecht and Tennessee Williams.

The Drama Centre

The Drama Centre was founded in 1963 by a group of teachers from the Central School who had become disillusioned by the kind of pragmatic training offered there and the stereotyped graduate it produced. It offers a three-year full-time course for actors where entrance is gained following an audition and interview. The Drama Centre is very particular about taking in students with the right attitude; the director, Christopher Fettes, remarks: 'I suppose what you're looking for is people who have within them a sense of poetry', and indicates that the kind of student who best seems to suit this form of training is a dedicated, thoughtful kind of person who 'in many ways prefers not to work at all than to work on rubbish'.[39] The Drama Centre is accredited by the NCDT and is a member of the CDS, although it does not receive a subsidy.[40]

The Drama Centre claims to be the only drama school in England offering a methodological approach based on a fusion of several major contributions to the development of European theatre in the twentieth century. This includes Stanislavski, Grotowski, Brecht, Laban and his influence on Michael Chekhov and the 'Method' in the United States together with a synthesis of Laban's achievements as determined by Yat Malmgren. It also claims to be the true heir of the Old Vic Theatre School in its merging of European and American theatre traditions: 'We attempt to create a school in which it is possible for British people to come and study something of the achievements of European and American theatre in the first thirty or forty years of this century.'[41]

The Drama Centre aims to provide the student actor with a systematic approach to the problems of acting which will lead to the eventual acquisition of learning how to bring feeling under control and how to confer form upon it. Its ultimate goal is to teach the actor how to work by himself on any role in any play.[42]

The acting class is the core of the systematic approach, which extends over two years and to which all other courses are closely related. A select group is invited back for a third year, in which they perform for an audience. Movement psychology, under the title of 'action', also plays a central role in the training which sets out to examine the relationship between feeling and form in drama. It is not concerned with dance, mime, eurhythmics or gymnastics and is only indirectly related to psychology. It employs exercises, a technique of relaxation and improvisation, to help the actor raise his consciousness and control the forces that determine the expressive qualities of movements, gestures and speech. A considerable time is spent on rehearsing plays from a wide variety of authors. Other subjects include play analysis, classical ballet, jazz ballet, voice, speech and music.

The aims of the voice and speech classes, as outlined in the prospectus, are as follows: 'To encourage an awareness of the expressive qualities of the voice and to bring them under control; to gain freedom and flexibility through breath control, note resonance and word; to remedy faulty speech habits and emotional impulses.'[43] According to voice and speech teacher Barbara Berkery, the day has long passed when one can have as models the rhetorical functions of language as demonstrated in the pulpit and in government. She bemoans the fact that the importance of speech is no longer in evidence, where 'language, bled white, appears to many lifeless, its functions in decay – only the poet or the actor can restore something of the erotic force that gave it life'.[44] Consequently, in her teaching she attempts to help her students to 'render the word afresh, to deliver it as though for the first time to each new audience'. Although the course is fully integrated with other classes, not as much time is spent on this subject as in other drama schools, owing to the time which mastering the 'Method' demands.

Following the survey which the Calouste Gulbenkian Foundation conducted in 1975, where the whole question of actor training was investigated and the state of training at existing drama schools examined, the following report was submitted regarding the subject 'Voice':

A great deal of importance is attached to the teaching of voice in drama schools and a high degree of expertise is required of teachers. Most principals admitted that it was even more difficult to get good voice teachers than good movement teachers. This is partly the result of certain social trends over the last thirty years that have rejected traditional views of elocution, the 'beautiful voice' and high standards of speech, in favour of the more scientific study of linguistics. This has made the teaching of the use of the voice more 'realistic' but tended to reduce the supply of experienced specialist teachers. Nowhere, however, did there appear any tendency to minimise the importance of the students working on their voice. Our members noted considerable emphasis on the physical aspect of voice production and were impressed, in the classes which they visited, by the amount of movement which took place in the training of the voice and the frequency with which students in movement classes were invited to break into sound.[45]

This random survey of drama schools gives some indication of the different attitudes to actor training and vocal delivery in Britain since Michel Saint-Denis revolutionized training practices for the theatre, with his plan for the training of the all-round actor, in which the way an actor moved had a relevance to the way he spoke.[46] This was a reaction to the conglomeration of classes, none of which had the slightest connection with each other, offered by drama schools up to the fifties. Since then, others have followed suit – rejecting traditional and conservative approaches to the training of the actor in their search for a new kind of theatre, more attuned to the new kind of society that has come into existence. Consequently, this new society in Britain brought with it new attitudes to voice and speech in general and to training practices in particular.

A DUALITY OF APPROACHES TO VOICE TRAINING

Voice and speech training underwent enormous changes in the fifties, when the theatre changed so radically in Britain with John Osborne's *Look Back in Anger* (1956). Suddenly and quite fundamentally, the whole question of accents and social classes disappeared and with it the need for an upper-class 'beautiful voice', according to Cicely Berry, who admitted to deliberately changing her approach to the demands which the new theatre made, where the emphasis was placed on 'what' was said rather than on 'how' it was said.[47] After many years' experience training actors and teachers at the Central School in London and at a private studio, Berry took up the position of voice director of the Royal Shakespeare Company, which she still holds. Love of language is the secret behind her method of working, and she admits she has received much support from the directors of the Royal Shakespeare Company, Trevor Nunn, Terry Hands and John Barton.[48] However, one of the greatest influences on her was working very closely with Peter Brook on *A Midsummer Night's Dream* in 1970, when his way of working with the actors gave her a 'kind of confidence in using particular exercises, about handing on language and so on'.[49]

Cicely Berry's approach to vocal delivery is based upon a thorough understanding of the text, irrespective of whether it is Shakespeare or a modern dramatist like Pinter or Beckett. Not that she regards the voice as unimportant. Rather, she believes that the meaning should inform the sound; consequently, the point of departure in her method is through the text. This principle was asserted in her first book on the subject which appeared in 1973: 'The vocal transformation of yourself into another character must come from the words and rhythms of the writing; if this leads you into a different way of speaking that is fair, providing no tension comes from it.'[50] It was repeated in her second book for actors in 1987: 'To fill another character we need to open ourselves to all the possibilities of the language, and this has to reach an audience not just by being loud enough, but by being filled with purpose.'[51]

Although her first book was mainly concerned with the general aspects of voice production, changes in the emphasis are apparent in her second one, where instead of 'making the voice free', it is chiefly about 'making the language organic, so that the words act as the spur to the sound, and so that flexibility and range are found because the words require them'.[52] It is for this reason that her approach today emphasizes reaching out through words, to make what is said remarkable to the hearer, and above all using language as 'thoughts in action'. The similarities to *sententiae* are undeniable.[53]

Practically speaking, her method demands that one does not simply make literal sense of the language of the text, in terms of its rhythm and phrasing, but that one also pays attention to the organic structure, the dynamic, of each word. In this respect all exercises for articulation are designed to explore just how the vowels and consonants are related to each other in each word, so that the thought is released through this physical activity. Similarly, breathing is linked with the structure of thought and phrasing, which implies that the actor who runs out of breath is really not exploring the structure of the thoughts efficiently.

In her work on Shakespeare, Cicely Berry advocates a thorough understanding of the rules of metre and form, not so that the actor feels bound by them in performance, but rather so that he will be able to make wiser decisions about when and why he might choose not to follow them. Her reasons for this are that the meaning is always contained in the structure of the thoughts which coincide with the metrical form, with the demands of the iambic pentameter and the use of the caesura, and that much of the energy of the thought is to be found in the stressed syllables. On this point, Cicely Berry believes that:

> there is in Shakespeare an energy which runs through the text which is not a naturalistic one; an energy which impels one word to the next, one line to the next, one thought to the next, one speech to the next, and one scene to the next. . . This is the action of the text, and this informs the style of speaking.[54]

For the actor this means that he must be aware of the sense of the continuum in the play, of knowing that whatever is said changes the moment and provokes the next thought, and that he must not drop this active thought process. She suggests a method of working on the text by systematically going through the following progression: discovering the energy through the text; working through the antithesis; exploring the substance of the word; discovering the movement of thought; finding the source of the imagery – its logic and its inquiry into nature; discovering the balance between argument and emotion; recognizing word games and patterns; examining the structure of speeches and soliloquies. Tuning in to the language in this way is designed to give the actor a certain awareness and freedom, but above all it should reinforce all he wants to do with the character.

The next step in her process is to proceed past the rehearsal stage of exploring the language – of feeling free and secure with it – to the presentation of it to an audience, where the emphasis should be on making 'what is spoken remarkable', rather than simply showing feelings. Innumerable exercises are suggested to help the actor integrate the motive and the speech, so that he can 'present' and 'be' at the same time. Many of these exercises are at odds with the character's obvious motives in a particular scene, and their general purpose can be interpreted as highlighting the character's need to communicate, his need to define his thoughts, or express specific feelings. They are mostly physical in nature, and are designed to help the actor release the physical vigour of the language in a specific way.

Cicely Berry does not believe in over-emphasizing the emotional side of the technique or of regarding the voice as an instrument. She regards singing as helping the voice to 'come out freely' but feels that there is a distinct difference between singing and acting, in that in singing 'the sound is the message' and the energy is in the resonance, whereas in acting the voice is an extension of the actor, for whom 'the word must impinge, as it is the word which contains the results of his feelings and his thought. It is therefore in the word that his energy must lie, and in the million ways of stressing, lengthening and inflecting it.'[55]

Rather than working on the voice for volume, she suggests that the actor should work for size, and this should include practice in the particular theatre space where he will perform. Although she recommends continual exercises for the voice, such as relaxation, and the Alexander technique for releasing tension, breathing for capacity and other exercises for developing resonance, she maintains that the verbal energy will be there if the thought behind the word is focused properly in the particular theatrical space. This space even dictates the particular pitch level which he should use and it should be given every consideration.

Cicely Berry calls the poet the 'super-realist' but warns the actor that the function of speech is to communicate his own needs, so however stylized or heightened the language is, the actor must find the 'need to speak and speak in just that fashion and with those particular words'.[56] Her method is applicable to all sorts of texts, both modern and classical, and is designed to help the actor to listen to the way the words are used and thereby make him more alive to the impulses contained in the text: 'The words may be those of absolutely ordinary, everyday speech, but the situation is special and those words and that rhythm are special to that character.'[57]

According to Cicely Berry, in the normal rehearsal of a Shakespeare play in Stratford so much talking has been done around the character and so many choices have been made, that how the language is used has to be made to fit what has already been decided before one has the experience of speaking it. To deal with this problem, she has directed language projects where the aims have been twofold:

To explore the movement of the language as fully as possible, the movement of thought, the imagery and rhetoric and relate this directly to the actors' process – i.e. the finding of motive, relationship and character. To try to find a way of making this process clear to an audience, not by teaching or demonstrating, but perhaps by putting them into a slightly different relationship with the action ... by trying to get them to listen with slightly different attention.[58]

In conclusion, it is her untiring dedication to finding ways of making people listen again to the music of language and to its poetry, and not only to grasp its literal meaning, that is so unique about Cicely Berry's contribution to vocal delivery in the modern theatre.

An approach of a completely different nature is advocated by Kirsten Linklater, who bemoans the fact that twentieth-century man has come to rely too much on the printed word, and as a result has lost some of the red-bloodedness which his language had 400 years ago.[59] After training as an actress at the London Academy of Music and Dramatic Art, she returned there to teach as assistant to Iris Warren, a reputedly remarkable teacher, who during the thirties moved the science of voice production for British actors forward into a new phase, by adding psychological understanding to the physiological principles which Elsie Fogerty had established in the first twenty-five years of this century, when she systematized a method of speech training based on accurate physical mechanics of the voice. In moving from 'external' controls to internal psychological ones, Iris Warren was able to help British actors avoid straining their voices when expressing strong emotions – by helping them 'unblock'. All this pioneering work ran counter to the 'voice beautiful' ideal of the day, but was supported by Michel Saint-Denis and movement teacher Litz Pisk, at the Old Vic Theatre School after the Second World War, when the main teaching direction was towards organic training.

Since 1963, Kristin Linklater has lived in the United States, where she has worked with professional theatre groups, such as Stratford Ontario with Tyrone Guthrie, and the Open Theatre with Joseph Chaikin. She has been Master Teacher of Voice at the New York University Theatre Program since 1966, and subsequently had workshops with the Royal Shakespeare Company during the 1972–3 season.

Her approach to voice training is based on psychotherapeutic principles, emphasizing that in order to unlock the mind, one must unlock the body. Building on the premise that the 'inner muscles of the body must be free to receive the sensitive impulses from the brain that create speech', she has evolved a system of vocal training, psycho-physical in nature, where the emphasis is placed on the relationship between mind and body. She has outlined her ideology as follows:

> Everyone possesses a voice capable of expressing through a two-to-four octave natural pitch range, whatever gamut of emotion, complexity of mood and subtlety of thought he or she experiences . . . the tensions acquired through living in this world, as well as defences, inhibitions and negative reactions to environmental influences, often diminish the efficiency of the natural voice to the point of distorted communication.[60]

In pursuing the ultimate neuro-muscular state of receptiveness which serves the need to communicate, Kristin Linklater insists that one must learn to undo tension in the whole body. Consequently, her whole method is totally dependent upon physical awareness, beginning with the spine and progressing throughout the body by systematically isolating, exercising and relaxing shoulders, arms, neck and head, so that the skeleton rather than the muscles do the work. In her working method, the voice is described metaphorically rather than scientifically. In this 'freed' state, the connection with the breath, which she refers to as 'the source of sound', can be made by releasing a 'sigh of relief'.

Once the speaker has discovered his 'centre' – that is, the energy centre of his body which houses breath, feelings and impulses – he is encouraged (again by use of metaphor) to imagine that he has a 'pool of vibrations' in the lower half of his torso, which he is encouraged to release on the sound 'huh' by manually jiggling the sound out.[61] This is called a 'touch of sound', and once established, is encouraged to be amplified by stimulating different areas of vibrations in the lips, cheeks, nose, forehead, top of skull, back of neck, throat and chest. The guiding principle behind all these exercises is that the speaker should 'personalize' the vibrations so that he may be pleasurably involved with them. Consequently, the method continues to embrace a 'stream of vibrations' by releasing tensions which can inhibit resonance throughout the body, by referring to the body as a resonating ladder – or house, whose 'cellar' is the centre and whose 'attic' is the skull resonators.

In terms of linking the voice to a text, emphasis is placed on: 'maintaining the relationship between impulse and muscular activity if the vocal and emotional apparatus are to develop simultaneously'.[62] Practically speaking, the desired state is to be arrived at by a method of 'panting in anticipation' on the emotions in the context of a speech or a scene. The following progression is suggested: visual images which should stimulate a feeling response, then words, and finally more demanding texts. All of these exercises are to be connected to the breath and each separate image should demand a change of breath. A great deal of 'rolling up and down' through the spine, hopping, 'bouncing out the sound', and other 'freeing processes' accompany work on the text, so that the impulse from mind to emotion (housed in the breath centre) will be unimpeded.

Kristin Linklater believes that theatre today needs to move towards a 'revitalized eloquence', and bemoans the fact that we no longer speak with 'force, fluency and appropriateness' because of the fact that 'fear of indulgence has virtually deprived us of a serviceable form through which to communicate'. She maintains that we have come to associate words too much with ideas and too little with instinct and is emphatic that 'we have to struggle for verbal expression because words seem to belong not in the body but in the head'.[63] In her opinion, human communication has steadily been deteriorating, becoming fragmented, weakened and even false, since the Elizabethan age, when rhetoric reached fantastic heights, where man could balance emotion, intellect and soul. She attributes this to the fact that words have become banished from the body, and for this reason sees that for a while emotion must be given precedence in order to put the balance right, 'words must be taken back to physical and emotional sources'.[64]

In her opinion, there should ideally be no need to specifically develop a technique for working on a text because, 'if the work to free the voice has been deeply absorbed, the person will be naturally freer; the person and the voice will be unified'.[65] Nevertheless, although she believes that the interpretation of a text must be released from within, it is the duty of every actor to understand every detail of what the text contains:

In finding out what the text contains, in the case of verse or heightened prose, an actor must learn about scansion, rhyme, rhythm, word-balances, puns, hyperbole, short and long vowels, voiced and un-voiced consonants, pace, volume and pitch, the meaning of forms and so on, but this should expand awareness and deepen understanding, not impose 'the correct way to say the text'. It is food for the intellect and develops the intellectual strength necessary to provide form for the content of emotion and imagination.[66]

Her practical advice for an actor is to hear and feel the text rather than simply see it, so that it can be transformed into sound; to do everything possible to develop a sensory and physical response to the text rather than an intellectual one. In conclusion, her attitude to work on a text is clarified by this statement:

Work on the text means letting the words of the text happen to you; finding ways to let the text impregnate you so that sensory, emotional, imaginative, physical and vocal discoveries are the foundation on which the intellect can build. This, in turn, becomes the foundation on which the speech, the sense, the character and the play are built.[67]

To sum up, Cicely Berry's approach to the vocal delivery of a classical text is principally through the text itself, whereby the actor is encouraged to involve himself actively in the structure of the thought at the moment of communication. Once having this security of meaning, he should then be able to determine how his voice or sound can best convey this thought. Only by following this line and by avoiding a heavy emotional involvement will he have a chance of sharing the structure of the text with the audience. Conversely, Kirsten Linklater's approach is based on the organic functioning of the voice, which, when liberated, receives its impulses from the senses and consequently informs the text. The words, or what is said, are regarded as a result of what is felt, and the freer the voice the more chance the actor has of conveying these feelings. Neither one of them believes in the 'correction of faults' and both of them are attempting some sort of integrated method – Cicely Berry through the text and Kirsten Linklater through the voice – whereby both what is said and how it is said should spring from the same source.

Is it feasible to conclude from this duality of approaches that one is better than the other? Guaranteed to achieve more startling results in performance? More suited to performing Shakespeare? That one is best suited to an 'orthodox' actor training and the other to an approach which is aligned with some special aesthetic which the teacher wishes to pursue in more detail?

Perhaps what is most significant for actor training is that as the voice is such a personal thing, different methods work for different people, depending upon how they feel about it. In addition, when the student actor enters the acting profession, he will have to work with directors who favour one particular style more than another. Without doubt the Shakespearean ideal in the English-speaking theatre has undergone enormous changes in the twentieth century and with it the approach to vocal delivery.

What seems to have become the real issue at stake is the whole question of what kind of actor one wishes to train, and for what theatre. Is it possible, or even desirable, to train an all-round actor for theatre today? There is no doubt that the acting ideal has also undergone enormous changes during the twentieth century as the theatre has advanced so rapidly, and the risk is that one is training an actor for a theatre which has become, or is on the way to becoming, obsolete. Another important consideration is that the world has become somewhat more homogenous, as distances have become smaller and influences are felt more rapidly than ever before from one country to another, particularly in the theatre. Therefore, it is important to compare English actor training with that of other countries, particularly the question of vocal training.

INTERNATIONAL COMPARISONS

Actor training was examined in detail during the sixties at a number of symposia organized by the International Theatre Institute, which dealt in turn with the following subjects: voice, body, improvisation, interpretation and style. As many as twenty different countries were represented (Britain included) and although the first symposium was concerned with body and voice training as constituting the instruments of the actor, they were never considered as ends in themselves.

In spite of the differences between each language, one essential and common point was apparent in the demonstrations at the 1963 symposium in Brussels: 'to connect voice training to a general

179

physical training and even to a psychic training. This everywhere implies the concern of teaching a pupil to get to know his body, the mastership of his breathing, to overcome individual or linguistic obstacles.'[68] Most of the exercises were concerned with liberation and relaxation, and the sincere, truthful voice was encouraged rather than the musical 'voice beautiful' one. This principle was carried over into the student's work on the text, where the personalized voice, which could easily carry emotion, was encouraged.

On the subject of style, which was debated at the Essen conference in 1965, many differences of opinion were apparent, as if any definition of this word itself would sterilize or mummify plays in the shackles of tradition. However, one thing became clear, and this was that there were many different styles – the style of the period, a national style and a personal style – and that the actor had a different understanding of this from the critic.[69] This is of prime importance for actor training particularly from the point of view of the understanding of language and its consequent delivery, as many of the participants pointed out, because this subject is aligned to the actor's training in eliciting the emotional aspects of his role (according to Stanislavski) and his ability to work with intelligence (according to Brecht).

Perhaps the most important finding came from the last of these symposia, in Stockholm in 1967, on the subject of interpretation, which was concerned with exploring 'the ways and means which enable the actor to grasp and assimilate the social and cultural atmosphere as related to the texts of different styles which he is called upon to interpret'.[70] There it was determined that in all true theatre education, culture is one of the main elements of the artist's equipment both on the level of his professional competence and on that of his inner wealth; that it is essential for his contact with the intellectual world and his fellow men provided that it is fertile; that the past appears with reference to the present and, above all, is necessary for shaping the future.

The findings of a second international seminar, concerned with the training of theatre teachers, in 1986 defined voice training for actors as 'the skill of using the voice, the articulation and the language in an expressive, communicative way when acting',[71] although the acquiring of different song skills was regarded as being outside the realm of voice training. It can be seen that at this time emphasis was placed on both the voice and the delivery of a text as well as on acting, which would suggest an integrated approach. However, there was never any suggestion about how all this should be taught. It became apparent that most actor training programmes still pursue a fragmented approach to acting, where the number of subjects offered is almost as numerous as the different parts of the body, although there have been attempts to integrate, or at least co-ordinate, the more obvious ones, such as movement and voice. This was revealed in the report to the Calouste Gulbenkian Foundation on professional training for drama (1975), which also called attention to the need for a more supportive approach to voice training for speech and for singing.[72]

A survey made on the performance of Shakespeare in Sweden from the mid-thirties to the mid-eighties revealed some interesting findings in terms of voice/text ratio, vocal delivery style, directors' interpretations and actor training.[73] A significant number of instances of a vocal delivery style which demonstrated a balancing of the sound element with the text occurred in the period of time from the mid-thirties to the mid-forties. At this time, directors showed a fascination with the structure of the text, while actor training was beginning to incorporate psychology. The style of vocal delivery changed radically in the next ten years (1945–55) to a predominantly natural one, which can be said to have demonstrated a de-emphasizing of the text and an interest in the 'subtext'. This gained support from the newly emergent psychological–realistic repertoire and from Stanislavski's teachings, which were translated into Swedish for the first time and which even affected the teaching of voice. During the next ten years (1955–64) there was a renewed interest in the classics, particularly Shakespeare, and an interest in vocal delivery as part of the creation of a role, as demonstrated by some directors. Verse was taught again at the drama schools and at this time training institutions for speech were founded. All this was reflected in the style of vocal delivery, which again demonstrated a balance between sound and text.

Changes in the social and political climate in Sweden (1965–74) were reflected in the Shakespeare productions at this time, particularly in the text, which was often drastically changed in order to support certain political platforms. Verse was regarded as bourgeois, and dispensed with, while the acting became very physical. This was supported by the acting programmes taught at the drama schools at that time, and by the kind of training offered by the newly instigated Free Group Movement, where the 'liberated' voice replaced all traces of the 'voice beautiful'. These trends continued into the eighties, when the vocal delivery styles demonstrated in Shakespeare productions (1975–85) showed a total dependence on the sound rather than the text and in particular a marked increase in the use of emotion.

One of the most debatable issues in actor training during the past twenty years has been concerned with voice teaching – whether the subject should be taught by a speech therapist or a speech teacher. The former has the medical training and expertise to help correct and cure damaged voices, whereas the latter is usually trained in literature, although with some training in the rudiments of voice production. The area of speech, or textual interpretation has been completely separated from voice training in Sweden, either because the therapist/voice teacher is not trained in textual interpretation or literature, or because the speech teacher is regarded as unqualified to tamper with the voice production side. This divided approach has consequently had repercussions, not only on actor training but ultimately on where the emphasis has been placed in performance. This is the situation in most American acting schools.

As has been shown, interest has been developing in the 'organic' approach to vocal delivery in the theatre and this has brought with it a different approach to this aspect of the actor's technique. Rather than seeking the services of speech therapists for the initial training, an increasing number of acting schools have attempted to bring their teaching more into line with practices in the professional theatre and have sought a 'liberated' approach, where the student is more often taught by 'metaphor' and suggestion rather than by corrective practices and drilling. This also has had repercussions on the quality of sound which is heard in performance – not only in terms of aesthetic beauty, but more importantly for the theatre, on the effectiveness of this aspect of vocal delivery to carry the para-linguistic function of language, which Roman Jakobson described as 'that part of vocalization able to evoke an immense range of emotional connotations, irrespective of the explicit semantic content of the utterance'.[74]

An example of this kind of approach can be seen in the work of Mirka Yemen Dzakis, the artistic leader of the theatre group Io, who visited Stockholm in 1989 with a performance of Aeschylus' *The Persians* in Old Greek. She applied her method of working with

182

voice in Peter Stein's production of *The Oresteia* in the late seventies at the Schaubühne in Berlin, and has also worked with Peter Brook and Robert Wilson. She believes that sound corresponds to different 'rooms' in the body and consequently to the different emotions, and that it functions as a symbol for the human condition. Regarding herself as a kind of mediator between Aeschylus and the audience, Yemen Dzakis assists her actors to use the Old Greek language as an expression for deep human emotions by helping them realize the corresponding physical forms for these sounds in their own bodies, which she refers to as 'resonance chambers for sounds which are thousands of years old'.[75] Her approach is not a psychological one, rather she advises using the body as a musical instrument via which the actor should be able to reach inside. The same attitude applies to the way she works on a text – through 'physiologizing the vowels and consonants in the body and through gymnastics where tone and text are explored together'.[76] She believes that the human body is capable of finding expressions which are capable of crossing the language and culture barrier.

The fruits of this approach were certainly obvious in the performance of *The Persians*, where the actors' voices were very musical, the rhythms varied and the tones exciting and evocative. Nevertheless, the whole production called so much attention to the sound that it resembled a musical score, deeply interwoven and dependent upon physical and vocal effects rather than characterization. However, her vocal work on Stein's *The Oresteia* was of a different calibre, as it supported themes and a directorial conception, and although even here the chorus's contribution was obviously structured along physical and musical lines, it probed much deeper than a mere exploration of demonic sound elements.

By placing the emphasis on the 'medium' rather than the 'message', vocal delivery seems to run the risk of losing its ability to activate an audience to think and thereby hold its attention – a dilemma which Aristotle was most aware of and which has been described in full in the first chapter. Whereas rhetoric developed its method of *sententia* in the Renaissance in order to combat an overdone expression and throw the emphasis back on to the text, modern-day vocal delivery practices have not been so successful in balancing the two. This has been particularly obvious in the performance of Shakespeare in the modern theatre in Britain: the 'ideal' has changed and consequently the style has undergone radical changes.

THE SHAKESPEAREAN IDEAL IN BRITAIN

Prior to the 1950s the staging practices of Shakespeare in Britain were traditional and class-bound. The proscenium-arch dominated and a theatre of illusion was the usual fare offered to the audience, which was often placed at a fair distance from the stage and consequently did not regard anything within this world as real. The central protagonists were star actors, whose characterizations were in line with a Victorian interpretation of the plays, where the extraordinary individual was emphasized in the tragedies and stylish frivolity in the comedies. Gielgud and Olivier epitomized the ideal vocal delivery style at this time, which was mainly rhetorical (see chapter 2).

The winds of change came mainly from two sources according to Nyberg: from the influence of continental theatre experimentation which Stanislavski, Brecht, Meyerhold and Craig had been doing, and from changes in the financial structure of the theatre in Britain.[77] The most important result of the democratizing of the theatre was the financial support which made it possible to establish open stages to replace the proscenium-arch ones, and institutions which could afford permanent or semi-permanent companies, which had time to explore the business of acting in the new spaces.

When Peter Hall established the Royal Shakespeare Company in 1964, he set about exploring the modern playwrights who had begun to appear in Britain after the war – the protagonists of the Theatre of the Absurd – and the results soon made themselves felt in a more realistic style of staging and acting. Open staging was, in Hall's opinion, the only social shape for a theatre of that time, and he championed it enthusiastically for Shakespeare:

> The audience is moulded into one group; it gets tremendous effects, but the interest which illusion can give should not be missing. Backdrops, screens or a flytower can be flown in and out. It is flexible rather than permanent. But in order to get the actor into 3D contact with his audience, this is obviously what Shakespeare needs.[78]

This kind of open staging was not accepted without some

misgivings by theatre critic Kenneth Tynan, who believed it put half the audience into a disadvantageous position, and as a result every member of the audience saw a different play. He was equally outspoken on the question of style and interpretation, maintaining that 'plays should be performed in the style of the period in which they are written'.[79]

Nevertheless, this realistic phase lasted until Peter Brook began his Theatre of Cruelty workshops at the Royal Shakespeare Company in 1963 together with Charles Marowitz, in order to investigate acting and staging techniques as different as possible from the realistic approach. In 1970, this culminated in Brook's production of *A Midsummer Night's Dream*, which revealed that the new criteria for acting Shakespeare should be sought in popular theatre forms.

In spite of the popularity of this production, it heralded the beginning of a phase where much criticism began to be levelled at directors, because it was believed they had assumed far too much power, and that productions were becoming far too interested in costly staging at the expense of the acting or the play. Directorial attempts to make the plays relevant by bringing them up to date were regarded with contempt and a general attitude was fostered in favour of returning to the basics of the theatre – to simple staging, where the actors and the text would be placed in the centre again. The production of *Macbeth* directed by Trevor Nunn in 1976 at the studio theatre of the Royal Shakespeare Company, The Other Place, was typical of the style for this kind of theatre. The actors decided to dispense with costumes altogether, although later costumes were chosen individually in order to denote rank and character and were decidedly modern; there was no scenery and the actors worked as an ensemble in an empty circle, almost without any properties, where they could make quick changes just as in a film, without the least difficulty. The acting style was mainly psychological–realistic in this intimate theatre. However it was combined with primitive ritual, which the ensemble regarded as a very important factor for audiences so used to naturalism and television. It was a tremendous success both with the critics and the audience and remained in the repertoire for two years. According to one critic, 'the text was spoken rather than declaimed; the words were given both a psychological truth and a poetic charge where the language together with the verse seemed to be created out of the dramatic situation'.[80]

Every age has its own Shakespearean ideal and the 1980s seems to offer a diversified approach at the Royal Shakespeare Company in Stratford. In a production of *Henry VIII* directed by Howard Davies in 1983 the vocal delivery style was more cerebral than emotional. The actors played with a distance to their text – communicating the ideas behind it clearly and rhythmically and even with musical accompaniment – particularly during the longer monologues, which seemed to provide a substitute for the emotion. A very different playing style and style of delivery was evident in Adrian Noble's production of *The Comedy of Errors*, included in the 1983 season. The production was conceived along *commedia dell'arte* lines and was performed at an alarmingly energetic tempo, with plenty of movement, acrobatics and fun. Music, movement, speech and song were all integrated with 'circus-like' sound effects to punctuate and highlight the comedy.

The modern theatre has witnessed an attempt at re-emphasizing the importance of the actor and simple staging rather than the frivolous and questionable flirtations which directors have made with Shakespeare in the past. Nevertheless, one thing has remained constant throughout this entire period of time, in spite of impulses which have come from so many different sources, and the many experiments which have been made with vocal delivery style, and that is an undeniable belief in the power of the word. The text had predominance in Shakespeare's own day, not because of its artistic beauty as poetic verse alone, but because of the intelligence and humanity which lay behind it, in that it had so much to tell about the human condition, about our weaknesses and our strengths: it is this aspect of Shakespeare which surely will defy all extraneous 'treatments' and survive all ages.

CONCLUSION

The discipline of rhetoric undoubtedly played an important part in establishing the principles upon which vocal delivery on the stage was based, from its early days in the ancient Greek theatre, where the directive had been mainly learning how to move and persuade an audience in the best possible manner. Taking their impetus from the teachings of Aristotle, actors learned early the importance of balancing voice, text and emotion. When later this ratio was altered by placing more emphasis on one or other of these factors, actors had further rhetorical guidelines to follow in observing the principles of *actio*, in which voice, facial expression, gestures and posture were to be in harmony with the text in order to lift out its contents and character. This was particularly relevant in the speaking of verse.

The long struggle between the classical ideal of vocal delivery, which advocated strict adherence to the verse metre and an orchestrated delivery, careful enunciation and attitudes derived by imitation of models, and the romantic approach, which recommended combining strong inner emotions, expressive face and varied tones, a careless diction, infrequent use of verse and overuse of gesture, indicates the dilemma whereby rhetoric found itself to be insufficient in a changing world, and fell into disuse.

In the twentieth century vocal delivery has witnessed a revival of interest in rhetoric's *actio* and *persuasio* particularly as demonstrated by advertising and propaganda. Their brain-washing effects via the mass media have stimulated a healthy disbelief in the meaning of the word. Consequently, voices have been raised advocating a revival of interest in poetics, whereby one should be better able to understand the theory and practice of reading and writing and thereby come closer to the elusive 'content'. One of the

187

greatest influences upon the analysis and performance of literature can be attributed to the concept of 'structuralism', which regarded the literary work as autonomous and had a significant bearing on the importance of the verse design for the delivery of verse. Further developments in 'semiotics' rejected the 'innocent reader' and threw the impetus back on the 'act of reading' as being important for giving life to a text, while at the same time questioning whether the code or the message was in fact most important for the theatre. This has led to a practice of 'deconstructing' the text in order to arrive at new meanings.

Dramatic language has also undergone enormous changes in the modern theatre, with new ideologies and experiments falling upon each other in rapid succession. Perhaps the most significant change has been the advent of the non-verbal as a replacement for the verbal text, where the language of words has been frequently replaced by a language of sounds. In the voice/text/emotion ratio, the text is the one that has been changing character and the impetus which has been thrown back on to voice and emotion has had considerable significance for vocal delivery practices in the twentieth century, particularly in the handling of verse.

Many theatre practitioners, following a structural method of analysis, regard the verse metre and design as being essential to the initial interpretation and delivery of Shakespeare in performance, maintaining that without adhering to these formal guidelines one misses much of what the writer intended. On the other hand, other schools of thought regard what the writer intended as unimportant for the theatre, preferring to freely cut and adapt in order to support a particular line of approach or ideology.

Similarly, the renewed interest in voice and emotion – not to mention the physical aspects of *actio* and *persuasio* – has made enormous demands on voice-training practices, which, although developing progressively this century along lines that are more scientifically sound, have been increasingly bombarded by methods of 'liberating' rather than training in technique, so that the person behind the voice would be able to invest his acting with more abandonment and hopefully more expression. A close look at a number of Hamlets reveals how this change in the balance of voice, text and emotion has been steadily emerging since the end of the last century to encompass a more emotion-filled delivery style, and takes into consideration its effect on audiences in the modern theatre.

Modern theatre theoreticians have taken over the role which rhetoric once played in shaping the actor's vocal delivery, by advocating different approaches to the voice/text/emotion ratio, use of *actio*, and in their attitudes to moving or persuading the audience. Stanislavski suggested ways of combining voice, text and emotion by using the 'subtext', although he was later to realize that in the performance of Shakespeare the 'subtext' alone would not suffice without coupling it to the verse's rhythm and tempo. Brecht rejected Stanislavski's idea of playing on the audience's emotions; rather, he endeavoured to make the audience think and become more socially aware. He advocated a thorough training in voice and use of verse metre, and believed in the use of a strong physical manifestation in order to convey the text. Artaud rejected the text completely and placed all emphasis on physical and vocal elements, where use of emotion was regarded as essential to awaken some response in the audience, and it is here we see the non-verbal begin to assume importance. Wolfsohn's followers, the Roy Hart Theatre, continued in this vein, recommending that by using the voice and emotion the performer's own personal inhibitions would be liberated. Here we see the origins of theatre as therapy. These principles encouraged Grotowski in his laboratory theatre workshops, to experiment with the body, by which he maintained vocal impulses could be stimulated and thereby the voice would be made more organically open. Brook has also moved away from the traditional use of the language of words and experimented with ways of exploring vocal impulses and communication through sound and fragmentation – although not entirely. In his productions, however, Brook is a tireless taskmaster, constantly challenging the actors to really explore the text with an open approach so that by combining emotion and intellect, the ordinary and literariness, they will be able to give life to it.

The modern theatre in Europe has been determined by the contribution of the director rather than the theoretician, the playwright or the actor, and this has clearly had an important bearing on vocal delivery and style. In his Shakespeare productions, Ingmar Bergman has shown a distinctive attitude to voice, text and emotion, where the text is not treated as verse; the poetic imagery is often eliminated and replaced by a visual imagery; the order of scenes is often rearranged; the auditive aspects are underplayed and the acting style is usually an emotional one. His predilection for red and black in the scenography in all his

Shakespeare productions would suggest a fascination for the 'dark' nightmarish aspects of these plays, which are momentarily explored and which disappear as 'worlds of illusion' only.

A different approach to vocal delivery is seen in Ariane Mnouchkine's Shakespeare productions, in which she has been concerned with finding in Shakespeare a relevance for today. This led her to experiment with form, mainly by borrowing from the East, in terms of movement, gesture, costuming and staging, thereby creating a heightened epic style of acting. However, the element which has most influenced the vocal delivery was the predominance of music underlying the text – which although it did not replace it, at times functioned as a kind of 'subtext' for the actors' emotions or intentions, in its use of rhythms and tones.

Although he has experimented freely with rearranging the text, and with the manner of vocal delivery, Peter Stein has demonstrated not only in his Shakespeare productions, but in his modern repertoire also, an ability to analyse the text with a ferocious exactness for extracting meaning. His is an ideological approach, which has encouraged him to examine each word for its actual meaning, and to refute all bourgeois sentiment. This has been demonstrated in his experiments with acting style, where the actors clearly have learned to master combining the epic style with psychological realism. Vocal experimentation has never been allowed to assume importance, rather it has been encouraged in order to offer wider connotations which have been text-based.

The postmodern approach to vocal delivery has certainly encouraged a more experimental use of voice and emotion, suitable gestures and ideas of persuading an audience than the previous directors have demonstrated. The work of Chaikin, Schechner, Foreman and Wilson have many factors in common: the text and discursive speech have been rejected in favour of other means of expression; the group has replaced the individual character actor; experiments in staging have often assaulted the usual boundaries existing between actor and audience; the physical/visual has taken precedence over the auditive; ritual has been reintroduced.

Chaikin's early search for another kind of theatre far removed from the naturalistic led him to evolve another style of acting, which was based on sound and movement and which was group-dependent. By their combined efforts, the group and not the individual created striking kinetic images which were intended to evoke striking echoes in the audience, and by this means persuade them, rather than attempting to reach them intellectually or ideologically. Here another kind of *actio* is demonstrated. Although writers were incorporated in the work of the Open Theatre, the text was the result of group improvisations rather than the point of departure, and the message usually topical.

Similarly, Schechner's experiments with group theatre and with 'characterless' performances led him to develop a particular style of acting with The Performance Group, where, through psychoanalysis and group therapy, the actor was encouraged to attain full emotional potential, whereby he could exercise a shamanistic power over the audience. Further experimentation with the theatrical space led to Schechner's environmental theatre practices whereby the audience became part of the staging. The text, which was totally disregarded or rewritten and adapted by the group according to their own personal fantasies, was very often delivered in sound-effects rather than words.

The productions of Richard Foreman and Robert Wilson differ in so far as they are concerned with the visual aspects of the production rather than the contribution of the group, and because of their own importance in the final realizations. Both of them have demonstrated an interest in a polyphonic theatre, where all the fragmented elements are made available for the audience to enjoy in a free way, without any strong emotional commitment, while allowing them to appreciate the theatrical playfulness.

Foreman's texts are mainly self-referential, and he is always present in their final realization, operating tape recordings and buzzers to interrupt the action and to 'create' each production live. The fact of the actors' delivery being recorded, without emotion, in rehearsal and replayed in performance to the accompaniment of their choreographed movements, has placed a different perspective on *actio* and *persuasio*. Foreman's use of framing devices to freeze pictures, and sound-effects to underline special moments are all intended to keep the audience on their toes and more observant.

Finally, Robert Wilson's theatre of visions has taken the role of language and vocal delivery in the modern theatre to its extreme. It indicates his total distrust of language as a means of communication, and has given utmost support for the fragmentary nature of what one has come to associate with postmodern theatre. Voice is used in all the myriad non-discursive ways possible in order to make sound pictures, and to communicate by non-verbal means. To support this, Wilson relies as heavily on visual imagery to externalize these interior experiences, preferring a dreamlike quality in the acting and a lack of emotion. The text has no importance for Wilson, who distributes lines at random, if he does not dispense with them altogether. The kind of acting style which he prefers is far removed from character acting, where the performers are encouraged to present themselves on stage without self-consciousness, performing actions as they would in everyday life, although in slow motion. In terms of *persuasio*, Wilson tries to distance the audience as much as possible from the theatrical event taking place, or from identification, rather he wants them to go on a journey of discovery where they will come out asking questions rather than having explanations given.

Although actor training has endeavoured to keep abreast of these changing attitudes to vocal delivery and the text, it has been shown that the problems facing the training institutions seem to be of a much more complex nature. Either they have been content to settle for a fragmented schema where a little of everything is taught, or they have adopted a special ideology or aesthetic line which has determined the training and consequently the kind of theatre which best suits the kind of training offered. Although training in vocal delivery for the classics, and this includes Shakespeare and the speaking of verse, appears to be sound in most acting school programmes, very few opportunities seem to have existed for experimentation of the nature which could encompass the kind of training necessary for contributing to the demands of the postmodern theatre. In spite of the changes in the Shakespeare ideal in the modern theatre, training in vocal delivery seems to have fluctuated between either a text-based approach or a liberated vocal approach, which has become very physical. At its best, a vocal delivery programme for a contemporary acting school should demonstrate an attitude of openness to the voice/text/ emotion ratio and to the question of *actio* and *persuasio* – where no one way is ever emphatically and dogmatically regarded as the only way, but where experimentation is encouraged. On the question of performing Shakespeare, this would, it is hoped, add new dimensions to old problems and question the verity of truths already known.

...tor. A Survey of Tragic Acting
...ertson, pp.370ff.
...ences of Henry Irving,

...d in Actors

...tralis.

...Quarterly

...Practice,

..., vol. 1,

...he Actor,

...pensate
..., no. 4,

...islavski

...Read-
1949,

...ol. 39,   ion of the elei
              ...formance, p. 35
...rnal   Theories of the
              the Present, p. 4
              ...hes, On Racine (
...es, op. cit., pp. 11
...153ff.
..154–5.
..., op. cit., p. 498.
..., 'Semiotics of Theat
..., no. 1, 1977, p. 110.
...nenie', or making strange
...is, 'Notes Toward a Sen
Dram...eview, T84, vol. 23, n
K. Ela...The Semiotics of Thea
45 A. Olsson, Den okände texten, pl
See M. Carlson, 'Psychic Poly
Criticism, Fall 1986, pp. 35–47.

1

NOTES

1 VOCAL DELIVERY IN HISTORICAL PERSPECTIVE

1 See G. Kennedy, *The Art of Persuasion in Greece*, pp. 8–9.
2 Aristotle's *Poetics* and *Rhetoric*, quoted in *Essays in Classical Criticism*, ed. T. A. Moxon and T. Twining, p. 80. The word 'belief' is of prime importance not only in terms of the early Greek civilization, but later, in contemplating the whole process of the effectiveness of speech on its hearer in further civilizations. Aristotle had studied this process carefully and arrived at some very clearly defined conclusions.
3 Ibid., p. 149ff.
4 See O. C. Brockett, *History of the Theatre*, pp. 27ff.
5 See G. Kennedy, *The Art of Rhetoric in the Roman World 300BC–AD300*, pp. 149ff.
6 Cicero, quoted in ibid., p. 223.
7 See *The Institutio Oratoria*, ed. E. Capps, T. E. Page and W. H. D. Rouse, p. 27.
8 Ibid., pp. 249ff.
9 Ibid., p. 277.
10 See Brockett, op. cit., pp. 78–9.
11 For a further explanation of Saint Augustine's *De Doctrina Christiana*, see G. Kennedy, *Classical Rhetoric and its Christian and Secular Tradition from Ancient to Modern Times*, pp. 27–33.
12 See B. Erbe, *En Undersøgelse af Byzantinsk Teater*, pp. 46–7.
13 See K. Young, *The Drama of the Medieval Church*, vols 1 and 2.
14 See G. Frank, *The Medieval French Drama*, pp. 18ff.
15 P. France, *Rhetoric and Truth in France from Descartes to Diderot*, pp. 23ff.
16 See B. Joseph, *Elizabethan Acting*, p. 1.
17 Ibid., pp. 60ff.
18 T. Heywood, *An Apology for Actors*, quoted in *Early Treatises on the Stage*, pp. 28–9.
19 J. Bulwer, *Chirologia . . . Chironomia*, p. 4.
20 See T. Cibber, 'Two Dissertations on the Theatres', quoted by C. Price, in *Theatre in the Age of Garrick*, pp. 15–42.

21 For a summarized
   eighteenth century
   Performance Practi
   International, Part I
   'The Hands', vol. ii
   1978.
22 T. Cibber, 'Two Di
   cit., p. 15.
23 For a fuller descript
   2.
24 See B. Joseph, *The T.*
   Burbage and Alleyn to
25 See F. Delsarte, 'Eler
   Acting, ed. T. Cole a

2 VOCAL DEL

1 See R. Barthes, 'Den
   ed. K. Aspelin and B.
2 D. C. Bryant, 'Rhetoric
   of Speech, vol. 39, no. 4,
3 Ibid., p. 417.
4 See H. A. Bosmajian, '
   of Speech, vol. 46, no. 4,
5 K. Johannesson, *Svensk*
   pp. 47ff.
6 See *The Institutio Oratori*
7 J. Culler, *Structuralist Po*
   Literature, quoted in T. I
8 See J. Piaget, *Structuralis*
9 See Hawkes, op. cit,. pp
10 Ibid., pp. 61ff.
11 Ibid., pp. 63ff.
12 V. Shklovsky, 'The Resu
   'Structuralism in Theatre
   Review, T72, vol. 20, no. 4
13 R. Jakobson, quoted in V
   p. 183.
14 J. Mukarovsky, 'Art as Se
   trans. J. Burbank and P. S
15 Hawkes, op. cit., p. 75.
16 J. Mukarovsky, 'Standard I
   Hawkes, op. cit., p. 75.
17 See P. Bogatyrev, 'Semiotic
   Semiotics of Art: Prague Sch
   Titunik, pp. 33ff.

46 E. Fischer-Lichte, 'Postmodern Literary Theory and Drama
   at the University of Stockholm, 17 April 1989.
47 See J. Martin and W. Sauter, 'Postmodernism in the
   Stockholm, Nordic Theatre Studies, Munksgaard (in press)
48 E. Fischer-Lichte, 'Performance Analysis – A Semiotic A
   lecture at the University of Stockholm, 19 April 1989.
49 See E. Fischer-Lichte, *Semiotik des Teaters. Das System der the*
   Zeichen, vol. 1.
50 P. N. Campbell, 'The Role of Language in the Theatre',
   Journal of Speech, vol. 68, no. 4, 1982, pp. 438–47.
51 Emile Zola, quoted in J. L. Styan, *Modern Drama in Theory and*
   vol. 1: *Realism and Naturalism*, pp. 10ff.
52 Ibid., p. 28.
53 See author's Preface to *Miss Julie* in *The Plays of Strindberg*
   introd. and trans. M. Meyer, pp. 99–112.
54 W. L. Sharp, *Language in Drama: Meanings for the Director and*
   p.118.
55 T. P. Adler, 'The Wesker Trilogy Revisited: Games to Com
   for the Inedaquacy of Words', *Quarterly Journal of Speech*, vol. 6
   1979.
56 J. L. Styan, *The Elements of Drama*, pp. 11–12.
57 C. Innes, *Holy Theatre: Ritual and the Avant Garde*, pp. 18ff.
58 M. Esslin, *The Theatre of the Absurd*, 3rd edn, p. 393.
59 J. Beck, quoted in J. Roose-Evans, *Experimental Theatre from Sta*
   to Peter Brook, p. 106.
60 See E. Bentley, *The Brecht Commentaries*, p. 65.
61 G. B. Shaw, quoted in G. R. Kernodle, 'Basic Problems i
   ing Shakespeare', *Quarterly Journal of Speech*, vol. 35, no. 1
   p. 36.
62 W. Mellers, 'Beyond the Sensual Speech', *Project Voice*, p. 7.
63 C. E. Burklund, 'Melody in Verse', *Quarterly Journal of Speech*,
   no. 1, 1953, p. 57.
64 J. Veilleux, 'Towards a Theory of Interpretation', *Quarterly Jo*
   Speech, vol. 55, no. 2, 1969, pp. 105–15.
65 R. Jakobson, 'Closing Statement: Linguistics and Poetics', qu
   Sebeok, op. cit., pp. 366–7.
66 See I. A. Richards, 'Poetic Process and Literary Analysis', qu
   Sebeok, op. cit., pp. 9–23.
67 D. R. Salper, 'The Sounding of a Poem', *Quarterly Journal of Speech*
   vol. 57, no. 1, 1971, pp. 133ff.
68 B. W. Long and M. F. Hopkins, *Performing Literature – An Introd*
   Oral Interpretation, pp. 251ff.
69 See Kernodle, op. cit., pp. 36–43.
70 R. Jakobson and L. G. Jones, *Shakespeare's Verbal Art in*
   Spirit, p. 32.
71 See H. Kökeritz's reading of Shakespeare's Sonnet no. 18 'Shall I
   compare thee to a summer's day' (L379), The National Archive o

*v*ing Images (ALB), Stockholm, which is
*s*earch into Elizabethan pronunciation. He has
*h*etic transcript and this clarifies many idiosyncrasies
with a Modern English pronunciation.
*R*obson and Jones, op. cit., pp. 32ff.
*B*arton, *Playing Shakespeare*, pp. 25ff.
Ibid.

75 See U. Eco, *A Theory of Semiotics*, pp. 269–70.
76 See I. McKellen, quoted in Barton, op. cit., p. 182.
77 Elam, op. cit., pp. 80ff.
78 See M. Garcia, 'Observations on Human Voice', quoted in D.F. Proctor, *Breathing, Speech and Song*, pp. 6–7.
79 See L. Browne, 'On Photography of the Larynx and Soft Palate', in Proctor, op.cit., p. 11.
80 See T. R. French, 'A Photographic Study of the Singing Voice', in Proctor, op. cit., p. 11.
81 See W. Rasmus, 'Voice and Diction in Historical Perspective', *Quarterly Journal of Speech*, vol. 47, no. 3, 1961, pp. 253–61.
82 See W. Russell, 'Ortophony or Voice Culture', *Quarterly Journal of Speech*, vol. 47, no. 3, 1961, p. 225.
83 See V. Anderson, 'A Modern View of Voice and Diction', *Quarterly Journal of Speech*, vol. 39, no. 1, 1953, pp. 25–32.
84 See Proctor, op. cit., pp. 39–42.
85 See Rasmus, op. cit., p. 255.
86 H. Sewall, 'On the Relation of Diaphragmatic and Costal Respiration with Particular Reference to Phonation', in Proctor, op. cit., pp. 82ff.
87 See C. T. Simon and F. Keller, 'An Approach to the Problem of Chest Resonance', *Quarterly Journal of Speech*, vol. 13, 1927, p. 432.
88 See J. Grotowski, *Towards a Poor Theatre*, pp. 147ff.
89 Proctor, op. cit., p. 117.
90 See C. Van Riper and J. V. Irwin, *Voice and Articulation*, pp. 296ff.
91 Ibid., pp. 297ff.
92 A. W. Mills, 'Some Contributions of Voice Science to Voice Training', *Quarterly Journal of Speech*, vol. 36, no. 3, 1959, p. 380.
93 V. S. Anderson, *Training the Speaking Voice*, pp. 66ff.
94 In an article by K. Parker entitled 'Goodbye, Voice Beautiful', *Plays and Players*, July 1985, two of Britain's leading voice teachers, Cicely Berry from the Royal Shakespeare Company and Patsy Rodenberg from the Guildhall School of Drama, discuss the fact that the voice beautiful ideal disappeared in the British theatre when it was found to be inadequate for the new wave of young playwrights who emerged after John Osborne's *Look Back in Anger*, and it became more important to encourage *what* was being said rather than *how* it was said. As a result they changed their training methods.
95 Anderson, 'A Modern View of Voice and Diction', op. cit., p. 28.
96 F. S. Brodnitz, 'The Holistic Study of the Voice', *Quarterly Journal of Speech*, vol. 48, no. 3, 1960, p. 283.

97 C. Scott, quoted in B. Joseph, *The Tragic Ac in England from Burbage and Alleyn to Forbes-Rob*

98 H. Cain, quoted in Bram Stoker, *Personal Reminis* vol. II, pp. 116ff.

99 H. Irving, Lecture delivered at Harvard University, quote *on Acting*, ed. T. Cole and H. Chinoy, p. 359.

100 Joseph, op. cit., pp. 582ff.

101 Ibid., p. 386.

102 Ibid., pp. 390ff.

103 Barnes, quoted in Joseph, op. cit., p. 391.

104 P. Brook, quoted in Cole and Chinoy, op. cit., p. 397.

105 See L. Olivier, *On Acting*, p. 44.

106 J. Agate, quoted in G. Brandreth, *John Gielgud. A Celebration*, p. 64.

107 Olivier, op. cit., p. 45.

108 P. Brook, quoted in Cole and Chinoy, op. cit., p. 424.

109 See J. C. Trewin, *Paul Scofield*, pp. 77ff.

110 J. Gielgud, quoted in R.L. Sterne, *John Gielgud Directs Richard Burton in 'Hamlet': A Journal of Rehearsals*, p. 158.

111 Ibid., p. 148.

112 H. Novack, quoted in J. L. Gibson, *Ian McKellen. A Biography*, p. 132.

113 I. McKellen, quoted in ibid., p. 24.

3 A SMORGASBORD OF IDEALS

1 See J. Benedetti, *Stanislavski: An Introduction*, ch. 4.

2 Stanislavski. quoted in S. H. Carnicke, 'An Actor Prepares. Rabota akterna nad soboi, Chast.'I: A Comparison of the English with the Russian Stanislavski', *Theatre Journal*, December 1984, p. 483.

3 Actors who were taught by Stanislavski brought with them 'The System' as it was to Stanislavski at that time. This, together with the late publication of *An Actor Prepares* (1936), *Building a Character* (1949) and *Creating a Role* (1961), together with heavy editing and many inconsistencies in the translation of basic terminology from original Russian to English, have contributed to the confusion. For further clarification, the reader is referred to H. Schnitzler's 'Truth and Consequences, or Stanislavski Misinterpreted', *Quarterly Journal of Speech*, vol. 40, April 1954, pp. 481–3.

4 Ibid., pp. 488–9.

5 See S. Moore, *The Stanislavski System: The Professional Training of an Actor: Digested from the teachings of Konstantin S. Stanislavski*, pp. 68–70.

6 K. Stanislavski, *Teatr*, p. 111.

7 See K.S. in a letter to Alexandre Benois. I am grateful to Jean-Norman Benedetti, who first told me this anecdote in a letter dated 25 January 1988. It subsequently appeared in his book *Stanislavski: A Biography*, London, Methuen, 1988, to which the reader is referred (pp. 213ff.).

8 The 'Method' as taught by Lee Strassberg in America is evidently based only on Stanislavski's Emotional Memory Period (after 1906)

before he had fully evolved his Method of Analysis through Physical Actions.

9 K. Stanislavski, quoted in Moore, op.cit., p. 68.
10 See C. Stanislavski, *Building a Character*, trans. E.R. Hapgood, pp. 82–108.
11 Ibid., p. 128.
12 Ibid., pp. 162–3.
13 Ibid., p. 239.
14 Ibid., pp. 240–1.
15 C. Stanislavski, quoted in Benedetti, *Stanislavski: An Introduction*, op. cit., p. 70.
16 Stanislavski, *Building a Character*, op. cit., p. 241.
17 See J.V. Morgan, *Stanislavski's Encounter with Shakespeare: The Evolution of a Method*, p. 79.
18 Gordon Craig, quoted in Morgan, op. cit., p. 128.
19 Ibid., p. 128.
20 C. Stanislavski, quoted in *Creating a Role*, trans. E. R. Hapgood, p. 261.
21 Ibid., p. 267.
22 See E. Bentley, *The Brecht Commentaries*, p. 32.
23 See B. Brecht, *Brecht on Theatre. The Development of an Aesthetic*, p. 213.
24 See B. Brecht, 'A New Technique of Acting' trans. Eric Bentley, *Theatre Arts*, April 1949, and cited in *Actors on Acting*, ed. T. Cole and H.K. Chinoy, pp. 308–11.
25 Following a trip to Moscow in 1935, Brecht came into contact with Viktor Shklovsky's term *'ostranenie'*, or making strange, which was part of Russian formalist literary theory. This no doubt can be seen as the meaning behind his translation and later use of the term *'Verfremdung'*.
26 B. Brecht, 'A Short Organum for the Theatre', quoted in *Brecht on Theatre*, op. cit., p. 193.
27 Ibid., p. 117.
28 Ibid., p. 248.
29 Ibid., p. 15.
30 Stanislavski, quoted in *Building a Character*, op. cit., pp. 173–4.
31 Brecht, quoted in *Brecht on Theatre*, op. cit., p. 195.
32 Ibid., p. 116.
33 See Cole and Chinoy, op. cit., pp. 314–16.
34 Brecht, quoted in *Brecht on Theatre*, op. cit., p. 200.
35 Ibid., pp. 201–2.
36 Ibid., p. 224.
37 See J. Willett, *Brecht in Context*, pp. 200–1.
38 A. Artaud, *The Theatre and its Double*, trans. M. C. Richards, pp. 12–13.
39 A. Artaud, 'The Alfred Jarry Theatre', quoted in Antonin Artaud *Collected Works*, vol. 2, pp. 30ff.
40 A. Artaud, 'The Theatre and the Plague', in *The Theatre and its Double*, op. cit., pp. 28ff.
41 Ibid., pp. 49ff.

42 Ibid., p. 46.
43 Artaud, *Collected Works*, vol. 4, p. 103.
44 See C. Innes, *Holy Theatre: Ritual and the Avant Garde*, pp. 64ff.
45 A. Artaud, 'The Conquest of Mexico', in *The Theatre and its Double*, op. cit., p. 128.
46 See A. Artaud, 'The Theatre and Cruelty', in *The Theatre and its Double*, op. cit., pp. 85ff.
47 Ibid., p. 94.
48 Ibid., p. 110.
49 Ibid., p. 94.
50 Ibid., p. 117.
51 See J. Roose-Evans, *Experimental Theatre from Stanislavski to Peter Brook*, pp. 74–90.
52 Innes, op. cit., p. 110.
53 See A. Wolfsohn, 'The Omnitone', *Time Magazine*, 19 March 1956, pp. 47ff.
54 See H. Kretzmer, *Daily Express*, 16 September 1969.
55 Wolfsohn, op. cit.
56 See Roose-Evans, op. cit., pp. 181ff.
57 See Wolfsohn, op. cit.
58 E. Pardo, 'The Work of the Roy Hart Theatre', *Project Voice*, November 1982, p. 15.
59 See O. Cook, Programme notes to 'Not So Much a Concert – More a Way of Voice', Stockholm City Theatre, December 1985.
60 O. Cook, Interview, 16 October 1985.
61 O. Cook, Voice demonstration, Stockholm University, Theatre Department, October 1985.
62 The Alexander technique, so called after its founder F.M. Alexander (1869–1955), is a systematic approach to voice training where the speaker learns 'not to do', that is, he learns to free the tensions which occur in his body during the speech act.
63 Cook, Interview, op. cit.
64 Pardo, op. cit., p. 16.
65 E. Pardo, quoted in A. Carpelan, 'Roy Hart Theatre: En chockartad upplevelse', *Scen och Salong*, no. 10–11, pp. 21–3.
66 S. Osten, director of the Unga Klara Teater in Stockholm, summed up the reactions of the audience to this production as those of 'fear based on social limitations'; quoted in Carpelan, op. cit., p. 23.
67 *Svenska Dagbladet*, July 1982.
68 M. Di Caro, 'Poesis of the Roy Hart. What Images, What Voices', *Giornale di Sicilia*, 26 April 1985.
69 Y.P., *Midi Libre*, 19 April 1985.
70 See T. Burzyński and Z. Osiński, *Grotowski's Laboratory*, pp. 13–21.
71 See J. Grotowski, 'He Wasn't Entirely Himself', in *Towards a Poor Theatre*, pp. 85–93.
72 Ibid., p. 115.
73 See figures 64 and 65 in ibid., p. 147.
74 J. Grotowski, quoted by J. Kumiega in *The Theatre of Grotowski*, p. 12.

75 Grotowski, *Towards a Poor Theatre*, op. cit., pp. 58ff.
76 A. Korewa, quoted in Kumiega, op. cit., p. 20.
77 T. Kudlinski, quoted in ibid., p. 24.
78 See Burzyński and Osiński, op. cit., pp. 16–17.
79 Ibid., p. 19.
80 Ibid., pp. 23ff.
81 Ibid., pp. 35–7.
82 E. Barba, quoted in Kumiega, op. cit., pp. 118–19.
83 Grotowski, *Towards a Poor Theatre*, op. cit., p. 151.
84 L. Flaszen, quoted in Kumiega, op. cit., p. 64.
85 A. Seymour, quoted in ibid., p. 69.
86 ibid., p. 77.
87 P. Feldman, 'On Grotowski', *Drama Review*, T46, vol. 14, no. 2, 1970, pp. 193ff.
88 J. Grotowski, quoted in Burzyński and Osiński, op. cit., p. 55.
89 J. Grotowski, quoted in *Drama Review*, T46, vol. 14, no. 2, p. 193.
90 J. Grotowski, quoted in Kumiega, op. cit., p. 90.
91 Ibid., p. 92.
92 P. Brook, quoted in Innes, op. cit., p. 129.
93 See P. Brook, *The Shifting Point: Theatre, Film, Opera 1946–1987*.
94 P. Brook, quoted in Cole and Chinoy, op. cit., pp. 422–9.
95 See P. Brook, *The Empty Space*, pp. 115ff.
96 Ibid., pp. 48–9.
97 Innes, op. cit., p. 185.
98 See Cole and Chinoy, op. cit., p. 429.
99 P. Brook, quoted in C. Berry, *Voice and the Actor*, p. 3.
100 See D. Selbourne, *The Making of 'A Midsummer Night's Dream': An Eyewitness Account of Peter Brook's Production from First Rehearsal to First Night*, pp. 33ff.
101 See S. Beauman, *The Royal Shakespeare Company   A History of Ten Decades*, pp. 268ff.
102 See Brook, op. cit., p. 122.
103 Ibid., p. 55.
104 See Innes, op. cit., p. 134.
105 Ibid., p. 135.
106 P. Brook, *Playscript 9 US: The Book of the Royal Shakespeare Theatre Production*.
107 Brook, *The Shifting Point*, op. cit., p. 108.
108 Ibid.
109 P. Brook's film of *The Tempest*, 1968.
110 P. Brook, quoted in Selbourne, op. cit., p. 23.
111 R. Peaslee, quoted in Roose-Evans, op. cit., p. 102.
112 See Innes, op. cit., pp. 139–40.
113 See J. Lahr, 'Knowing What to Celebrate', *Plays and Players*, March 1976, pp. 17–19.
114 See M. Shevtsova, 'Peter Brook Adapts the Tragedy of Carmen', *Theatre International*, vol. 2, no. 10, 1983, pp. 38–55.
115 See Brook, *The Shifting Point*, op. cit., p. 163.

116 Ibid., p. 85.
117 Ibid., p. 43.

4 DIRECTORIAL VISIONS

1 I. Bergman, quoted in L.-L. Marker and F.J. Marker, *Ingmar Bergman: Four Decades in the Theatre*, Directors in Perspective Series, p. 6.
2 I. Bergman, quoted by H. Sjögren, 'Ingmar Bergmans teater – rörelser i rummet', in *Perspektiv på teater ur svensk regi- och iscensättningshistoria*, Documents and Studies collected by U. Gran and U.-B. Laggeroth, pp. 83ff.
3 Ibid., p. 139.
4 I. Bergman, quoted in Marker and Marker, op. cit., p. 97.
5 Ibid., p. 97.
6 H. Grevenius, quoted in ibid., p. 34.
7 'Göteborgs Handels- och Sjöfartstidning', quoted in Marker and Marker, op. cit., p. 36.
8 Grevenius, op. cit., p. 36.
9 Bergman, quoted in Marker and Marker, op. cit., p. 37.
10 See J. Martin, 'Eloquence is Action: A Study of Form and Text's Influence on the Vocal Delivery Style of Shakespeare in Sweden 1934–1985', doctoral dissertation, University of Stockholm, 1987.
11 See H. Sjögren, *Stage and Society in Sweden*, pp. 23–41.
12 Bergman, quoted in ibid., p. 61.
13 E. Törnquist, quoted in Marker and Marker, op. cit., p. 73.
14 See Martin, op. cit.
15 L. Zern. 'Ingen förstår Shakespeare', *Dagens Nyheter*, 13 January 1985.
16 T. Baeckström, *Göteborgs Handels-och Sjöfartstidning*.
17 B. Jahnsson, *Aftonbladet*, 5 May 1979.
18 See H. Granville-Barker, *Prefaces to Shakespeare*, vols 1 and 2.
19 I. Bergman, Preface to *Kung Lear*.
20 See M. Lagercrantz, 'Dramat i Smyckesskrinet – Kung Lear på Dramaten 1984', unpublished thesis, University of Stockholm, 1985, pp. 18–29.
21 See Martin, op. cit., pp. 106–8.
22 I. Björkstén, 'Fenomenalt bildskapande och teatermagi', *Svenska Dagbladet*, 10 March 1984, and B. Jahnsson, 'Stor tragedi med matt slut', *Dagens Nyheter*, 10 March 1984.
23 Zern, op. cit.
24 Bergman, Preface to *Kung Lear*, op. cit.
25 See I. Bergman, *Svenska Dagbladet*, 12 December 1986.
26 I. Bergman, *Arbetet*, 12 December 1986.
27 See I. Björkstén, *Svenska Dagbladet*, 21 December 1986.
28 T. Ellefsen, *Dagens Nyheter*, 21 December 1986.
29 L. Zern, *Expressen*, 21 December 1986.
30 Björkstén, op. cit. (see n. 27).
31 See M. and U. Sörenson, *Teater i Paris*, pp. 8–9.

32 See A. Mnouchkine, 'Le Théâtre ou la vie', *Fruits: en plein soleil*, no. 2/3, June 1984, pp. 202–23.
33 See S. Moscoso, 'Notes de répétitions: Le Théâtre du Soleil Shakespeare 2 partie', *Double Page*, no. 32, 1984.
34 See I. Glanzelius, 'Théâtre du Soleil dödförklaras ständigt', *Dagens Nyheter*, 15 May 1983.
35 See G. Wirén, 'Åter till Shakespeare', *Dagens Nyheter*, 1 April 1984.
36 Sörenson, op. cit., pp. 12–13.
37 Shakespeare, *The Tragedy of King Richard II*, act II, scene i.
38 Moscoso, op. cit.
39 Ibid.
40 Sörenson, op. cit., pp. 12–13.
41 Ibid., p. 16.
42 G. Sandier, *Lettres/Arts*, 19 December 1981.
43 See Wirén, op. cit.
44 Moscoso, op. cit.
45 Sörenson, op. cit.
46 Ibid.
47 Ibid., pp. 8–9.
48 Moscoso, op. cit.
49 See Sörenson, op. cit.
50 See Wirén, op. cit.
51 See Moscoso, op. cit.
52 J-J. Lemêtre, 'Mesure pour mesure', *Fruits: en plein soleil*, no. 2/3, June, 1984, pp. 188–9.
53 C. Lee, quoted in *Fruits: en plein soleil*, no. 2/3, June, 1983, p. 198.
54 G. Bigot, 'Ourselves We Do Not Owe', in *Fruits: en plein soleil*, no. 2/3, June, 1984, p. 124.
55 See Mnouchkine, op. cit., p. 208.
56 Wirén, op. cit.
57 M. Patterson, *Peter Stein: Germany's Leading Theatre Director*, pp. 1–2.
58 Ibid., p. 4.
59 Ibid., p. 8.
60 P. Stein, quoted by P. Lackner, 'Stein's Path to Shakespeare', *Drama Review*, T74, vol. 21, no. 2, 1977, pp. 80–102.
61 I. Nagel, *Tasso-Regiebuch*, pp. 184–5; quoted in Patterson, op. cit., pp. 23–4.
62 P. Stein, quoted by B. Dort, *Drama Review*, T74, vol. 21, no. 2, pp. 91–2.
63 P. Stein, quoted in Patterson, op. cit., p. 72.
64 See V. Canaris, *Theater Heute*, no. 13, 1971, p. 32; quoted in Patterson, op. cit., p. 75.
65 Stein, quoted in Patterson, op. cit., p. 108.
66 See G. Jäger, *Theater Heute*, no. 7, 1974; quoted in Patterson, op. cit., p. 109.
67 Lackner, op. cit., pp. 79–102.
68 Patterson, op. cit., p. 130.
69 B. Hinrichs, *Die Zeit*, 31 December 1976; quoted in Patterson, op. cit.

70 D. Z. Mairowitz, 'As They Like It', *Plays and Players*, no. 290, 1977, p. 18.
71 P. Stein, Protocol no. 450. quoted in Patterson, op. cit., p. 142.
72 J. Warren, Review of *The Hairy Ape*, *Plays and Players*, no. 406, July 1987, pp. 19–20.
73 See B. Skawonius, 'Generationen från 1968 har satt sig på de unga', *Dagens Nyheter*, 21 March 1982.
74 R. Lysell, 'Scenisk opera utan musik: Peter Stein's Fedra', *Nya Teatertidningen*, no. 41, 1988.
75 F.X. Kroetz, Play text *Nicht Fish Nicht Fleish*, Swedish trans. U. Olsson and H. Grevenius, *Varken fågel eller fisk*, Royal Dramatic Theatre, Stockholm, 1981.
76 L. Zern, 'Teater i Europa', *Nya teatertidningen*, op. cit., pp. 22–7.

5 THE POSTMODERN APPROACH

1 See J. Martin and W. Sauter, 'Postmodernism in the Theatre', Stockholm, Nordic Theatre Studies, Munksgaard (in press).
2 J. Chaikin, quoted in J. Roose-Evans, *Experimental Theatre from Stanislavski to Peter Brook*, pp. 106ff.
3 J. Chaikin, quoted in J. Lahr, *Acting out America: Essays on Modern Theatre*, pp. 122–35.
4 R. Pasolli, *A Book on the Open Theatre*, pp. 61–9.
5 J. Chaikin, quoted in Lahr, op. cit., pp. 133–4.
6 Ibid.
7 Pasolli, op. cit., p. 80.
8 J. Grotowski, quoted in Pasolli, op. cit., p. 115.
9 Ibid., p. 124.
10 J.C. van Itallie, quoted in Lahr, op. cit., p. 128.
11 Pasolli, op. cit., pp.125ff.
12 J. Chaikin, quoted in Lahr, op. cit., p. 130.
13 Pasolli, op. cit., p. 126.
14 J. Chaikin, quoted in Roose-Evans, op. cit., pp. 128–9.
15 See C. Innes, *Holy Theatre. Ritual and the Avant Garde*, p. 181.
16 Ibid., p. 182.
17 See R. Schechner, *The End of Humanism: Writings on Performance*, p. 98.
18 See Innes, op. cit., p. 57.
19 R. Schechner, 'Actuals: Primitive Ritual and Performance Theory, an Anthropological Approach to Modern Experimental Theatre', *Theatre Quarterly*, vol. 1, no. 2, 1971, p. 61.
20 See R. Schechner, 'Post Proscenium', in *American Theatre 1969–70*, New York, International Theatre Institute of the USA, 1970, p. 29.
21 Ibid., p. 24.
22 Innes, op. cit., p. 181.
23 Lahr, op. cit., pp. 24–5.
24 See A. Sainer, *The Radical Theatre Notebook*, p. 27.
25 Schechner, *American Theatre*, op. cit., pp. 27ff.
26 See Schechner, 'Actuals', op. cit., p. 63.

NOTES

1 VOCAL DELIVERY IN HISTORICAL PERSPECTIVE

1 See G. Kennedy, *The Art of Persuasion in Greece*, pp. 8–9.
2 Aristotle's *Poetics* and *Rhetoric*, quoted in *Essays in Classical Criticism*, ed. T. A. Moxon and T. Twining, p. 80. The word 'belief' is of prime importance not only in terms of the early Greek civilization, but later, in contemplating the whole process of the effectiveness of speech on its hearer in further civilizations. Aristotle had studied this process carefully and arrived at some very clearly defined conclusions.
3 Ibid., p. 149ff.
4 See O. C. Brockett, *History of the Theatre*, pp. 27ff.
5 See G. Kennedy, *The Art of Rhetoric in the Roman World 300BC–AD300*, pp. 449ff.
6 Cicero, quoted in ibid., p. 223.
7 See *The Institutio Oratoria*, ed. E. Capps, T. E. Page and W. H. D. Rouse, p. 27.
8 Ibid., pp. 249ff.
9 Ibid., p. 277.
10 See Brockett, op. cit., pp. 78–9.
11 For a further explanation of Saint Augustine's *De Doctrina Christiana*, see G. Kennedy, *Classical Rhetoric and its Christian and Secular Tradition from Ancient to Modern Times*, pp. 27–33.
12 See B. Erbe, *En Undersøgelse af Byzantinsk Teater*, pp. 46–7.
13 See K. Young, *The Drama of the Medieval Church*, vols 1 and 2.
14 See G. Frank, *The Medieval French Drama*, pp. 18ff.
15 P. France, *Rhetoric and Truth in France from Descartes to Diderot*, pp. 23ff.
16 See B. Joseph, *Elizabethan Acting*, p. 1.
17 Ibid., pp. 60ff.
18 T. Heywood, *An Apology for Actors*, quoted in *Early Treatises on the Stage*, pp. 28–9.
19 J. Bulwer, *Chirologia . . . Chironomia*, p. 4.
20 See T. Cibber, 'Two Dissertations on the Theatres', quoted by C. Price, in *Theatre in the Age of Garrick*, pp. 15–42.

21 For a summarized overview of these books on the art of acting in the eighteenth century, the reader is referred to D. Barnett's 'The Performance Practice of Acting: The 18th Century', *Theatre Research International*, Part I: 'Ensemble Acting', vol. ii, no. 3, 1977; Part II: 'The Hands', vol. iii, no. 1, 1977; Part III: 'The Arms', vol. iii, no. 2, 1978.

22 T. Cibber, 'Two Dissertations on the Theatres', quoted in Price, op. cit., p. 15.

23 For a fuller description of semiotics, the reader is referred to chapter 2.

24 See B. Joseph, *The Tragic Actor: A Survey of Tragic Acting in England from Burbage and Alleyn to Forbes-Robertson*, p. 393.

25 See F. Delsarte, 'Elements of the Delsarte System', quoted in *Actors on Acting*, ed. T. Cole and H. K. Chinoy, pp. 187–90.

2 VOCAL DELIVERY IN THE TWENTIETH CENTURY

1 See R. Barthes, 'Den retoriska analysen', quoted in *Form och Struktur*, ed. K. Aspelin and B.A. Lundberg, p. 270.

2 D. C. Bryant, 'Rhetoric: Its Functions and Its Scope', *Quarterly Journal of Speech*, vol. 39, no. 4, 1953, p. 413.

3 Ibid., p. 417.

4 See H. A. Bosmajian, 'The Nazi Speaker's Rhetoric', *Quarterly Journal of Speech*, vol. 46, no. 4, 1960, pp. 365–71.

5 K. Johannesson, *Svensk retorik från Stockholms blodbad till Almedalen*, pp. 47ff.

6 See *The Institutio Oratoria*, ed. E. Capps *et al.*, Book II.i.

7 J. Culler, *Structuralist Poetics: Structuralism, Linguistics and the Study of Literature*, quoted in T. Hawkes, *Structuralism and Semiotics*, p. 160.

8 See J. Piaget, *Structuralism*, quoted in Hawkes, op.cit., p. 16.

9 See Hawkes, op. cit,. pp. 20ff.

10 Ibid., pp. 61ff.

11 Ibid., pp. 63ff.

12 V. Shklovsky, 'The Resurrection of the World', quoted by F. Deák, 'Structuralism in Theatre: The Prague School Contribution', *Drama Review*, T72, vol. 20, no. 4, 1976, pp. 82–94.

13 R. Jakobson, quoted in V. Erlich, *Russian Formalism: History–Doctrine*, p. 183.

14 J. Mukarovsky, 'Art as Semiotic Fact', in *Structure, Sign and Function*, trans. J. Burbank and P. Steiner, p. 84.

15 Hawkes, op. cit., p. 75.

16 J. Mukarovsky, 'Standard Language and Poetic Language', quoted in Hawkes, op. cit., p. 75.

17 See P. Bogatyrev, 'Semiotics in the Folk Theatre', trans. B. Kochis, in *Semiotics of Art: Prague School Contributions*, ed. L. Matejka and I. Titunik, pp. 33ff.

18 P. Bogatyrev, 'Forms and Functions of Folk Theatre', in Matejka and Titunik, op. cit., p. 44.
19 J. Honzl, 'Dynamics of Sign in the Theatre', in Matejka and Titunik, op. cit., p. 91.
20 See J. Honzl, 'The Hierarchy of Dramatic Devices', in Matejka and Titunik, op. cit., p. 123.
21 Ibid., p. 118.
22 See J. Veltrusky, 'Man and Object in the Theatre', trans. P. Garvin, in *A Prague School Reader on Esthetics, Literary Structure and Style*, pp. 106–7.
23 See J. Veltrusky, 'Dramatic Text as a Component of Theatre', in Matejka and Titunik, op. cit., p. 94.
24 Veltrusky, op. cit., p. 109.
25 Ibid., pp. 115ff.
26 R. Jakobson, 'Fundamentals of Language', in Hawkes, op. cit., p. 79.
27 R. Jakobson, 'Closing Statement: Linguistics and Poetics', in *Style in Language*, ed. T. A. Sebeok, p. 377.
28 Ibid., p. 353. In this paper, Jakobson shows that when orientation is directed towards the *context*, then the referential function dominates; the emotive or expressive function focused on the *addresser* (and he referred to the actor of Stanislavski's Moscow Art Theatre, who in an audition successfully managed to make forty different messages from 'This evening' by changing its expressive tint); orientation towards the *addressee* emphasized the connative or imperative function; orientation on the *contact*, the phatic; on the *code*, itself, the metalingual and on the *message*, the poetic function of the language.
29 Ibid., p. 357.
30 Ibid., p. 359.
31 Ibid., p. 360.
32 Ibid., pp. 364f.
33 Ibid., p. 366.
34 A full description of the elements of dynamic iconography are given in J. Hilton, *Performance*, p. 35.
35 M. Carlson, *Theories of the Theatre: A Historical and Critical Survey from the Greeks to the Present*, p. 414.
36 See R. Barthes, *On Racine (Sur Racine)*, trans. R. Howard, p. 148.
37 See Hawkes, op. cit., pp. 114ff.
38 Ibid., pp. 153ff.
39 Ibid., pp. 154–5.
40 Carlson, op. cit., p. 498.
41 U. Eco, 'Semiotics of Theatrical Performance', *Drama Review*, T21, vol. 30, no. 1, 1977, p. 110. (Compare 'ostension' with the term '*ostranenie*', or making strange, which the Russian formalists used.)
42 P. Pavis, 'Notes Toward a Semiotic Analysis: Languages of the Stage', *Drama Review*, T84, vol. 23, no. 4, 1982, pp. 165–77.
43 K. Elam, *The Semiotics of Theatre and Drama*, p. 159.
44 A. Olsson, *Den okände texten*, pp. 59ff.
45 See M. Carlson, 'Psychic Polyphony', *Journal of Dramatic Theory and Criticism*, Fall 1986, pp. 35–47.

46 E. Fischer-Lichte, 'Postmodern Literary Theory and Drama', lecture at the University of Stockholm, 17 April 1989.

47 See J. Martin and W. Sauter, 'Postmodernism in the Theatre', Stockholm, Nordic Theatre Studies, Munksgaard (in press).

48 E. Fischer-Lichte, 'Performance Analysis – A Semiotic Approach', lecture at the University of Stockholm, 19 April 1989.

49 See E. Fischer-Lichte, Semiotik des Teaters. Das System der theatralischen Zeichen, vol. 1.

50 P. N. Campbell, 'The Role of Language in the Theatre', Quarterly Journal of Speech, vol. 68, no. 4, 1982, pp. 438–47.

51 Emile Zola, quoted in J. L. Styan, Modern Drama in Theory and Practice, vol. 1: Realism and Naturalism, pp. 10ff.

52 Ibid., p. 28.

53 See author's Preface to Miss Julie in The Plays of Strindberg, vol. 1, introd. and trans. M. Meyer, pp. 99–112.

54 W. L. Sharp, Language in Drama: Meanings for the Director and the Actor, p.118.

55 T. P. Adler, 'The Wesker Trilogy Revisited: Games to Compensate for the Inedaquacy of Words', Quarterly Journal of Speech, vol. 65, no. 4, 1979.

56 J. L. Styan, The Elements of Drama, pp. 11–12.

57 C. Innes, Holy Theatre: Ritual and the Avant Garde, pp. 18ff.

58 M. Esslin, The Theatre of the Absurd, 3rd edn, p. 393.

59 J. Beck, quoted in J. Roose-Evans, Experimental Theatre from Stanislavski to Peter Brook, p. 106.

60 See E. Bentley, The Brecht Commentaries, p. 65.

61 G. B. Shaw, quoted in G. R. Kernodle, 'Basic Problems in Reading Shakespeare', Quarterly Journal of Speech, vol. 35, no. 1, 1949, p. 36.

62 W. Mellers, 'Beyond the Sensual Speech', Project Voice, p. 7.

63 C. E. Burklund, 'Melody in Verse', Quarterly Journal of Speech, vol. 39, no. 1, 1953, p. 57.

64 J. Veilleux, 'Towards a Theory of Interpretation', Quarterly Journal of Speech, vol. 55, no. 2, 1969, pp. 105–15.

65 R. Jakobson, 'Closing Statement: Linguistics and Poetics', quoted in Sebeok, op. cit., pp. 366–7.

66 See I. A. Richards, 'Poetic Process and Literary Analysis', quoted in Sebeok, op. cit., pp. 9–23.

67 D. R. Salper, 'The Sounding of a Poem', Quarterly Journal of Speech, vol. 57, no. 1, 1971, pp. 133ff.

68 B. W. Long and M. F. Hopkins, Performing Literature – An Introduction to Oral Interpretation, pp. 251ff.

69 See Kernodle, op. cit., pp. 36–43.

70 R. Jakobson and L. G. Jones, Shakespeare's Verbal Art in Th'Experience of Spirit, p. 32.

71 See H. Kökeritz's reading of Shakespeare's Sonnet no. 18 'Shall I compare thee to a summer's day' (L379), The National Archive of

Recorded Sound and Moving Images (ALB), Stockholm, which is
based upon his research into Elizabethan pronunciation. He has
produced a phonetic transcript and this clarifies many idiosyncrasies
which arise with a Modern English pronunciation.

72 See Jakobson and Jones, op. cit., pp. 32ff.
73 J. Barton, *Playing Shakespeare*, pp. 25ff.
74 Ibid.
75 See U. Eco, *A Theory of Semiotics*, pp. 269–70.
76 See I. McKellen, quoted in Barton, op. cit., p. 182.
77 Elam, op. cit., pp. 80ff.
78 See M. Garcia, 'Observations on Human Voice', quoted in D.F.
   Proctor, *Breathing, Speech and Song*, pp. 6–7.
79 See L. Browne, 'On Photography of the Larynx and Soft Palate', in
   Proctor, op.cit., p. 11.
80 See T. R. French, 'A Photographic Study of the Singing Voice', in
   Proctor, op. cit., p. 11.
81 See W. Rasmus, 'Voice and Diction in Historical Perspective',
   Quarterly Journal of Speech, vol. 47, no. 3, 1961, pp. 253–61.
82 See W. Russell, 'Ortophony or Voice Culture', *Quarterly Journal of
   Speech*, vol. 47, no. 3, 1961, p. 225.
83 See V. Anderson, 'A Modern View of Voice and Diction', *Quarterly
   Journal of Speech*, vol. 39, no. 1, 1953, pp. 25–32.
84 See Proctor, op. cit., pp. 39–42.
85 See Rasmus, op. cit., p. 255.
86 H. Sewall, 'On the Relation of Diaphragmatic and Costal Respiration
   with Particular Reference to Phonation', in Proctor, op. cit., pp. 82ff.
87 See C. T. Simon and F. Keller, 'An Approach to the Problem of Chest
   Resonance', *Quarterly Journal of Speech*, vol. 13, 1927, p. 432.
88 See J. Grotowski, *Towards a Poor Theatre*, pp. 147ff.
89 Proctor, op. cit., p. 117.
90 See C. Van Riper and J. V. Irwin, *Voice and Articulation*, pp. 296ff.
91 Ibid., pp. 297ff.
92 A. W. Mills, 'Some Contributions of Voice Science to Voice
   Training', *Quarterly Journal of Speech*, vol. 36, no. 3, 1959, p. 380.
93 V. S. Anderson, *Training the Speaking Voice*, pp. 66ff.
94 In an article by K. Parker entitled 'Goodbye, Voice Beautiful', *Plays
   and Players*, July 1985, two of Britain's leading voice teachers, Cicely
   Berry from the Royal Shakespeare Company and Patsy Rodenberg
   from the Guildhall School of Drama, discuss the fact that the voice
   beautiful ideal disappeared in the British theatre when it was found to
   be inadequate for the new wave of young playwrights who emerged
   after John Osborne's *Look Back in Anger*, and it became more
   important to encourage *what* was being said rather than *how* it was
   said. As a result they changed their training methods.
95 Anderson, 'A Modern View of Voice and Diction', op. cit.,
   p. 28.
96 F. S. Brodnitz, 'The Holistic Study of the Voice', *Quarterly Journal of
   Speech*, vol. 48, no. 3, 1960, p. 283.

97 C. Scott, quoted in B. Joseph, *The Tragic Actor. A Survey of Tragic Acting in England from Burbage and Alleyn to Forbes-Robertson*, pp.370ff.
98 H. Cain, quoted in Bram Stoker, *Personal Reminiscences of Henry Irving*, vol. II, pp. 116ff.
99 H. Irving, Lecture delivered at Harvard University, quoted in *Actors on Acting*, ed. T. Cole and H. Chinoy, p. 359.
100 Joseph, op. cit., pp. 582ff.
101 Ibid., p. 386.
102 Ibid., pp. 390ff.
103 Barnes, quoted in Joseph, op. cit., p. 391.
104 P. Brook, quoted in Cole and Chinoy, op. cit., p. 397.
105 See L. Olivier, *On Acting*, p. 44.
106 J. Agate, quoted in G. Brandreth, *John Gielgud. A Celebration*, p. 64.
107 Olivier, op. cit., p. 45.
108 P. Brook, quoted in Cole and Chinoy, op. cit., p. 424.
109 See J. C. Trewin, *Paul Scofield*, pp. 77ff.
110 J. Gielgud, quoted in R.L. Sterne, *John Gielgud Directs Richard Burton in 'Hamlet': A Journal of Rehearsals*, p. 158.
111 Ibid., p. 148.
112 H. Novack, quoted in J. L. Gibson, *Ian McKellen. A Biography*, p. 132.
113 I. McKellen, quoted in ibid., p. 24.

3 A SMORGASBORD OF IDEALS

1 See J. Benedetti, *Stanislavski: An Introduction*, ch. 4.
2 Stanislavski, quoted in S. H. Carnicke, 'An Actor Prepares. Rabota akterna nad soboi, Chast.'I: A Comparison of the English with the Russian Stanislavski', *Theatre Journal*, December 1984, p. 483.
3 Actors who were taught by Stanislavski brought with them 'The System' as it was to Stanislavski at that time. This, together with the late publication of *An Actor Prepares* (1936), *Building a Character* (1949) and *Creating a Role* (1961), together with heavy editing and many inconsistencies in the translation of basic terminology from original Russian to English, have contributed to the confusion. For further clarification, the reader is referred to H. Schnitzler's 'Truth and Consequences, or Stanislavski Misinterpreted', *Quarterly Journal of Speech*, vol. 40, April 1954, pp. 481-3.
4 Ibid., pp. 488-9.
5 See S. Moore, *The Stanislavski System: The Professional Training of an Actor: Digested from the teachings of Konstantin S. Stanislavski*, pp. 68-70.
6 K. Stanislavski, *Teatr*, p. 111.
7 See K.S. in a letter to Alexandre Benois. I am grateful to Jean-Norman Benedetti, who first told me this anecdote in a letter dated 25 January 1988. It subsequently appeared in his book *Stanislavski: A Biography*, London, Methuen, 1988, to which the reader is referred (pp. 213ff.).
8 The 'Method' as taught by Lee Strassberg in America is evidently based only on Stanislavski's Emotional Memory Period (after 1906)

before he had fully evolved his Method of Analysis through Physical Actions.

9 K. Stanislavski, quoted in Moore, op.cit., p. 68.
10 See C. Stanislavski, *Building a Character*, trans. E.R. Hapgood, pp. 82–108.
11 Ibid., p. 128.
12 Ibid., pp. 162–3.
13 Ibid., p. 239.
14 Ibid., pp. 240–1.
15 C. Stanislavski, quoted in Benedetti, *Stanislavski: An Introduction*, op. cit., p. 70.
16 Stanislavski, *Building a Character*, op. cit., p. 241.
17 See J.V. Morgan, *Stanislavski's Encounter with Shakespeare: The Evolution of a Method*, p. 79.
18 Gordon Craig, quoted in Morgan, op. cit., p. 128.
19 Ibid., p. 128.
20 C. Stanislavski, quoted in *Creating a Role*, trans. E. R. Hapgood, p. 261.
21 Ibid., p. 267.
22 See E. Bentley, *The Brecht Commentaries*, p. 32.
23 See B. Brecht, *Brecht on Theatre. The Development of an Aesthetic*, p. 213.
24 See B. Brecht, 'A New Technique of Acting' trans. Eric Bentley, *Theatre Arts*, April 1949, and cited in *Actors on Acting*, ed. T. Cole and H.K. Chinoy, pp. 308–11.
25 Following a trip to Moscow in 1935, Brecht came into contact with Viktor Shklovsky's term '*ostranenie*', or making strange, which was part of Russian formalist literary theory. This no doubt can be seen as the meaning behind his translation and later use of the term '*Verfremdung*'.
26 B. Brecht, 'A Short Organum for the Theatre', quoted in *Brecht on Theatre*, op. cit., p. 193.
27 Ibid., p. 117.
28 Ibid., p. 248.
29 Ibid., p. 15.
30 Stanislavski, quoted in *Building a Character*, op. cit., pp. 173–4.
31 Brecht, quoted in *Brecht on Theatre*, op. cit., p. 195.
32 Ibid., p. 116.
33 See Cole and Chinoy, op. cit., pp. 314–16.
34 Brecht, quoted in *Brecht on Theatre*, op. cit., p. 200.
35 Ibid., pp. 201–2.
36 Ibid., p. 224.
37 See J. Willett, *Brecht in Context*, pp. 200–1.
38 A. Artaud, *The Theatre and its Double*, trans. M. C. Richards, pp. 12–13.
39 A. Artaud, 'The Alfred Jarry Theatre', quoted in *Antonin Artaud Collected Works*, vol. 2, pp. 30ff.
40 A. Artaud, 'The Theatre and the Plague', in *The Theatre and its Double*, op. cit., pp. 28ff.
41 Ibid., pp. 49ff.

42 Ibid., p. 46.
43 Artaud, *Collected Works*, vol. 4, p. 103.
44 See C. Innes, *Holy Theatre: Ritual and the Avant Garde*, pp. 64ff.
45 A. Artaud, 'The Conquest of Mexico', in *The Theatre and its Double*, op. cit., p. 128.
46 See A. Artaud, 'The Theatre and Cruelty', in *The Theatre and its Double*, op. cit., pp. 85ff.
47 Ibid., p. 94.
48 Ibid., p. 110.
49 Ibid., p. 94.
50 Ibid., p. 117.
51 See J. Roose-Evans, *Experimental Theatre from Stanislavski to Peter Brook*, pp. 74–90.
52 Innes, op. cit., p. 110.
53 See A. Wolfsohn, 'The Omnitone', *Time Magazine*, 19 March 1956, pp. 47ff.
54 See H. Kretzmer, *Daily Express*, 16 September 1969.
55 Wolfsohn, op. cit.
56 See Roose-Evans, op. cit., pp. 181ff.
57 See Wolfsohn, op. cit.
58 E. Pardo, 'The Work of the Roy Hart Theatre', *Project Voice*, November 1982, p. 15.
59 See O. Cook, Programme notes to 'Not So Much a Concert – More a Way of Voice', Stockholm City Theatre, December 1985.
60 O. Cook, Interview, 16 October 1985.
61 O. Cook, Voice demonstration, Stockholm University, Theatre Department, October 1985.
62 The Alexander technique, so called after its founder F.M. Alexander (1869–1955), is a systematic approach to voice training where the speaker learns 'not to do', that is, he learns to free the tensions which occur in his body during the speech act.
63 Cook, Interview, op. cit.
64 Pardo, op. cit., p. 16.
65 E. Pardo, quoted in A. Carpelan, 'Roy Hart Theatre: En chockartad upplevelse', *Scen och Salong*, no. 10–11, pp. 21–3.
66 S. Osten, director of the Unga Klara Teater in Stockholm, summed up the reactions of the audience to this production as those of 'fear based on social limitations'; quoted in Carpelan, op. cit., p. 23.
67 *Svenska Dagbladet*, July 1982.
68 M. Di Caro, 'Poesis of the Roy Hart. What Images, What Voices', *Giornale di Sicilia*, 26 April 1985.
69 Y.P., *Midi Libre*, 19 April 1985.
70 See T. Burzyński and Z. Osiński, *Grotowski's Laboratory*, pp. 13–21.
71 See J. Grotowski, 'He Wasn't Entirely Himself', in *Towards a Poor Theatre*, pp. 85–93.
72 Ibid., p. 115.
73 See figures 64 and 65 in ibid., p. 147.
74 J. Grotowski, quoted by J. Kumiega in *The Theatre of Grotowski*, p. 12.

75 Grotowski, *Towards a Poor Theatre*, op. cit., pp. 58ff.
76 A. Korewa, quoted in Kumiega, op. cit., p. 20.
77 T. Kudlinski, quoted in ibid., p. 24.
78 See Burzyński and Osiński, op. cit., pp. 16–17.
79 Ibid., p. 19.
80 Ibid., pp. 23ff.
81 Ibid., pp. 35–7.
82 E. Barba, quoted in Kumiega, op. cit., pp. 118–19.
83 Grotowski, *Towards a Poor Theatre*, op. cit., p. 151.
84 L. Flaszen, quoted in Kumiega, op. cit., p. 64.
85 A. Seymour, quoted in ibid., p. 69.
86 ibid., p. 77.
87 P. Feldman, 'On Grotowski', *Drama Review*, T46, vol. 14, no. 2, 1970, pp. 193ff.
88 J. Grotowski, quoted in Burzyński and Osiński, op. cit., p. 55.
89 J. Grotowski, quoted in *Drama Review*, T46, vol. 14, no. 2, p. 193.
90 J. Grotowski, quoted in Kumiega, op. cit., p. 90.
91 Ibid., p. 92.
92 P. Brook, quoted in Innes, op. cit., p. 129.
93 See P. Brook, *The Shifting Point: Theatre, Film, Opera 1946–1987*.
94 P. Brook, quoted in Cole and Chinoy, op. cit., pp. 422–9.
95 See P. Brook, *The Empty Space*, pp. 115ff.
96 Ibid., pp. 48–9.
97 Innes, op. cit., p. 185.
98 See Cole and Chinoy, op. cit., p. 429.
99 P. Brook, quoted in C. Berry, *Voice and the Actor*, p. 3.
100 See D. Selbourne, *The Making of 'A Midsummer Night's Dream': An Eyewitness Account of Peter Brook's Production from First Rehearsal to First Night*, pp. 33ff.
101 See S. Beauman, *The Royal Shakespeare Company – A History of Ten Decades*, pp. 268ff.
102 See Brook, op. cit., p. 122.
103 Ibid., p. 55.
104 See Innes, op. cit., p. 134.
105 Ibid., p. 135.
106 P. Brook, *Playscript 9 US: The Book of the Royal Shakespeare Theatre Production*.
107 Brook, *The Shifting Point*, op. cit., p. 108.
108 Ibid.
109 P. Brook's film of *The Tempest*, 1968.
110 P. Brook, quoted in Selbourne, op. cit., p. 23.
111 R. Peaslee, quoted in Roose-Evans, op. cit., p. 102.
112 See Innes, op. cit., pp. 139–40.
113 See J. Lahr, 'Knowing What to Celebrate', *Plays and Players*, March 1976, pp. 17–19.
114 See M. Shevtsova, 'Peter Brook Adapts the Tragedy of Carmen', *Theatre International*, vol. 2, no. 10, 1983, pp. 38–55.
115 See Brook, *The Shifting Point*, op. cit., p. 163.

116 Ibid., p. 85.
117 Ibid., p. 43.

4 DIRECTORIAL VISIONS

1 I. Bergman, quoted in L.-L. Marker and F.J. Marker, *Ingmar Bergman: Four Decades in the Theatre*, Directors in Perspective Series, p. 6.
2 I. Bergman, quoted by H. Sjögren, 'Ingmar Bergmans teater – rörelser i rummet', in *Perspektiv på teater ur svensk regi- och iscensättningshistoria*, Documents and Studies collected by U. Gran and U.-B. Laggeroth, pp. 83ff.
3 Ibid., p. 139.
4 I. Bergman, quoted in Marker and Marker, op. cit., p. 97.
5 Ibid., p. 97.
6 H. Grevenius, quoted in ibid., p. 34.
7 'Göteborgs Handels- och Sjöfartstidning', quoted in Marker and Marker, op. cit., p. 36.
8 Grevenius, op. cit., p. 36.
9 Bergman, quoted in Marker and Marker, op. cit., p. 37.
10 See J. Martin, 'Eloquence is Action: A Study of Form and Text's Influence on the Vocal Delivery Style of Shakespeare in Sweden 1934–1985', doctoral dissertation, University of Stockholm, 1987.
11 See H. Sjögren, *Stage and Society in Sweden*, pp. 23–41.
12 Bergman, quoted in ibid., p. 61.
13 E. Törnquist, quoted in Marker and Marker, op. cit., p. 73.
14 See Martin, op. cit.
15 L. Zern. 'Ingen förstår Shakespeare', *Dagens Nyheter*, 13 January 1985.
16 T. Baeckström, *Göteborgs Handels-och Sjöfartstidning*.
17 B. Jahnsson, *Aftonbladet*, 5 May 1979.
18 See H. Granville-Barker, *Prefaces to Shakespeare*, vols 1 and 2.
19 I. Bergman, Preface to *Kung Lear*.
20 See M. Lagercrantz, 'Dramat i Smyckesskrinet – Kung Lear på Dramaten 1984', unpublished thesis, University of Stockholm, 1985, pp. 18–29.
21 See Martin, op. cit., pp. 106–8.
22 I. Björkstén, 'Fenomenalt bildskapande och teatermagi', *Svenska Dagbladet*, 10 March 1984, and B. Jahnsson, 'Stor tragedi med matt slut', *Dagens Nyheter*, 10 March 1984.
23 Zern, op. cit.
24 Bergman, Preface to *Kung Lear*, op. cit.
25 See I. Bergman, *Svenska Dagbladet*, 12 December 1986.
26 I. Bergman, *Arbetet*, 12 December 1986.
27 See I. Björkstén, *Svenska Dagbladet*, 21 December 1986.
28 T. Ellefsen, *Dagens Nyheter*, 21 December 1986.
29 L. Zern, *Expressen*, 21 December 1986.
30 Björkstén, op. cit. (see n. 27).
31 See M. and U. Sörenson, *Teater i Paris*, pp. 8–9.

32 See A. Mnouchkine, 'Le Théâtre ou la vie', *Fruits: en plein soleil,* no. 2/3, June 1984, pp. 202–23.
33 See S. Moscoso, 'Notes de répétitions: Le Théâtre du Soleil Shakespeare 2 partie', *Double Page,* no. 32, 1984.
34 See I. Glanzelius, 'Théâtre du Soleil dödförklaras ständigt', *Dagens Nyheter,* 15 May 1983.
35 See G. Wirén, 'Åter till Shakespeare', *Dagens Nyheter,* 1 April 1984.
36 Sörenson, op. cit., pp. 12–13.
37 Shakespeare, *The Tragedy of King Richard II,* act II, scene i.
38 Moscoso, op. cit.
39 Ibid.
40 Sörenson, op. cit., pp. 12–13.
41 Ibid., p. 16.
42 G. Sandier, *Lettres/Arts,* 19 December 1981.
43 See Wirén, op. cit.
44 Moscoso, op. cit.
45 Sörenson, op. cit.
46 Ibid.
47 Ibid., pp. 8–9.
48 Moscoso, op. cit.
49 See Sörenson, op. cit.
50 See Wirén, op. cit.
51 See Moscoso, op. cit.
52 J-J. Lemêtre, 'Mesure pour mesure', *Fruits: en plein soleil,* no. 2/3, June, 1984, pp. 188–9.
53 C. Lee, quoted in *Fruits: en plein soleil,* no. 2/3, June, 1983, p. 198.
54 G. Bigot, 'Ourselves We Do Not Owe', in *Fruits: en plein soleil,* no. 2/3, June, 1984, p. 124.
55 See Mnouchkine, op. cit., p. 208.
56 Wirén, op. cit.
57 M. Patterson, *Peter Stein: Germany's Leading Theatre Director,* pp. 1–2.
58 Ibid., p. 4.
59 Ibid., p. 8.
60 P. Stein, quoted by P. Lackner, 'Stein's Path to Shakespeare', *Drama Review,* T74, vol. 21, no. 2, 1977, pp. 80–102.
61 I. Nagel, *Tasso-Regiebuch,* pp. 184–5; quoted in Patterson, op. cit., pp. 23–4.
62 P. Stein, quoted by B. Dort, *Drama Review,* T74, vol. 21, no. 2, pp. 91–2.
63 P. Stein, quoted in Patterson, op. cit., p. 72.
64 See V. Canaris, *Theater Heute,* no. 13, 1971, p. 32; quoted in Patterson, op. cit., p. 75.
65 Stein, quoted in Patterson, op. cit., p. 108.
66 See G. Jäger, *Theater Heute,* no. 7, 1974; quoted in Patterson, op. cit., p. 109.
67 Lackner, op. cit., pp. 79–102.
68 Patterson, op. cit., p. 130.
69 B. Hinrichs, *Die Zeit,* 31 December 1976; quoted in Patterson, op. cit.

70 D. Z. Mairowitz, 'As They Like It', *Plays and Players*, no. 290, 1977, p. 18.

71 P. Stein, Protocol no. 450. quoted in Patterson, op. cit., p. 142.

72 J. Warren, Review of *The Hairy Ape*, *Plays and Players*, no. 406, July 1987, pp. 19–20.

73 See B. Skawonius, 'Generationen från 1968 har satt sig på de unga', *Dagens Nyheter*, 21 March 1982.

74 R. Lysell, 'Scenisk opera utan musik: Peter Stein's Fedra', *Nya Teatertidningen*, no. 41, 1988.

75 F.X. Kroetz, Play text *Nicht Fish Nicht Fleish*, Swedish trans. U. Olsson and H. Grevenius, *Varken fågel eller fisk*, Royal Dramatic Theatre, Stockholm, 1981.

76 L. Zern, 'Teater i Europa', *Nya teatertidningen*, op. cit., pp. 22–7.

5 THE POSTMODERN APPROACH

1 See J. Martin and W. Sauter, 'Postmodernism in the Theatre', Stockholm, Nordic Theatre Studies, Munksgaard (in press).

2 J. Chaikin, quoted in J. Roose-Evans, *Experimental Theatre from Stanislavski to Peter Brook*, pp. 106ff.

3 J. Chaikin, quoted in J. Lahr, *Acting out America: Essays on Modern Theatre*, pp. 122–35.

4 R. Pasolli, *A Book on the Open Theatre*, pp. 61–9.

5 J. Chaikin, quoted in Lahr, op. cit., pp. 133–4.

6 Ibid.

7 Pasolli, op. cit., p. 80.

8 J. Grotowski, quoted in Pasolli, op. cit., p. 115.

9 Ibid., p. 124.

10 J.C. van Itallie, quoted in Lahr, op. cit., p. 128.

11 Pasolli, op. cit., pp.125ff.

12 J. Chaikin, quoted in Lahr, op. cit., p. 130.

13 Pasolli, op. cit., p. 126.

14 J. Chaikin, quoted in Roose-Evans, op. cit., pp. 128–9.

15 See C. Innes, *Holy Theatre. Ritual and the Avant Garde*, p. 181.

16 Ibid., p. 182.

17 See R. Schechner, *The End of Humanism: Writings on Performance*, p. 98.

18 See Innes, op. cit., p. 57.

19 R. Schechner, 'Actuals: Primitive Ritual and Performance Theory, an Anthropological Approach to Modern Experimental Theatre', *Theatre Quarterly*, vol. 1, no. 2, 1971, p. 61.

20 See R. Schechner, 'Post Proscenium', in *American Theatre 1969–70*, New York, International Theatre Institute of the USA, 1970, p. 29.

21 Ibid., p. 24.

22 Innes, op. cit., p. 181.

23 Lahr, op. cit., pp. 24–5.

24 See A. Sainer, *The Radical Theatre Notebook*, p. 27.

25 Schechner, *American Theatre*, op. cit., pp. 27ff.

26 See Schechner, 'Actuals', op. cit., p. 63.

24 *Going on Stage*, op. cit., p. 10.
25 See T. Lubbock, 'A Life in the Day of Rose Bruford College of Speech and Drama', *Plays and Players*, no. 368, May 1984. pp. 8–11.
26 *The Rose Bruford College of Speech and Drama, Prospectus*, 1984.
27 Ibid., pp. 3–4.
28 See Lubbock, May 1984, op. cit., p. 9.
29 See *Rose Bruford College, Prospectus*, op. cit., p. 4.
30 See Rea, op. cit., pp. 64–7.
31 Ibid., p. 62.
32 See T. Lubbock, 'A Life in the Day of East 15 Acting School', *Plays and Players*, no. 370, July 1984, pp. 18–21.
33 Rea, op. cit., p. 61.
34 See J. Clark, 'The Work of the National Institute of Dramatic Art (Australia) in Relation to Canadian, British and some European Theatre Schools', unpublished report, 1972, p. 79.
35 Rea, op. cit., p. 21.
36 *East 15 Acting School, Prospectus*, 1984.
37 Ibid.
38 See Rea, op. cit., p. 62.
39 C. Fettes, quoted in Rea, op. cit., p. 63.
40 See *Going on Stage*, op. cit., p. 83.
41 Rea, op. cit., p. 62.
42 Ibid., p. 63.
43 *Drama Centre London, Prospectus*, 1983/4, p. 12.
44 Ibid., p. 12.
45 *Going on Stage*, op. cit., pp. 48–9.
46 See C. Matthew, 'Tuning the Instruments: A Theatregoer Asks: Are Drama Schools Really Necessary?', in *Theatre 73*, S. Morley (ed.), pp. 140–53.
47 C. Berry, quoted by K. Parker, 'Goodbye, Voice Beautiful', *Plays and Players*, no. 382, July 1985, pp. 32–3.
48 The reader is referred to chapter 2, in the section entitled 'A structural approach to the text', where John Barton's approach is explained in detail.
49 C. Berry, quoted in Parker, op. cit., p. 33.
50 C. Berry, *Voice and the Actor*, p. 132.
51 C. Berry, *The Actor and his Text*, p. 22.
52 Ibid., p. 11.
53 The reader is referred to chapter 1, where the Renaissance practice of *sententia* is discussed more fully.
54 Berry, *The Actor and His Text*, op. cit., p. 82.
55 Berry, *Voice and the Actor*, op. cit., p. 16.
56 Ibid., p. 121.
57 Ibid., p. 135.
58 C. Berry, *The King Lear Project*, pp. 6–7.
59 See K. Linklater, *Freeing the Natural Voice*, pp. 209ff.
60 Ibid., p. 1.
61 Ibid., p. 80.
62 Ibid., p. 129.

63 Ibid., p. 172.
64 Ibid., p. 175.
65 Ibid., p. 184.
66 Ibid., p. 186.
67 Ibid., p. 191.
68 G. Sion, *Synthesis of Five International Symposia on the Professional Training of the Actor*, trans. U. Crowley, ITI Paris, p. 5.
69 Ibid., pp. 12–18.
70 Ibid., pp. 25–30.
71 J. Martin, *Training Theatre Teachers*, ITI Stockholm, pp. 7–11.
72 See *Going on Stage*, p. 49.
73 See J. Martin, 'Eloquence is Action: A Study of Form and Text's Influence on the Vocal Delivery Style of Shakespeare in Sweden 1934–1985', doctoral dissertation, University of Stockholm, 1987.
74 R. Jakobson, quoted in K. Elam, *The Semiotics of Theatre and Drama*, pp. 82–3.
75 M. Yemen Dzakis conducted her own workshop at the Orion Teater in Stockholm, 6 February 1989, where she demonstrated her manner of working on the voice and explained her reasons for so doing. This was further clarified by a performance of *The Persians*, which her group, Io, gave at this theatre.
76 Yemen Dzakis workshop, Stockholm, 6 February 1989.
77 L. Nyberg, 'The Shakespearean Ideal: Shakespeare Production and the Modern Theatre in Britain', doctoral dissertation, University of Uppsala, 1988, p. 125.
78 P. Hall, 'Theatre – A Discussion', recorded by Argo, London, 1962.
79 K. Tynan, 'Theatre – A Discussion', op. cit.
80 J. Dench and I. McKellen, interviewed in *Shakespeare's teater* (L22), National Archive of Recorded Sound and Moving Images (ALB), Stockholm.

BIBLIOGRAPHY

Adler, T. P., 'The Wesker Trilogy Revisited: Games to Compensate for the Inadequacy of Words', *Quarterly Journal of Speech*, vol. 65, no. 4, 1979.

Anderson, V., 'A Modern View of Voice and Diction', *Quarterly Journal of Speech*, vol. 39, no. 1, 1953.

Anderson, V. S., *Training the Speaking Voice*, 3rd edn, New York, Oxford University Press, 1977.

Aristotle, 'Aristotle's *Poetics* and *Rhetoric*', in T. A. Moxon and T. Twining (eds), *Essays in Classical Criticism*, London, Dent, 1953.

Artaud, A., *The Theatre and its Double*, trans. M.C. Richards, New York, Grove Press, 1958.

Artaud, A., 'The Alfred Jarry Theatre', in Antonin Artaud, *Collected Works*, vols. 2 and 4, London, Caldar and Boyars, 1974.

Aspelin, K. and Lundberg, B. A. (eds), *Form och Struktur*, Stockholm, Pan/Nordstedts, 1971.

Baeckström, T., *Göteborgs Handels- och Sjöfartstidning*, 21 March 1975.

Barnett, D., 'The Performance Practice of Acting: The 18th Century', *Theatre Research International*, vol. ii, no. 3, 1977; vol. iii no. 1, 1977; vol. iii, no. 2, 1978.

Barthes, R., *On Racine (Sur Racine)*, trans. R. Howard, New York, Hill and Wang, 1964.

Barthes, R., 'Den retoriska analysen', in K. Aspelin and B.A. Lundberg (eds), *Form och Struktur*, Stockholm, Pan/Nordstedts, 1971.

Barton, J., *Playing Shakespeare*, London, Methuen, 1984.

Beauman, S., *The Royal Shakespeare Company – A History of Ten Decades*, Oxford, Oxford University Press, 1982.

Benedetti, J., *Stanislavski: An Introduction*, New York, Theatre Arts Books, 1982.

Benedetti, J., *Stanislavski: A Biography*, London, Methuen, 1988.

Bentley, E., *The Brecht Commentaries*, London, Methuen, 1981.

Bergman, I., Preface to W. Shakespeare's *Kung Lear (King Lear)*, trans. B. G. Hallquist, Stockholm, Kungliga Dramatiska Teatern and Ordfronts, 1984.

Bergman, I., *Arbetet*, 12 December 1986.

Bergman, I., *Svenska Dagbladet*, 12 December 1986.

Berry, C., *Voice and the Actor*, London, Harrap, 1973.

Berry, C., *The Actor and his Text*, London, Harrap, 1987.

Berry, C., *The King Lear Project*, Royal Shakespeare Company, Education Department, Stratford-upon-Avon, 1988.

Bigot, G., 'Ourselves We Do Not Owe', *Fruits: en plein soleil*, no. 2/3, June, Paris, 1984.

Björkstén, I., 'Fenomenalt bildskapande och teatermagi', *Svenska Dagbladet*, 10 March 1984.

Björkstén, I., *Svenska Dagbladet*, 21 December 1986.

Bogatyrev, P., 'Semiotics in the Folk Theatre' (1938), trans. B. Kochis, in L. Matejka and I. Titunik (eds), *Semiotics of Art: Prague School Contributions*, Cambridge, Mass., MIT Press, 1976.

Bogatyrev, P., 'Forms and Functions of Folk Theatre' (1940), in L. Matejka and I. Titunik (eds), *Semiotics of Art: Prague School Contributions*, Cambridge, Mass., MIT Press, 1976.

Bosmajian, H.A., 'The Nazi Speaker's Rhetoric', *Quarterly Journal of Speech*, vol. 46, no. 4, 1960.

Brandreth, G., *John Gielgud. A Celebration*, London, Pavilion, 1984.

Brecht, B., 'A New Technique of Acting', in T. Cole and H.K. Chinoy (eds), *Actors on Acting*, New York, Crown, 1970.

Brecht, B., *Brecht on Theatre: The Development of an Aesthetic*, J. Willett (trans. and ed.), London, Eyre Methuen, 1979.

Brecht, B., 'A Short Organum for the Theatre', in J. Willett (trans. and ed.), *Brecht on Theatre: The Development of an Aesthetic*, London, Eyre Methuen, 1979.

Brecht, S., *The Theatre of Visions: Robert Wilson*, Frankfurt-am-Main, Suhrkamp, 1978.

Brockett, O. C., *History of the Theatre*, Boston, Allyn and Bacon, 1982.

Brodnitz, F. S., 'The Holistic Study of the Voice', *Quarterly Journal of Speech*, vol. 48, no. 3, 1960.

Brook, P., *Playscript 9 US: The Book of the Royal Shakespeare Theatre Production*, London, Caldar and Boyars, 1968.

Brook, P., *The Empty Space*, London, Penguin, 1968.

Brook, P., *The Shifting Point: Theatre, Film, Opera 1946–1987*, New York, Harper and Row, 1987.

Browne, L., 'On Photography of the Larynx and Soft Palate', in D. F. Proctor, *Breathing, Speech and Song*, Vienna, Springer, 1980.

Bryant, D. C. 'Rhetoric: Its Functions and its Scope', *Quarterly Journal of Speech*, vol. 39, no. 4, 1953.

Bullwer, J., *Chirologia: Or the Natural Language of the Hand . . . Whereunto is added Chironomia: Or, the Art of Manualle Rhetoricke*, London, 1644.

Burke, K., *Rhetoric of Motives*, New York, Prentice Hall, 1950.

Burklund, C. E., 'Melody in Verse', *Quarterly Journal of Speech*, vol. 39, no. 1, 1953.

Burzyński, T. and Osiński, Z., *Grotowski's Laboratory*, Warsaw, Interpress, 1979.

Campbell, P. N., 'The Role of Language in the Theatre', *Quarterly Journal of Speech*, vol. 68, no. 4, 1982.

Canaris, V., *Theater Heute*, no. 13, 1971.

Capps, E., Page, T. E. and Rouse, W. H. D. (eds), *The Institutio Oratoria*, trans. H.E. Butler, London, Heinemann, 1922.

Carlson, M., 'Psychic Polyphony', *Journal of Dramatic Theory and Criticism*, New York, Fall 1986.

Carlson, M., *Theories of the Theatre: A Historical and Critical Survey from the Greeks to the Present*, New York, Cornell University Press, 1986

Carnicke, S. H., 'An Actor Prepares. Rabota akterna nad soboi, Chast.' I: A Comparison of the English with the Russian Stanislavski', *Theatre Journal*, December 1984.

Carpelan, A., 'Roy Hart Theatre: En chockartad upplevelse', *Scen och Salong*, no. 10–11, Stockholm, 1982.

Central School of Speech and Drama, Prospectus, 1984.

Cibber, T., 'Two Dissertations on the Theatres' (1756), in C. Price, *Theatre in the Age of Garrick*, Oxford, Blackwell, 1973.

Cicero, *De Oratore*, in G. Kennedy, *The Art of Rhetoric in the Roman World 300BC–AD300*, New Jersey, Princeton University Press, 1972.

Clark, J., 'The Work of the National Institute of Dramatic Art (Australia) in Relation to Canadian, British and some European Theatre Schools', unpublished report, Sydney, 1972.

Clifford Turner, J., *Voice and Speech in the Theatre*, London, Pitman, 1950.

Cole, T. and Chinoy, H. K. (eds), *Actors on Acting*, New York, Crown, 1970.

Cook, O., Programme notes to 'Not So Much a Concert – More a Way of Voice', Stockholm City Theatre, December 1985.

Culler, J., *Structuralist Poetics: Structuralism, Linguistics and the Study of Literature*, London, Routledge and Kegan Paul, 1975.

Davy, K., 'Foreman's PAIN(T) and Vertical Mobility', *Drama Review*, T62, vol. 18, no. 1974.

Deák, F., 'The Byrd Hoffman School of Byrds', *Drama Review*, T62, vol. 18, no. 2, 1974.

Deák, F., 'Structuralism in Theatre: The Prague School Contribution', *Drama Review*, T72, vol. 20, no. 4, 1976.

Delsarte, F., *Delsarte System of Oratory: Containing all the Literary Remains of Francois Delsarte* (Given in his own Words), trans. A.L. Alger, New York, Edgar S. Werner, 1893.

Di Caro, M., 'Poesis of the Roy Hart: What Images, What Voices', *Giornale di Sicilia*, 26 April 1985.

Diderot, D., *Paradoxe sur le comédien*, in P. Vernière, *Oeuvres estétiques*, Paris, Classiques Garnier (no publication date).

Drama Centre, London, Prospectus, 1983/4.

East 15 Acting School, Prospectus, 1984.

Eco, U., *A Theory of Semiotics*, Bloomington, Indiana University Press, 1976.

Eco, U., 'Semiotics of Theatrical Performance', *Drama Review*, T21, vol. 30, no. 1, 1977.

Edberg, U. B., *Svenska Dagbladet*, 6 September 1987.

Elam, K., *The Semiotics of Theatre and Drama*, London, Methuen, 1980.

Ellefsen, T., *Dagens Nyheter*, 21 December 1986.

Erbe, B., *En Undersøgelse af Byzantinsk Teater*, Oslo, Norwegian University Press, 1973.

Erlich, V., *Russian Formalism: History–Doctrine*, revised edn, The Hague, Mouton,1965.

Esslin, M., *The Theatre of the Absurd*, 3rd edn, London, Pelican, 1968.

Feldman, P., 'On Grotowski', *Drama Review*, T46, vol. 14, no. 2, 1970.

Fischer-Lichte, E., *Semiotik des Teaters. Das System der theatralischen Zeichen*, vol. 1, Tübingen, Gunter Narr and Francke, 1983.

Foreman, R., 'Ontological-Hysterical Manifesto II', *Drama Review*, T63, vol. 18, no. 3, 1974.

Foreman, R., Programme notes to Teater Aurora's *Kärlek och vetenskap*, Stockholm, 1987.

France, P., *Rhetoric and Truth in France from Descartes to Diderot*, Oxford, Clarendon Press, 1972.

Frank, G., *The Medieval French Drama*, London, Oxford University Press, 1954.

French, T. R., 'A Photographic Study of the Singing Voice', in D.F. Proctor, *Breathing, Speech and Song*, Vienna, Springer, 1980.

Garcia, M., 'Observations on Human Voice', in D.F. Proctor, *Breathing, Speech and Song*, Vienna, Springer, 1980.

Gibson, J. L., *Ian McKellen: A Biography*, London, Weidenfeld and Nicolson, 1986.

Girrard, G., Quellet, R. and Rigault, C., *L'Univers du théâtre*, Paris, Presses Universitaires de France, 1978.

Glanzelius, I., 'Théâtre du Soleil dödförklaras ständigt', *Dagens Nyheter*, 15 May 1983.

Going on Stage: A Report to the Calouste Gulbenkian Foundation on Professional Training for Drama, Kent, Bishop and Sons, 1975.

Gran, U., and Laggerroth, U.-B., *Perspektiv på teater: ur Svensk regi- och iscensättningshistoria*, Uddevalla, Rabén and Sjögren, 1971.

Granville-Barker, H., *Prefaces to Shakespeare*, vols 1 and 2, London, Batsford, 1958.

Grotowski, J., *Towards a Poor Theatre*, London, Methuen, 1975.

Guildhall School of Music and Drama (The), Prospectus, 1985/6.

Hawkes, T., *Structuralism and Semiotics*, London, Methuen, 1986.

Helbo, A., 'Le Code théâtral', in A. Helbo (ed.), *Sémiologie de la représentation*, Brussels, Editions Complexe, 1975.

Heywood, T., *An Apology for Actors* (1612), in *Early Treatises on the Stage*, London, Shakespeare Society, 1853.

Hill, J., *The Actor: A Treatise on the Art of Playing*, London, 1750.

Hilton, J., *Performance* (New Directions in Theatre Series), London, Macmillan, 1987.

Hinrichs, B., *Die Zeit*, 31 December 1976.

Honzl, J., 'Dynamics of Sign in the Theatre' (1943), in L. Matejka and I. Titunik (eds), *Semiotics of Art: Prague School Contributions*, Cambridge, Mass., MIT Press, 1976.

Honzl, J., 'The Hierarchy of Dramatic Devices' (1940), in L. Matejka and I. Titunik (eds), *Semiotics of Art: Prague School Contributions*, Cambridge, Mass., Harvard University Press, 1976.

Innes, C., *Holy Theatre: Ritual and the Avant Garde*, Cambridge, Cambridge University Press, 1981.

Irving, H., Lecture delivered at Harvard University, in T. Cole and H. Chinoy (eds), *Actors on Acting*, New York, Crown, 1970.

Jahnsson, B., *Aftonbladet*, 5 May 1979.

Jahnsson, B., 'Stor tragedi med matt slut', *Dagens Nyheter*, 10 March 1984.

Jakobson, R., 'Closing Statement: Linguistics and Poetics', in T.A. Sebeok (ed.), *Style in Language*, Cambridge, Mass., MIT Press, 1960.

Jakobson, R., 'Fundamentals of Language' (1956), in T. Hawkes, *Structuralism and Semiotics*, London, Methuen, 1986.

Jakobson, R. and Jones, L. J., *Shakespeare's Verbal Art in Th'Experience of Spirit*, The Hague, Mouton, 1970.

Johannesson, K., *Svensk retorik från Stockholms blodbad till Almedalen*, Malmö, Nordstedt, 1983.

Joseph, B., *Elizabethan Acting*, London, Oxford English Monographs, 1951.

Joseph, B., *The Tragic Actor: A Survey of Tragic Acting in England from Burbage and Alleyn to Forbes-Robertson*, London, Routledge and Kegan Paul, 1959.

Jäger, G., *Theater Heute*, no. 7, 1974.

Kennedy, G., *The Art of Persuasion in Greece*, New Jersey, Princeton University Press, 1963.

Kennedy, G., *The Art of Rhetoric in the Roman World 300BC–AD300*, New Jersey, Princeton University Press, 1972.

Kennedy, G., *Classical Rhetoric and its Christian and Secular Tradition from Ancient to Modern Times*, London, Croom Helm, 1980.

Kernodle, G.R., 'Basic Problems in Reading Shakespeare', *Quarterly Journal of Speech*, vol. 35, no. 1, 1949.

King Lear Project (The), Royal Shakespeare Company, Education Department, Stratford upon Avon, 1988.

Kirby, M., 'Ontological-Hysteric Theatre', *Drama Review*, T58, vol. 17, no. 2, 1973.

Kowzan, T., 'The Sign in the Theatre', *Diogenes*, no. 61, 1968.

Kretzmer, H., *Daily Express*, 16 September 1968.

Kroetz, F.X., *Nicht Fisch Nicht Fleish*, Swedish trans. U. Olsson and H. Grevenius, *Varken fågel eller fisk*, Royal Dramatic Theatre, Stockholm, 1981.

Kumiega, J., *The Theatre of Grotowski*, London, Methuen, 1985.

Lackner, P., 'Stein's Path to Shakespeare', *Drama Review*, T74, vol. 21, no. 2, 1977.

Lagercrantz, M., 'Dramat i Smyckesskrinet – Kung Lear på Dramaten 1984', unpublished thesis, University of Stockholm, 1985.

Lahr, J., *Acting Out America: Essays on Modern Theatre*, Harmondsworth, Pelican, 1972.

Lahr, J., 'Knowing What to Celebrate', *Plays and Players*, no. 269, March 1976.

Langton, B., 'Journey to Ka Mountain', *Drama Review*, T58, vol. 17, no. 2, 1973.

Lee, C., *Fruits: en plein soleil*, no. 2/3, June, 1983.

Le Faucheur, *Traité de l'action de l'orateur ou de la prononciation et du geste par M. Conrat*, Paris, 1657.

Lemêtre, J-J., 'Mesure pour mesure', *Fruits: en plein soleil*, no. 2/3, June, 1984.

Linklater, K., *Freeing the Natural Voice*, New York, Drama Book Specialists, 1976.

Long, B.W. and Hopkins, M.F., *Performing Literature – An Introduction to Oral Interpretation*, New York, Prentice-Hall, 1982.

Lubbock, T., 'A Life in the Day of R.A.D.A.', *Plays and Players*, no. 367, April 1984.

Lubbock, T., 'A Life in the Day of Rose Bruford College of Speech and Drama', *Plays and Players*, no. 368, May 1984.

Lubbock, T, 'A Life in the Day of Central School of Speech and Drama', *Plays and Players*, no. 369, June 1984.

Lubbock, T., 'A Life in the Day of East 15 Acting School', *Plays and Players*, no. 370, July 1984.

Lysell, R., 'Scenisk opera utan musik: Peter Stein's Fedra', *Nya teatertidningen*, no. 41, 1988.

Mairowitz, D.Z., 'As They Like It', *Plays and Players*, no. 290, December 1977.

Marker, L.L. and Marker, F.J., *Ingmar Bergman: Four Decades in the Theatre* (Directors in Perspective Series), Cambridge, Cambridge University Press, 1982.

Martin, J., *Training Theatre Teachers*, International Seminar in Stockholm, 7–11 January 1986, Stockholm, International Theatre Institute.

Martin, J., 'Eloquence is Action: A Study of Form and Text's Influence on the Vocal Delivery Style of Shakespeare in Sweden 1934–1985', doctoral dissertation, University of Stockholm, 1987.

Martin, J. and Sauter, W., 'Postmodernism in the Theatre', paper given at the International Symposium, *Beyond New Criticism and Nouvelle Critique: Trends in Cultural Theory and Practice*, Stockholm, organized by the Department of English, University of Stockholm 1988; Nordic Theatre Studies, Munksgaard (in press).

Matejka, L. and Titunik, I. (eds), *Semiotics of Art: Prague School Contributions*, Cambridge. Mass., MIT Press, 1976.

Matthew, C., 'Tuning the Instruments. A Theatregoer Asks: Are Drama Schools Really Necessary?', in S. Morley (ed.), *Theatre 73*, London, Hutchinson, 1973.

Mellers, W., 'Beyond the Sensual Speech', *Project Voice*, Cardiff Laboratory Theatre, November, 1982.

Mills, A. W., 'Some Contributions of Voice Science to Voice Training', *Quarterly Journal of Speech*, vol. 36, no. 3, 1959.

Mnouchkine, A., 'Le Théâtre ou la vie', *Fruits: en plein soleil*, no. 2/3, June 1984.

Moore, S., *The Stanislavski System: The Professional Training of an Actor: Digested from the Teachings of Konstantin S. Stanislavski*, New York, Penguin, 1976.

Morgan, J. V., *Stanislavski's Encounter with Shakespeare: The Evolution of a Method*, Michigan, UMI Research Press Theatre and Dramatic Studies no. 14, Ann Arbor, 1984.

Moscoso, S., 'Notes de répétitions: le Théâtre du Soleil, Shakespeare, 2 partie', *Double Page*, no. 32, 1984.

Moxon, T. A. and Twining, T. (eds), *Essays in Classical Criticism*, London, Dent, 1953.

Mukarovsky, J., 'Standard Language and Poetic Language', in *A Prague School Reader on Esthetics, Literary Structure and Style*, selected and trans. P. L. Garvin, Washington, DC, Georgetown University Press, 1964.

Mukarovsky, J., 'Art as Semiotic Fact', in *Structure, Sign and Function*, trans. J. Burbank and P. Steiner, New Haven, Yale University Press, 1978.

Nyberg, L., 'The Shakespearean Ideal. Shakespeare Production and the Modern Theatre in Britain', doctoral dissertation, University of Uppsala, 1988.

Olivier, L., *On Acting*, London, Weidenfeld and Nicolson, 1986.

Olsson, A., *Den okände texten*, Stockholm, Bonniers, 1987.

Pardo, E., 'The Work of the Roy Hart Theatre', *Project Voice*, Cardiff, November, 1982.

Parker, K., 'Goodbye Voice Beautiful', *Plays and Players*, no. 382, July 1985.

Pasolli, R., *A Book on the Open Theatre*, New York, Bobbs-Merrill Company, 1970.

Patterson, M., *Peter Stein: Germany's Leading Theatre Director*, New York, Cambridge University Press, 1981.

Pavis, P., *Problèmes de sémiologie théâtrale*, Montreal, Presse de l'Université de Quebec, 1976.

Pavis, P., 'Notes Toward a Semiotic Analysis: Languages of the Stage', *Drama Review*, T84, vol. 23, no. 4, 1979.

Piaget, J., *Structuralism*, London, Routledge and Kegan Paul, 1971.

Price, C., *Theatre in the Age of Garrick*, Oxford, Blackwell, 1973.

Proctor, D.F., *Breathing, Speech and Song*, Vienna, Springer, 1980.

Quintilian, *De Institutione Oratoria*, in E. Capps, T.E. Page and W.H.D. Rouse (eds), *The Institutio Oratoria*, trans. H.E. Butler, London, Heinemann, 1922.

Rasmus, W., 'Voice and Diction in Historical Perspective', *Quarterly Journal of Speech*, vol. 47, no. 3, 1961.

Rea, K., 'Drama Training in Britain Part 1', *Theatre Quarterly*, vol. 10, no. 39, 1981.

Richards, I. A., 'Poetic Process and Literary Analysis', in T. A. Sebeok (ed.), *Style in Language*, Cambridge, Mass., MIT Press, 1960.

Richards, I. A., *The Philosophy of Rhetoric*, 2nd edn, New York, Oxford University Press, 1965.

Roose-Evans, J., *Experimental Theatre from Stanislavski to Peter Brook*, London, Routledge and Kegan Paul, 1984.

Rose Bruford College of Speech and Drama (The), Prospectus, 1984.

Royal Academy of Dramatic Art (The), Prospectus, 1984.

Russell, W., 'Ortophony or Voice Culture', *Quarterly Journal of Speech*, vol. 47, no. 3, 1961.

Sainer, A., *The Radical Theatre Notebook*, New York, Avon Books, 1975.

Sainte-Albine, P.-R. de, *Le Comédien*, Paris, 1747.

Saint Augustine, *De Doctrina Christiana*, in G. Kennedy, *Classical Rhetoric and its Christian and Secular Tradition from Ancient to Modern Times*, London, Croom Helm, 1980.

Saint-Denis, M., *Training for the Theatre*, New York, Theatre Arts Books, 1982.

Salper, D.R., 'The Sounding of a Poem', *Quarterly Journal of Speech*, vol. 57, no. 1, 1971.

Sandier, G., *Lettres/Arts*, 19 December 1981.

Schechner, R., 'Post Proscenium', in *American Theatre 1969–70*, New York, International Theatre Institute of the USA, 1970, p. 29.

Schechner, R., 'Actuals: Primitive Ritual and Performance Theory, an Anthropological Approach to Modern Experimental Theatre', *Theatre Quarterly*, vol. 1, no. 2, 1971.

Schechner, R., 'Drama, Script, Theatre, Performance', *Drama Review*, R59, vol. 17, no. 3, 1973.

Schechner, R., *Environmental Theatre*, New York, Hawthorne, 1973.

Schechner, R., *The End of Humanism. Writings on Performance*, New York, Performing Arts Journal Press, 1982.

Schechner, R., 'Richard Foreman on Richard Foreman: An Interview by Richard Schechner', *Drama Review*, T116, vol. 31, no. 4, 1987.

Schnitzler, H., 'Truth and Consequences, or Stanislavski Misinterpreted', *Quarterly Journal of Speech*, vol. 40, April 1954.

Sebeok, T. A. (ed.), *Style in Language*, Cambridge, Mass., MIT Press, 1960.

Selbourne, D., *The Making of 'A Midsummer Night's Dream': An Eyewitness Account of Peter Brook's Production from First Rehearsal to First Night*, London, Methuen, 1982.

Sewall, H., 'On the Relation of Diaphragmatic and Costal Respiration with Particular Reference to Phonation', in D. F. Proctor, *Breathing, Speech and Song*, Vienna, Springer, 1980.

Shakespeare, W., *Kung Lear (King Lear)*, trans. B. G. Hallquist, Stockholm, Kungliga Dramatiska Teatern and Ordfronts, 1984.

Sharp, W. L., *Language in Drama: Meanings for the Director and the Actor*, Scranton, Pennsylvania, Chandler, 1970.

Shevtsova, M., 'Peter Brook Adapts the Tragedy of Carmen', *Theatre International*, vol. 2, no. 10, 1983.

Simmer, B., 'Robert Wilson and Therapy', *Drama Review*, T69, vol. 21, no. 1, 1976.

Simon, C. T. and Keller, F., 'An Approach to the Problem of Chest Resonance', *Quarterly Journal of Speech*, vol. 13, June 1927.

Sion, G., *Synthesis of Five International Symposia on the Professional Training of the Actor*, trans. U. Crowley, Paris, Institut International du Théâtre (no publishing date).

Sjögren, H., 'Ingmar Bergmans teater – rörelser i rummet', in *Perspektiv på teater ur svensk regi- och iscensätningshistoria*, Documents and Studies collected by U. Gran and U-B. Laggeroth, Uddevalla, Rabén and Sjögren, 1971.

Sjögren, H., *Stage and Society in Sweden*, Uddevalla, The Swedish Institute, 1979.

Skawonius, B., 'Generationen från 1968 har satt sig på de unga', *Dagens Nyheter*, 21 March 1982.

Sörenson, M. and U., *Teater i Paris*, Kristianstad, Liber, 1983.

Stanislavski, C., *An Actor Prepares*, trans. E. R. Hapgood, New York, Theatre Art Books, 1936.

Stanislavski, K., *Teatr*, Moscow, 1940.

Stanislavski, C., *My Life in Art*, trans. J. J. Robbins, Boston, New York, Theatre Art Books, 1952.

Stanislavski, C., *Building a Character*, trans. E. R. Hapgood, London, Eyre Methuen, 1979.

Stanislavski, C., *Creating a Role*, trans. E. R. Hapgood, London, Methuen, 1983.

Sterne, R.L., *John Gielgud Directs Richard Burton in 'Hamlet': A Journal of Rehearsals*, New York, Random House, 1962.

Stevens, D., 'A Surprising Saint-Sébastien', *International Herald Tribune*, 6 April 1988.

Stoker, B., *Personal Reminiscences of Henry Irving*, vol. II, London, Heinemann, 1906.

Strindberg, A., *Miss Julie*, in *The Plays of Strindberg*, vol. 1, introd. and trans. M. Meyer, New York, Vintage Books, 1964.

Styan, J.L., *The Elements of Drama*, London, Cambridge University Press, 1960.

Styan, J.L., *Modern Drama in Theory and Practice*, vol.1: *Realism and Naturalism*, Cambridge, Cambridge University Press, 1981.

Trebizond, G., *Rhetoric in Five Books*, in G. Kennedy, *Classical Rhetoric and its Christian and Secular Tradition from Ancient to Modern Times*, London, Croom Helm, 1980.

Trewin, J.C., *Paul Scofield*, Rockliff, Theatre World Monographs, 1956.

Trilling, O., 'Robert Wilson's Ka Mountain and Guardenia Terrace', *Drama Review*, T58, vol. 17, no. 2, 1973.

Ubersfeld, A., *Lire le théâtre*, Paris, Editions Sociales, 1977.

Van Riper, C. and Irwin, J.V., *Voice and Articulation*, New Jersey, Pitman Medical, 1959.

Veilleux, J., 'Towards a Theory of Interpretation', *Quarterly Journal of Speech*, vol. 55, no. 2, 1969.

Veltrusky, J., 'Dramatic Text as a Component of Theatre' (1941), in L. Matejka and I. Titunik (eds), *Semiotics of Art: Prague School Contributions*, Cambridge, Mass., MIT Press, 1976.

Veltrusky, J., 'Man and Object in the Theatre', trans. P. Garvin, in *A Prague School Reader on Esthetics, Literary Structure and Style*, Washington DC, Georgetown University Press, 1955.

Warren, J., Review of *The Hairy Ape*, *Plays and Players*, no. 406, July 1987.

Willett, J., *Brecht in Context*, London, Methuen, 1984.

Wilson, R., Lecture at the Nobel Symposium, 24–7 May 1988, Royal Dramatic Theatre, Stocholm.

Wirén, G., 'Åter till Shakespeare', *Dagens Nyheter*, 1 April 1984.

Yemen Dzakis, M., Demonstration Workshop at the Orionteatern, Stockholm, 6 February 1989.

Young, K., *The Drama of the Medieval Church*, vols 1 and 2, Oxford, Clarendon Press, 1933.

Y.P., *Midi Libre*, 19 April 1985.

Zern, L., 'Ingen förstår Shakespeare', *Dagens Nyheter*, 13 January 1985.

Zern, L., *Expressen*, 21 December 1986.

Zern, L., 'Teater i Europa', *Nya teatertidningen*, no. 41, 1988.

Zich, O., *Estetika dramatického umeni* (Aesthetics of Dramatic Art), Prague, Melantrich, 1931.

INDEX

219

3833